From The Ashes:
The REAL Story of Cardiff City Football Club

By the same author:

Into the Dragon's Lair: A Supernatural History of Wales
Apartment 14F: An Oriental Ghost Story
Dead of Night
Devil's Island
Rainbow's End

From The Ashes:
The REAL Story of Cardiff City Football Club

Christian Saunders

First published in 2013

© Christian Saunders

© Llygad Gwalch 2013

ISBN: 978-1-84524-213-8

Cover photographs: Myrddin ap Dafydd
Cover design: Eleri Owen
Photographs pages 49-64: Getty Images

Published by Llygad Gwalch,
12 Iard yr Orsaf, Llanrwst, Wales LL26 0EH
tel: 01492 624031
fax: 01492 641502
email: books@carreg-gwalch.com
internet: www.carreg-gwalch.com

Contents

Introduction

From the Ashes . . .

After a succession of near misses, on finally achieving promotion to the Promised Land of the Premier League, Cardiff City is, in 2013, arguably the biggest and most successful football club in Wales. It was the first to achieve 'Championship' status within the new League structure, boasts a squad peppered with highly rated international players, and is now beginning to live up to its time-honoured 'sleeping giant' tag.

But this has not always been the case.

After an initial blaze of glory, during which they became (and still remain) the only non-English club ever to win the coveted FA Cup and came within a whisker of winning the old First Division title, Cardiff City began a slow, painful descent down the footballing hierarchy into relative obscurity. A combination of limited income, high running costs and bad management ensured a grim existence of perpetual struggle, which was blighted still further by the rise, fall and rise again of football hooliganism, a phenomenon that has sadly become synonymous with the club. To some, Cardiff City Football Club always was an unnecessary burden and a right royal pain in the nether-regions. In the grand scheme of things the club is a black sheep, to play on one of the tiresome insults used week-in week-out, up and down the country by unimaginative anti-Welsh philistines ... I mean, fellow football supporters.

It isn't too hard to work out why the Bluebirds ruffle so many feathers. Even before its inception the mere notion of founding a football club in the Rugby Union heartland of south Wales was unthinkable, and controversy reigned from that moment on. In October 2004 figures released by the Home Office revealed that Cardiff City officially had the worst behaved set of supporters in the entire country, with more arrests and banning orders than any other League club. Interpret this as you may, but it has to be at least in part due to the passion and conviction the club stirs in its supporters. Even the most hardened cynic has to admit that the willingness to shed blood for any chosen cause is admirable, however inconsequential it may seem to outsiders. Obviously, it would be wrong to condone violence of any kind, especially if this book is to avoid the stereotypical pre-planned response that has greeted so many others of its ilk.

Football literature first hit the mainstream over a decade ago when a plethora of writers began exploiting a frustrated new generation's blood-lust and a rash of ex-hooligans began recounting their memoirs. As Colin Ward maintains in his contemporary classic *Steaming In*, the hooligan element forced out of the game by the establishment had grown up and moved on. Evidently a large percentage took up writing, while a surprising amount also took to spinning vinyl in DJ booths. Some critics of the genre point at the recent influx of books and the accompanying mainstream movies allegedly 'glamorizing' hooliganism. It isn't just football. There are far more serious and pressing issues to address than the odd post-match flare-up, most of which are blown out of all proportion by the media. But that's a job for the politicians of this world, the people we elect to serve us. In defence of the much-maligned modern football hooligan, I can vouch for the fact that it is extremely difficult to turn the other cheek (never mind stand back and applaud!) while your club, country and cultural identity is routinely defiled and ridiculed. Sometimes you can't help but take it personally. It's just that most of us know where to draw the line.

For the hard core, Cardiff City is much more than just a football club, it's a movement, akin to those once instigated by the likes of Owen Glyndŵr, only with slightly less bloodshed. It evokes certain emotions that simply cannot be controlled, especially when the issue of national pride is raised. The traditional rivalry between England and Wales has been well documented and manifests itself in many forms, the football pitch being just one. In effect, virtually every game is a country versus country affair, while rare local derbies take on even more significance. It's easy to see how emotions can sometimes get the better of people. The above is intended as nothing more than a tentative explanation, put forward in an effort to promote empathy and understanding. It is not an excuse.

Far from simply being a sport, for some, football is the be-all and end-all. It is also a notoriously unpredictable and fickle business. Players routinely come and go, their form ebbs and dips, prizes are won and lost, clubs and individuals rise and fall. There are power struggles, money wrangles, tantrums, scandals and a multitude of other issues to consider that are not directly related to football, but nevertheless have a huge influence. Heroes are made and men are broken in the blink of an eye. Whole football empires can be brought crashing down in the space of 90 minutes. More often than not it takes years, even decades, as the club you affiliate yourself with, for better or for worse, is slowly run down into a wanton state of stagnation and dereliction. And there you linger in quiet desperation, waiting for the receivers to call. Years of bad results take their toll, and the club you love now resembles a severely beaten punch-drunk boxer waiting for the referee to step in and end his misery. You look on helplessly as your man is battered from pillar to post, and what makes it even worse is that you know how good that guy used to be. He even held a title for a little while.

Sometimes, however, miracles do happen, and you watch in awe as your man rises Lazarus-like from the canvas, dusts himself down, and taps into a reservoir of inner strength even you didn't know he had. In no time at all he's on the road to silverware once again. Reprieved, refreshed and revitalised.

Cardiff City's latest miracle that lifted them off the canvas came in the form of a mysterious man from the east. A man of courage, wealth, and with a passion for football. Football, like life, often runs in cycles. Birth, death, and rebirth was the mantra of the ancient Celts, the colourful, enigmatic race of warmongers that once laid claim to most of Wales. This is the inspirational story of the birth, death, and subsequent rebirth of a football club. This is the REAL story of Cardiff City. Unauthorised and unofficial.

This book has been written without the input of Cardiff City Football Club, or of the club's representatives. All views contained herein are those of the author.

Christian Saunders
Summer 2013

1

All Gentlemen Together
(1899-1910)

In the late nineteenth century, the mass exportation of coal and iron from south Wales to the rest of the world triggered an economic boom. Workers moved in from England, Scotland, Ireland and further afield to settle in the region's sparse valleys and coastal towns. Because of its huge docks and convenient location, many people also settled in Cardiff, which quickly developed into the biggest coal-exporting port in the world. This influx of predominantly young men into the area resulted in a melting pot of contrasting views and cultures, and quite possibly the only thing that many of them had in common, apart from a desire to forge a better life, was a love of football. This alone immediately put some of them at odds with the natives of south Wales who, at the time, were traditionally staunch Rugby Union fanatics.

By then, football in England and Scotland had become a defining element of working class culture. Rugby Union was considered to be the sport of the middle and upper classes, and championed by the prestigious universities. Strangely, this rule did not seem to apply in south Wales, where rugby was historically a working-class sport. In direct contrast to their southern counterparts, natives of north Wales traditionally favoured 'the dribbling' code, a sentiment reflected by the formation of the Football Association of Wales (FAW) in Wrexham as early as 1876. It wasn't until 1893 that a separate organisation, the South Wales and Monmouthshire Football Association (SWMFA), was formed in an attempt to govern the game in the southern territories.

Cardiff City Football Club began life in the summer of 1899 as Riverside AFC, which was initially little more than an imprint of an amateur cricket club from the Riverside district of Cardiff. In an admirable display of loyalty and camaraderie, the cricketers took it upon themselves to find a pastime that would both enhance their fitness and keep them together socially over the winter months. Somewhat surprisingly, with south Wales being a traditional Rugby Union outpost, they opted to try their collective hand at association football.

The driving force behind the club's formation was 29-year-old Walter Bartley 'Bart' Wilson, who had moved to Cardiff from Bristol in 1897. Although partially disabled, he was a great sportsman. In particular he was a football fanatic, and had witnessed first-hand the enthusiasm and raw passion the game could muster in his native West Country city, as two successful professional clubs (Bristol City and Bristol Rovers) had formed there shortly before he left. It was Bart who assumed the role of club secretary, and took it upon himself to organize meetings and partake in the necessary behind-the-scenes dealings required to establish a functioning football club. He is now recognised as the club's founding father.

Riverside AFC played their first matches at Sophia Gardens near Cardiff castle (ironically, now the home of Glamorgan County cricket club) in their chosen strip of brown and amber quartered jerseys and black shorts, losing their very first fixture (on Saturday 7 October 1899) 1-9 to Barry West End. However, the defeat didn't deter them. With an inexperienced playing staff largely made up of committee members and frustrated cricket enthusiasts, they persevered with a succession of friendly matches against local opposition, often fielding two XIs simultaneously against different teams, eventually being accepted into the Cardiff and District League the following year. In 1902 they merged with another local team, Riverside Albion, a move which strengthened their ranks and their standing considerably, and three years later they won their first-ever piece of silverware, the Bevan Shield, a local amateur competition sanctioned by the SWMFA.

On 28 October 1905, in recognition of its increasing importance to the Principality, Cardiff was officially declared a city, and the committee of Riverside AFC sought to change the name of their blossoming club to Cardiff City Football Club. The request was initially refused unless the club agreed to participate in the South Wales League, one of the strongest Leagues in existence at the time, the concern being that the club were not playing at a high enough level to properly represent a city. In the wake of this disappointment, rumours abounded amongst disgruntled members of the FA that the club had jumped the gun and had already started calling themselves Cardiff City without proper authorisation. There was also the small matter that a club called Cardiff AFC had already been formed back in 1890, though it no longer existed. In due course, Riverside applied for election into the South Wales League and were accepted. Subsequently, following a meeting with the SWMFA on 5 September 1908 at Alexandra Hotel, Queen Street, Cardiff, they were finally allowed to change their name to Cardiff City on the understanding that 'if a professional team should be started in Cardiff in the near future, they would relinquish the name.'

The nickname 'the Bluebirds' is believed to have arisen when Cardiff was chosen over many other major cities to host a version of the famous play *The Bluebird* by Belgian writer Maurice Maeterlinck in 1908. The play was made into a popular silent movie two years later. A contributing factor could also have been the high volume of seagulls around the city.

It was hoped that the newly-formed club would capitalise on a sharp upturn in fortune of the national team, which had raised the profile of Welsh football immeasurably by winning their first-ever Home International Championship in the 1906-07 season. The competition was then in its twenty-fourth year, and had previously been dominated by England and Scotland. As a measure of how much the national team had improved, Wales' 1-0 victory at Wrexham on 4 March was their third consecutive victory against the Scots, opponents they had not beaten in the thirty meetings before that!

It was decided to arrange a short series of friendly matches for Cardiff City AFC, mainly as a means to gauge public interest in the club, with Crystal Palace of the Southern League visiting on 5 October 1909. In order to satisfy the huge public demand for tickets the match, which ended in a 3-3 draw, was played at Cardiff Arms Park, ironically the spiritual home of Welsh Rugby Union. Total gate receipts of £33 were deemed impressive, and more games were hastily arranged.

As luck would have it, around this time the Southern League, which had been in existence since 1890, was in the process of setting up a second division. Cardiff City was approached with a view to joining along with a number of other Welsh clubs, but in the event were refused entry on the basis that not only were they not yet professional, but they didn't even have a designated ground on which to play. In order to rectify the situation the committee began negotiations with the eminent Bute Estate, eventually acquiring a seven-year lease on a piece of disused waste ground between Sloper Road and the Taff Vale Railway embankment on the outskirts of the city centre. Two conditions of the lease were that neither betting nor the consumption of alcohol was to be allowed on the site, two cornerstones on which modern association football was built!

The club was now seen as being committed to professionalism, and was conditionally accepted into Division Two of the Southern League for the season commencing in 1910. The single-division Football League had already turned down several proposals of a merger with the Southern League, which was in danger of stagnating, so they decided to expand and introduce promotion and relegation between two divisions. South Wales was the logical area to target, as football was mushrooming in popularity in the region in proportion with the population. As rules dictated, a prospectus was filed with the registrar of Joint Stock Companies under the name of Cardiff City Football Club Ltd, and it was officially incorporated on 21 April 1910.

The first registered office was at 9 Park Place, Cardiff, an address from where one of the club members, Norman Robertson, practised as a solicitor. Lord Rhondda then became the first acknowledged non-board shareholder, and Lloyds was chosen as club banker. As soon as everything was in place the club was floated to attain some capital, and a board of directors was elected, with Sid H. Nicholls (brother of the famous Welsh international rugby player Gwyn) acting as the first chairman. As a gesture of appreciation, all twenty-six founding members of Riverside AFC were automatically made life members of Cardiff City and given four half-sovereign shares each.

The work on the club's soon-to-be home ground was carried out by scores of eager volunteers and good-natured corporation workers. In time, a suitable playing area was levelled and surfaced, the pitch enclosed with a white picket fence, and a small wooden grandstand erected on the Sloper Road side. To the left of the stand was a small building that housed the changing rooms and club offices. The new ground was all set to be called 'Sloper Park', but when guarantors were required, Lord Ninian Crichton-Stuart, the second son of the Marquis of Bute, stepped forward to offer his considerable financial support, and out of gratitude the club decided to name the ground Ninian Park.

All that was then needed was a selection of decent players, and again it was Bart who gleefully assumed the responsibility. His first professional signing was a Welsh-speaking left-winger called Jack Evans, whom he acquired from Cwmparc-and-Treorchy. Evans, who had originally gone south to look for work as a printer after badly injuring his shoulder playing for Wrexham, reportedly received the princely sum of 6 shillings as a signing-on fee, and 35 shillings a week in wages. Wilson then appointed Davy McDougall from Glasgow Rangers as team captain and player/manager, who in turn helped recruit a number of players from Scotland and the north of England, two footballing territories of which he had gleaned extensive personal knowledge during his career.

Obtaining this collection of journeymen proved to be both expensive and problematic, but was seen as an essential step in the development of the club if it was to be in any way successful. As the second division of the Southern League consisted of only twelve teams, meaning a season total of just twenty-two matches, the decision was made to compete in the Glamorgan League simultaneously. The former competition consisted of clubs like Merthyr Town and Treharris Athletic, alongside such contemporary stalwarts as Reading, Stoke and Walsall, while the latter included Tredegar, Maerdy and Cwmparc. Cardiff City was not the only club to contest both Leagues at the same time; Ton Pentre, Treharris Athletic, Merthyr and Aberdare Athletic also attempted the feat.

A prestigious friendly was arranged to officially open Ninian Park on Thursday 1 September 1910. The match was considered absolutely vital; consistently high attendance figures were deemed essential as the club faced a huge wage bill after recruiting so heavily. The visitors were Aston Villa, one of the biggest clubs in England and reigning Football League champions. Bizarrely, the actual kick-off was performed by Lord Ninian Crichton-Stuart himself!

The Cardiff team took to the field in a new strip of blue jerseys, white shorts, and blue socks, which (thankfully!) soon became their registered colours. The historic line-up that afternoon, more than half of whom were Scottish, consisted of: Ted Husbands (a goalkeeper hailing from Wrexham who had been plucked from Liverpool's reserves), James McKenzie, John Duffy, Bob Lawrie, Jack Ramsay, Davy McDougall, James McDonald, Tom Abley, Jim Malloch, Billy Watts and Jack Evans.

Before an estimated crowd of around 7,000, Villa narrowly won the tie 2–1, with Evans having the distinction of scoring Cardiff's first-ever goal at Ninian Park. It would be the first of many. Bart Wilson's dream of bringing professional football to Cardiff was now a reality, and the achievement was reflected in the local press, which had been very supportive throughout:

> Cardiff City Association Football Club has every reason to congratulate itself on the success of the inaugural match with Aston Villa yesterday. Not only did the players give an excellent account of themselves, but they managed to raise the enthusiasm of some 7,000 spectators. There were many

prominent people among the spectators, as well as a number of Welsh rugby players, who evinced much interest in the game.

Western Mail, 2 September 1910

A few weeks after the match Harry Bradshaw, secretary of the Southern League, inspected Ninian Park and was (reportedly) moved to comment, 'I am simply astounded with what has been accomplished. It is already a fine ground and it is nothing to what you can make of it. I see endless possibilities.' This rave endorsement was more than enough to convince his employers that Cardiff should figure in their future plans.

2

Professionalism and War
(1910–20)

1910–11 season

Cardiff City FC's first competitive match was away at Ton
Pentre in the Glamorgan League on 5 September 1910,
where they won 3-2 with a hat-trick by Welsh centre-
forward Bob Peake. Ironically enough, their first Southern
League Division Two match was against the same
opponents and ended in a similar result, Peake (2), Jack
Evans, and Billy Watt all scoring in a 4-1 victory before a
crowd of around 8,000. Even though it was vastly inferior to
the elite Football League, the Southern League was the
competition that the players, staff and fans most wanted to
perform well in because it represented the biggest chance of
recognition.

As word of Cardiff's mini-achievements spread, a
grandstand was erected at Ninian Park to satisfy public
demand for seats. Unthinkable in the twenty-first century,
the stand was built almost entirely by a section of supporters
and some of the players themselves.

The victories against Ton Pentre and successive draws at
Treharris and Aberdare set City on their way to a successful
Southern League programme, much of which was spent
amongst the promotion contenders. The club's decision to
invest in experienced players was paying dividends, but the
canny McDougall acknowledged the need to strengthen the
side further. Shortly after the Potteries club had demolished
City 5-0 in what would be their worst defeat of the season,
Welsh international defender George Latham was signed

from Stoke as player/coach. Unfortunately, the transfer coincided with a slight dip in form as City lost at home to Reading and then to Latham's former employers, condemning them to fourth place in their inaugural season in the Southern League with an impressive total of twelve wins and four draws from twenty-two games. Their biggest win came at the expense of hapless Chesham, whom they beat 7-1 on their own turf on 14 January 1911, and the top scorer was 'Little' Bob Peake, who notched twenty-nine goals in all competitions.

After beating Bath in the preliminary round of the FA Cup, City lost out to League rivals Merthyr Town in the first qualifying round before their biggest crowd of the season at Ninian Park, which numbered around 12,000. Meanwhile, in the Welsh Cup, they lost a third round replay to Ton Pentre after defeating Maerdy and Tredegar in earlier rounds. City also performed well in the Glamorgan League, losing just three of the eighteen matches played. The fact that Glamorgan League matches were regularly attracting attendance figures to rival those of the Southern League came as a shock to the sizeable Rugby Union-playing fraternity in south Wales. It was one of the first signs that fans were beginning to switch allegiances, with many opting to follow football as it was often seen as more exciting. That March also saw the first international football match ever held at Ninian Park, a 2-2 draw between Wales and Scotland.

At the end of the 1910-11 season it was agreed that the club as a whole would benefit from the appointment of a full time secretary/manager. The position was advertised in the press, and the successful applicant was Fred Stewart, a 38-year old who had previously occupied a similar position at Stockport County. He was initially appointed on a three-year agreement at £4 a week, plus bonuses.

After much debate, Cardiff then withdrew from the Glamorgan League, opting to fill any blanks in their calendar with a succession of friendly games. The appointment of Stewart sparked a period of hectic transfer activity at the club, while work continued behind the scenes to raise the overall standards at Ninian Park. In stark contrast to today's mega deals, in 1911 most Cardiff City players picked up just £2 per week, the exception being George Burton, a highly-rated forward signed from Middlesbrough, who earned £3.

1911–12 season

City started their second season in Division Two of the Southern League with a 3-1 win against Kettering Town on 2 September 1911, secured with a much-changed line-up of Ted Husbands, Arthur Waters, Bob Leah, Bob Lawrie, Eddie Thompson, Billy Hardy, Harry Tracey, Jack Burton, Harry Featherstone, Tom Abley and Jack Evans. They overcame a surprise defeat in the next match at Pontypridd by embarking on a run that was marred by just one loss in thirteen games. Ultimately, however, the season ended in disappointment as they finished in third place behind Portsmouth and eventual champions Merthyr, who could then, temporarily at least, legitimately claim to be the best football team in Wales. To underline their superiority Merthyr also dumped City out of the FA Cup, again after a hard-fought replay in the latter qualifying stages. However, despite the setbacks, the season was a historic one for Cardiff as they lifted the Welsh Cup in only their second season in the competition. A new ground record of 18,000 people turned up to watch them contest a goalless final with Pontypridd on 8 April 1912, and a similar number were there when they finished the job by winning the replay 3-0.

1912–13 season

That summer saw more hectic transfer activity at the club, sparked by McDougall leaving to take the post of player/manager with Newport County and taking goalkeeper Husbands with him. Stewart responded by signing a clutch of new players that included replacement goalkeeper Jack Kneeshaw from Colne, and a young prospect called Fred Keenor from Cardiff amateur side Roath Wednesdays. Keenor would go on to become a legend, though he didn't figure when City kicked off the 1912–13 campaign on 7 September at the Vetch Field against Swansea Town, who were newcomers to the Southern League and playing their first professional season. The game finished 1-1, with Burton netting for City and set Cardiff off on an unbeaten League run that lasted until Boxing Day, when they were eventually defeated 2-0 at Kenilworth Road by Luton Town.

Amazingly, that defeat proved to be City's only loss of the season as they bounced back on New Years Day 1913 with a merciless 5-0 thrashing of Llanelli. Two weeks later they achieved a club record-breaking 9-0 win over old rivals Ton Pentre at Ninian Park. Billy Devlin, a shrewd signing from Stockport, notched a hat-trick, while Jack Evans also got on the score sheet. The blossoming Evans, City's first professional signing, was having a good year, having been the first-ever Cardiff player selected to represent Wales at international level.

At that stage, City were undoubtedly the form team in the division and Stewart, eager to maintain momentum, paid Newport £100 for their prized winger Andy Holt. As the team went from strength to strength on the pitch, so their support grew. They were now averaging gates of 8,000–9,000. An estimated 25,000, another new attendance record, packed into Ninian Park on 21 March to see City beat Luton 3–0, thereby exacting full revenge for the Boxing Day defeat. The win meant that City won the championship hands-down with three games to spare. The League table made for impressive reading, with City notching eighteen wins and five draws from twenty-four games.

While they were practically untouchable in the League, they didn't fare quite so well elsewhere. City were the only non-English representatives in another short-lived League-formatted tournament called the Southern Alliance, which included such clubs as Southampton, Millwall, Brighton & Hove Albion, Portsmouth and Luton. Against such powerful opposition City struggled badly, and eventually finished rock bottom after sixteen games despite fielding their strongest line-up at virtually every fixture. After crushing Merthyr 5-1 in the preliminary round of the FA Cup, with Devlin becoming the first Cardiff player to score a hat trick in the competition, they subsequently went on to defeat Pontypridd, Llanelli and Exeter, before bowing out at home to Southend. Their grip on the Welsh Cup was also lost, as they crashed out to Swansea in the semi-finals. This controversial and bad-tempered encounter marked the start of a long and fractious association between the south Wales rivals.

Stewart recruited heavily again in the summer of 1913, most notably bringing in forwards Jim Henderson and George West (from Scotswood and Wallsend respectively) and Joe Clark from Hebburn Argyle. However, when the season started he largely kept faith with the players who had won him the championship a few short months earlier, believing consistency and continuity to be the twin routes to success.

1913-14 season
Unfortunately, Stewart's philosophy backfired badly. City lost their first five games, each by a single goal, a run that saw

them clinging to the foot of the table. They also tumbled out of the FA Cup at the fourth qualifying stage at the gleeful hands of Swansea, who were fast becoming Cardiff's nemesis. Stewart rang the changes, urging his side not to panic and introducing several of his new signings who had been patiently waiting in the wings. City gradually began to acclimatize to the higher standard of football and, with good results against Coventry City, Watford, Norwich City and Gillingham, steadily began to climb the table.

Both West and Keenor made their Cardiff debuts in a 1-1 home draw with Exeter on 6 December. West impressed enough to keep his place in City's attack and proved a great acquisition for the struggling Bluebirds, while Keenor was slower to develop and found himself temporarily dumped back in the reserves. One of Stewart's best signings during that period was talented right-back Charlie Brittan from Tottenham Hotspur of Division One for the sum of £1,000, which was a new club record. The transfer was seen by both the national and local media as a major coup for Cardiff. The super-skilled and composed Brittan made an impressive debut in City's first away win of the season, a 2-1 at Swindon Town on 20 December.

In an error that would never be allowed to happen in today's game, City were scheduled to play two matches on the same day on 3 January 1914. Consequently, the first team travelled to Southampton where they went down 2-0, while a reserve team was sent to play a Welsh Cup third round tie at Owestry Town where they lost 2-1, ending their involvement in the competition for another year. By this time City had improved as a team, though their away form remained slightly patchy. The much-touted arrival of Brittan added some steel to the defensive line, which showed as they managed to keep clean sheets in five of the last six games to finish a respectable tenth in the League.

After overturning that difficult start, the club had given a good account of themselves and despite their questionable form on the pitch, by the end of the 1913–14 season Cardiff were generally regarded as the best supported team in Britain outside the Football League and the Scottish equivalent.

That season was also notable for the introduction of modern-style match-day programmes, courtesy of the Imperial Printing Company. The very first featuring Cardiff was priced at 1d, and was produced for a Southern Alliance match against Newport that took place on 3 September. Amongst other things, the birth of the football programme paved the way for all manner of advertisers and would-be sponsors to get involved in the game. Much of the embryonic programme adopted a humorous stance and included anecdotes, jokes and contributions from regular columnists such as 'Fels Naptha', who took his nom de plume from a brand of industrial-strength soap and regularly served as unofficial spokesman for the fans.

1914–15 season

Stewart recruited two more experienced professionals in the closed season; George Beare, a right-winger from First Division Everton, and full-back Arthur Lever from Middlesbrough. Lever had starred in the Aston Villa team that had officially opened Ninian Park four years earlier. Both players were drafted straight into the side to open the 1914–15 League programme away to Watford, where defender Pat Cassidy scored City's goal in a 2-1 reverse.

Another shaky start to the season prompted Stewart to invest in Liverpool's Arthur Goddard, a veteran of twelve years and over 400 games for the Anfield outfit. His arrival was a revelation and Cardiff's fortunes changed dramatically as the goals began to flow, especially at home where they rattled off seven straight wins. Possibly the most inspiring result of all was a 7-0 thrashing of Bristol Rovers, which Bart Wilson must have watched with mixed emotions having been born and bred in the West Country industrial city. The run lifted the Bluebirds up to the lofty heights of third, and they were now regularly attracting home attendances of over 10,000.

A key game was played on New Year's Day 1915, when Watford, the eventual champions, were the visitors to the Welsh capital. In front of a sparse crowd of less than 2,000 (due to a lack of public transport and atrocious weather conditions) City went down 2-3, their goals coming from Beare and Evans. This game proved to be a turning point, however, as it was Cardiff's last home defeat of the season.

In stark contrast, their away form was less than spectacular, a fact compounded by a 0-2 defeat by Bristol City at Ashton Gate on 9 January 1915 that saw Cardiff tumble out of the FA Cup at the first time of asking. Both Bristol's goals were scored by Edwin Burton, who would later lose his life in the Great War.

Sometime at the beginning of 1915, Cardiff City voluntarily withdrew from the Welsh Cup, probably to concentrate on the League, though the official reason and precise date of this somewhat surprising course of action have long since been lost in the mists of time. They eventually finished third in the League, behind Reading and champions Watford, but above such footballing superpowers as Portsmouth, Southampton, Millwall and West Ham.

Most clubs, City included, managed to complete the 1914–15 season without suffering too many ill effects from the conflict that had been raging in Belgium and beyond since August 1914, apart from severe disruption to the railways, then the main means by which players, fans and officials travelled to away games in the days before luxury coaches and short-haul flights. However, the summer of 1915 saw the Forces' recruitment drive intensified, and with no foreseeable end to the hostilities, the Football League hierarchy decided to terminate all sanctioned fixtures to enable players to enlist to help the ongoing war effort. Clubs were still allowed, if not encouraged, to play friendly matches and even participate in small regional mini-Leagues, but all were affected severely by the loss of players, staff and supporters. Hence, in the run up to Christmas 1915, Cardiff City contested only a succession of low-key friendly games, primarily as morale boosters, even playing (and beating) old rivals Merthyr on Christmas Day.

In the New Year, the Bluebirds agreed to participate in a South–West combination League against such clubs as both Bristol teams, Newport and Southampton. They enjoyed a few notable victories but the drain on resources, along with severe travel restrictions, poor crowds, and turmoil amongst the playing staff, rendered the 'League' ultimately futile.

As the War raged on there was criticism directed at Cardiff from sections of the press and, in turn, the public, who questioned whether people should be enjoying football whilst others faced the horrors of the trenches. The rugby-playing fraternity of south Wales seized the opportunity to belittle the round ball game in an effort to prise back some lost support, and publicly slammed the decision to play on through the early stages of the War. In reality however, Cardiff probably did more than their fair share to help the war effort; seven players went off to fight (later rising to nine); all those left behind volunteered for home defence duty, each subscribed weekly to the war fund, and Ninian Park itself was offered to the military for drilling and training use.

1915–1917

Some players continued in City's service throughout, but for the most part Stewart was reduced to selecting disparate teams from a selection of enthusiastic amateurs, guests, visitors, and players home on leave from the forces. Most concerned parties agreed that the situation was intolerable, and at the end of the 1915–16 'season-that-never-was,' Cardiff withdrew from competitive fixtures for the duration of the war. Over the next two years they played only a handful of low-profile friendlies, including, on 28 April 1917, a satisfying 4-1 rout of Swansea.

1918

After the signing of the Armistice on 11 November 1918, the demobilization of the British Army resulted in players gradually filtering back to their respective clubs. By Christmas of that year Stewart was in a position to assess his playing staff, and another series of friendly matches were agreed to aid in the slow rehabilitation of the sport. It was decided that competitive football would resume the following August.

Despite the bloodshed of World War I, Cardiff's playing ranks were largely unscathed, with only two registered players being killed in the hostilities: Tom Witts and James McKenzie. The most significant loss to hit the club was that of Lord Ninian Crichton-Stuart, a leading patron, who was killed in action in Belgium in October 1915. 'Fels Naptha' spoke for many grateful fans in a later programme saying, 'He died the death of a brave soldier and a gallant gentleman'.

Several others sustained wounds, notably Fred Keenor, who was injured in the leg whilst serving with the 17th Middlesex ('Footballers') Battalion and Bart Wilson lost his son John, who was killed in France whilst serving with the

17th Welsh regiment. Throughout the war Fred Stewart had remained in Cardiff, building up his corn and coal merchant businesses whilst overseeing sporadic work on Ninian Park designed to further enhance spectator facilities, and the board of directors had kept the club alive mainly with money from their own pockets. During the war years, the football authorities had decided to help the smaller clubs by limiting players' future earning potential to a maximum of £156 per year (compared to a previous £208). Clubs were warned that if they exceeded this figure it could constitute making illegal payments, and they would be punished accordingly.

1919–20 season

Eventually, most of the playing staff circa 1915 were reinstated and a modest kitty made available for new signings. Inside-forward Billy Grimshaw was bought from Bradford City and fullback Alex Stewart was recruited from Watford. Irishman E. E. 'Bert' Smith also arrived when he left the army, and local amateur sides were scoured in the search for new talent. The hunt uncovered the soon-to-be-legendary Len Davies, along with Eddie Jenkins, Charlie Jones and Harold Beadles. Beadles was released following a trial period and joined Liverpool, only to be signed (at considerable extra cost) back from the Anfield club five years later. The re-vamped Cardiff line-up that returned to League action proper, away to Reading on 30 August 1919, featured no fewer than eight players from the team that had finished the 1914–15 season, as well as Fred Keenor, who was just beginning to force himself into the reckoning. They lost. Clearly, some fine-tuning was required.

The fading Cassidy was replaced with new boy Bert Smith and Billy Hardy returned from active duty to resume his playing career. Utility forward Billy Cox arrived from

Clydebank and scored the winner against Exeter on his home debut, thus paving the way for crowd favourite Billy Devlin to move to Newport. Arthur Cashmore also signed from Darleston, and he too scored on his home debut in a victory against Crystal Palace on 6 December. From there, Stewart's managerial tinkering began to pay off as the Bluebirds embarked on an unbeaten League run of fifteen games that lifted them to third in the table. This admirable run of success, coupled with a widespread sense of post-war relief and optimism amongst the general public, pushed the average attendance figure at Ninian Park over the 12,000 mark for the first time. Some matches attracted in excess of 25,000 people, astounding figures for a club that was still essentially a non-League outfit.

The crowds also turned out in the FA Cup, where City performed heroically to knock out Oldham Athletic and Wolverhampton Wanderers, the latter match being played before a partisan crowd of Wolves fans numbering almost 38,000, before going out to Bristol City. They were also in irresistible form in the Welsh Cup that term, inflicting heavy defeats on Merthyr and Chester in the early rounds and cruising towards a semi-final showdown with arch-rivals Swansea.

Midway through the season the Football League announced preliminary plans to introduce a Third Division to the existing set-up consisting primarily of the larger Southern League clubs. The Cardiff board were quick to realize the potential benefits such a move could have for the club and lodged a formal application, which was held over 'in abeyance' until such a time as the technicalities and logistics could be finalized. In support of the application, influential sports publication the Athletic News rightly asked, 'Why should South Wales, now a hot-bed of soccer, be outside the pale?'

Soon after the League's announcement, work began on the all-seated Canton stand at Ninian Park, possibly to fulfil a condition of entry into the League, though no records exist to validate this assumption. In any case, the ground capacity would be increased substantially, and that would lead to greater revenue. By now the club was finally in a position to reward those players that had stayed with them and often gone without pay through the lean war years. The families of those players killed in action also received generous cheques.

An interesting incident happened during a match against Southampton at the Dell on 17 January 1920, which would seem to dispel the myth that football hooliganism is a modern phenomenon. The Southampton supporters, dismayed at being behind on their own turf and disappointed at the way the game was going, took to throwing bricks and bottles at the City players. While he was engaged in the act of taking a corner, Jack Evans was hit squarely in the back by a chunk of masonry, and the Saints came back to claim a 2-2 draw. This could well have been the first documented incident where the subject of football hooliganism reared its ugly head in connection with Cardiff. It wouldn't be the last.

Back to the football, and by the end of March, City's form had dipped considerably as they coughed and spluttered their way through a run of six League games without a win, scoring only one goal in the process. Following that, the only bright spot was a 2–1 home win over Swansea in the semi-final Welsh Cup that saw them through to the final where they met Wrexham on 21 April. They won the competition to take the trophy to Ninian Park for a second time, but had to settle for fourth position in the League.

On 31 May 1920 the Football League decided to accept

both Leeds United and Cardiff into a restructured Second Division, with City polling twenty-three votes and Leeds thirty-one. The Bluebirds therefore became the first non-English club ever to be accepted into the English Football League proper, a feat reputedly achieved by just half an hour, as their Southern League rivals Swansea, Merthyr and Newport were also soon elected as members of the new Third Division. They were joined by Grimsby Town, who had been demoted from Division Two to accommodate Cardiff. Certified Second Division status was a far better result than even Fred Stewart and his board of directors had hoped for, even if the move did incur a £500 fine from the Southern League for 'insufficient notice of withdrawal.'

It was understood that if the club was to compete at the higher level Cardiff would need to strengthen their ranks considerably before the start of the new season. To this end Stewart was given the green light to sign 26-year-old forward Jimmy Gill from Sheffield Wednesday (then known as 'The Wednesday') for £750, defender Jack Page from Everton, and goalkeeper Ben Davies from Middlesbrough. The club also scoured the local amateur leagues for fresh (and relatively cheap) talent, a policy that had paid handsome dividends in the past. Via this route Stewart landed, amongst others, Herbie Evans, who would go on to make a sizeable impression in the Welsh capital. With new players recruited, the Canton stand completed, and an expectant throng of feverishly loyal support, Cardiff City AFC were ready to take their bow in the Football League after barely a decade as a professional club.

3

Glory Days
(1920–29)

1920–21 season

The newly restructured League consisted of three divisions, each of twenty-two teams, with automatic end of season promotion and relegation for two clubs between Divisions One and Two, and one between Divisions Two and Three. Cardiff City FC played their first-ever fixture in Division Two of the Football League proper at Edgeley Park on 28 August 1920, where they faced Fred Stewart's former employers Stockport County. The team that took to the field in that historical encounter was: Jack Kneeshaw, Charlie Brittan, Arthur Layton, Billy Hardy, E. E. 'Bert' Smith, Fred Keenor, Billy Grimshaw, Jimmy Gill, Arthur Cashmore, George West and Jack Evans. Stockport scored early, sending the home crowd into raptures, but then Gill made an instant impact by scoring City's first-ever goal in League football, on his debut, to equalise. He scored again before half time, and further strikes from Grimshaw, Keenor and Jack Evans gifted City an emphatic 5-2 opening day victory.

Cardiff's first home game was against Clapton Orient two days later. The game drew a crowd estimated at 25,000, but unfortunately City couldn't break down a stubborn defence and the match finished goalless. Cashmore has the distinction of scoring Cardiff's first League goal at Ninian Park, which came in a 3-0 win over Stockport on 4 September. City were then brought crashing back down to earth in the return match two days later, where they suffered their first-ever defeat in the Football League. However, the loss only served to galvanise the team, and they knuckled down to grind out an unbeaten run of eight games, during which time Gill scored six goals and attendance figures averaged 29,000. Their encouraging start to the season, and the support the club was getting from the Welsh public, persuaded the Board to fork out yet more cash to enable Stewart to sign Scottish international full-back Jimmy Blair from League rivals Wednesday for £3,500, at the time a record fee for a full-back. By Christmas, the Bluebirds had done the double over Wednesday and inflicted significant defeats on Blackpool, Bury and Coventry City, to force themselves into contention at the top of the table.

In the New Year a George Beare goal gave them a first round FA Cup win over Sunderland, and they continued to hold their own in the League programme. On 22 January 1921 they were again expected to fulfil two matches on the same day, and succeeded in beating Bristol City 1-0 at Ninian Park in the League before a colossal crowd of 43,000, but surrendered possession of the Welsh Cup by going down 3-1 away to minnows Pontypridd. That defeat didn't concern anyone too much, Cardiff had bigger things on their minds, especially after Cashmore put them into the third round of the much more attractive FA Cup at the expense of Brighton & Hove Albion.

Their next opponents in the competition were Southampton, on the south coast, who were duly despatched by a Gill goal on 19 February. In the next round they faced London giants Chelsea at Ninian Park before a crowd approaching 48,000, easily the biggest crowd the ground had ever catered for. An early Cashmore strike and 85 minutes-plus of resolute defending ensured that the Bluebirds progressed to the semi-final of the oldest and most revered football competition in the world for the first time in their history. Realising that the club was on the brink of something special, Stewart splashed the cash again to land forwards Harry Nash from Coventry and Fred Pagnam from Arsenal, the latter scoring on his home League debut in a 3-2 victory over Barnsley that took the Bluebirds soaring up to second place.

History was made on 19 March 1921 when King George V and Queen Mary watched the FA Cup semi-final against Wolverhampton Wanderers at Liverpool's Anfield (a neutral ground), the first time a reigning British monarch had attended a football match. However, both sides failed to rise to the occasion and the match ended goalless. The replay was at Old Trafford, Manchester, four days later where, by all accounts, City fell victim to some questionable refereeing decisions and bowed out of the competition. In total, almost 90,000 fans had attended the two games. For the record, Cardiff had their revenge on Wolves by completing a double over the Black Country boys in the last two games of the season that saw them claim runner-up spot behind Birmingham City. At the finish, City missed out on the top spot mathematically, on goal average, having finished level on points with the Midlanders. At the end of the day Birmingham's superior fire-power was the difference; they scored an awesome fifty-five goals in twenty-one home games compared to City's twenty-seven. Cardiff would have loved to have been crowned Second Division champions in their debut season in the Football League, but automatic promotion was the next best thing.

1921–22 season
The Bluebirds were then faced with the frightening prospect of First Division football after only one season of League experience. Stewart recruited shrewdly during the closed season, the only additions of note to the already large and seemingly well-equipped squad being Jimmy Nelson from

Belfast Crusaders and Frank Mason from Coventry. City got off to the worst possible start to life in the First Division, succumbing to six consecutive defeats. Their first match was against FA Cup holders and then-football superpower Tottenham Hotspur at Ninian Park on 27 August. They lost by a goal to nil in front of a crowd officially numbering 50,000, though an estimated further 10,000 forced entry into the ground, some of whom hijacked the scoreboard for use as a vantage point!

In the coming weeks Cardiff lost to Spurs again, and twice each to Aston Villa and Oldham Athletic, a sequence of results that rooted them to the foot of the table. The only high point was defender Bert Smith scoring their first-ever goal in the top division in a 2–1 defeat at Villa on 29 August. Yet another defeat was expected on 24 September, when League leaders Middlesbrough visited the Welsh capital, but the critics were confounded when Gill (2) and Nash conspired to give the Bluebirds a 3-1 win. Two weeks later the team notched their first away win in the First Division when a Gill brace put paid to a spirited challenge from Bolton Wanderers. October saw a flurry of transfer activity as Stewart paid £1,500 for Everton's skilful inside-forward Joe Clennell to compensate for the misfiring Fred Pagnam, who would soon be off-loaded to Watford. Arthur Cashmore and George Beare also found themselves surplus to requirements and were sold to Notts County and Bristol City respectively. The mercurial Len Davies was reinstated and immediately found the goal trail. City improved dramatically during the winter months to embark on a run of just one defeat in twenty-two League and Cup games. They had seemingly acclimatized to the higher standard of football and, after a questionable start, bridged the gap between Second and First Division football with apparent ease.

On 2 January 1922, 42-year-old trainer George Latham became the oldest League debutant in Cardiff's history after an overnight illness ravaged the team and he was called upon to play against Blackburn Rovers at Ewood Park. The record is unlikely ever to be bettered! Then, on 21 January, the Bluebirds met Bradford City at Ninian Park and triumphed 6-3 – this match is worthy of note because during the game Len Davies became the first Cardiff City player to score a Football League hat-trick.

In March, Spurs needed a replay to dump the Bluebirds out of the FA Cup at the fourth-round stage (the equivalent to a quarter-final berth), but City managed to maintain their good League form and carried it over into April when they also booked a place in the Welsh Cup final at the expense of Pontypridd. City's biggest defeat of the season came against eventual League champions Liverpool at Anfield, where they were hammered 5-1. However, they restored some pride a week later in the return fixture at Ninian Park by beating the Anfield outfit 2–0, with goals by Gill and Davies. Cardiff's last two games of the season were both against Manchester United; they earned a draw at Old Trafford on 29 April followed up with a handsome 3-1 victory at Ninian Park a week later. It is safe to assume that the Bluebirds played a significant role in relegating the Red Devils who, unthinkable as it may now seem, finished rock bottom of the League with a pitiful haul of twenty-eight points. Sandwiched between the two United games was the Welsh Cup final where City lifted the trophy again with a comfortable 2-0 win over Ton Pentre. In-form front men Davies and Gill were again on the scoresheet, putting paid to the Rhondda team's slim hopes of winning Wales' premier competition.

In their debut season amongst England's footballing elite, Cardiff gave a good account of themselves, finishing in a highly respectable fourth place below champions

Liverpool, runners-up Spurs, and a solitary point behind Burnley. Despite several large industrial strikes that blighted south Wales, the average attendance for League games at Ninian Park was around 33,000, compared to the League average of 28,000. Public interest in football was mushrooming across Wales partly because it offered an attractive way to spend the increased disposable income that years of wartime had brought. In the south alone there were twenty-three registered professional football clubs, five of which played in the Football League. The clubs had sprung up in most fair-sized towns, most notably in places like Aberdare and Merthyr Tudful. Post-war, attendances at professional matches were at an all-time high, and regularly exceeded those drawn by club Rugby Union, which was considered sub-standard by many critics as it lacked the structure and competitive edge of football. This explosion of interest was a national phenomenon that led to an expansion and split in the Third Division, which soon became Division Three (south) and Division Three (north) meaning that the total number of League clubs in England and Wales virtually doubled in the space of two years.

1922–23 season

As he had done before, for the start of the 1922–23 season Stewart opted to keep faith with the team that had performed so admirably the previous campaign and recruited only a handful of potential first-teamers from local Leagues as back up, the most notable of which being Jimmy Jones. City drew the first match at Spurs, and followed it up with an impressively one-sided 3-0 win over Villa with Joe Clennell (2) and Billy Grimshaw doing the damage, before losing a titanic battle 3-2 to Spurs in front of a seething crowd of 50,000-plus at Ninian Park. They recovered well after this defeat to beat both Villa (again) and Arsenal, but then self-destructed and lost six games on the bounce, conceding sixteen goals in the process.

Future dual-Irish international Tom Farquharson made his debut in goal for the Bluebirds on 14 October in a home defeat by Sunderland. Signed from Abertillery, Farquharson had fled to the valleys to escape the troubles in his native Ireland and rumour had it that he carried a handgun in his kitbag. The gloom surrounding Ninian Park didn't lift until the Bluebirds thrashed Liverpool, the reigning League champions, 3-0 on 28 October with goals from Grimshaw, McDonald and Clennell to end their barren run and send the 40,000 spectators into delirium. However, that was as good as things got for a while. After the Liverpool win City's form nose-dived and they didn't win again until December. Stewart moved to sign Fergus Aitken from Blackburn Rovers and George Reid from Walsall in an effort to turn things around, but City's form remained erratic. They badly needed to put a run together, and it was undoubtedly the re-emergence of crowd favourite Len Davies, who had suffered a dip in form after a promising start at Ninian Park, and had consequently lost his place in the team to the new signing Reid, that saved Cardiff that season. He came out of his shell to bang in sixteen goals in just twelve League and Cup games between 27 January and 14 March 1923, including hat-tricks in a 6-1 demolition of Chelsea at Ninian Park and a 10–0 rout of Owestry in a Welsh Cup tie. He also scored braces in successive 5-0 home wins over Blackburn and Newcastle United. During this remarkable run, Jimmy Gill also discovered the form of his life, notching eleven goals in eight League games as well as successive Welsh Cup hat tricks against Rhymney and poor Owestry.

In eleven home matches between Christmas and the end of the season, Cardiff remained unbeaten and conceded a miserly four goals. Unfortunately however, old adversaries

Spurs knocked them out of the FA Cup at the third round stage while Swansea awaited them in the semi-finals of the Welsh Cup. City powered to a dramatic 3-2 win and returned to the Vetch on 3 May to face Aberdare Athletic in the final, where goals from Grimshaw, Gill and Davies ensured that the Bluebirds retained the trophy. Ultimately, inconsistency cost them dear and they finished in ninth place in the League, while Liverpool retained their League title. As an indication of just how far the club had progressed, six Cardiff players were selected for international duty that season: Len Davies, Jack Evans and Fred Keenor turned out for Wales against Ireland, who had Bert Smith and Tom Farquharson in their side, while Jimmy Blair represented Scotland.

1923–24 season
City began the next season very much where they had left off, with new signings Harry Wake and Alfie Hagan from Newcastle United and Elvet Collins from Rhymney Town in tow. Bolton Wanderers opened the League program on 25 August at Ninian Park and were sent packing on the end of a 3-2 defeat. Two days later they entertained Sunderland, who were duly dispatched 2-1. It seemed to all that a Cardiff team that had promised so much in previous seasons but consistently failed to deliver was now ready to start doing the business. Len Davies kept up the momentum by handing the Bluebirds one-goal victories over West Ham and Newcastle as City embarked on a run that was tainted by just one defeat (away to Preston North End) in 22 matches. En route Davies set a new individual club scoring record when he netted all four goals in a 4-2 win at West Bromwich Albion on 10 November as City marched relentlessly to the top of the League, completing a League double over reigning champs Liverpool on the way.

To increase his options Stewart moved to sign winger Dennis Lawson from St Mirren, thus allowing Billy Grimshaw to leave for title hopefuls Sunderland. Grimshaw had been a consistent performer and a virtual ever-present for four years, and his loss disrupted the team more than anyone could have thought. Even so, it was not until the very last match of 1923 that City tasted defeat for the second time that season, a 2-1 reverse at Villa, in front of a Midlands crowd believed to be around 70,000. They lost to the Villains again less than a week later, before recovering their poise to register a League double over Arsenal. The Bluebirds also knocked the Gunners out of the FA Cup, the three games being played over three consecutive Saturdays.

In a unique situation on 16 February 1924, two Cardiff players captained their countries on the international stage against each other, ironically enough at Ninian Park, Keenor for Wales and Blair for Scotland. Keenor's men were the victors with a 2-0 victory that gave them the British Championship, a feat they achieved without dropping a single point making it the footballing equivalent of a Rugby Union Grand Slam. On the same day, a weakened City team drew their First Division match with Spurs 1-1 at White Heart Lane.

After the Arsenal games, the Bluebirds self-destructed again, succumbing to four League defeats on the bounce. The Cups were no picnic either; after seeing off Bristol City in round three of the FA Cup they went out at the next stage to Manchester City. A crowd of 76,166, saw the first game end goalless at Maine Road; Manchester's Welsh wizard, 50-year old Billy Meredith, set up the winner in the replay in Cardiff. The Bluebirds fared no better in the latter stages of the Welsh Cup after being drawn against neighbours Newport County. With neither side able to deliver a killer blow the tie extended to an unbelievable four matches, and ended with the Division Three (south) club inflicting a damaging 3-0 defeat on Stewart's men.

Despite the four League defeats, Cardiff were still in a good position to stake a claim for the title. However, when two games against Everton both ended goalless the pressure was on. City were faced with three home matches in a row in a straight race for the title. Bogey team Spurs were the first visitors, and went down 2-1. Next up were Burnley, who were beaten 2-0. Finally, it was the turn of their closest League rivals, Huddersfield Town, who held out stubbornly for yet another goalless draw. Those dropped points would prove vital.

Cardiff travelled to Burnley on 19 April, where Gill and Davies duly ensured a comfortable 2-0 victory. The results kept coming, until everything hinged on the very last game of the season at Birmingham on the 3 May. Unbelievably, City began the day as First Division leaders, with a point advantage over Herbert Chapman's Huddersfield. Simply put, the situation was that if the Bluebirds could win they would be crowned champions, but if they lost or drew, Huddersfield could claim the title with a 3-0 win. In a fraught, tension-filled match of epic proportions, City were handed a golden opportunity from the penalty spot just after the hour mark. Other senior players declined the invitation to take it so up stepped leading scorer Len Davies with his very first senior penalty kick ... and promptly missed. The match stayed goalless. Meanwhile, Huddersfield roared to the 3-0 win they needed to wrestle the title from City's grasp in the most heartbreaking fashion. They had scored four goals fewer than Cardiff, but, crucially, had conceded one less. At the final count, City lost out on goal average by just 0.024. No other club in history has missed out on a championship by such a small margin.

When *Athletic News* asked Stewart to explain his success

he said, 'We get players of decent ability, and each man does his best, with unity of feeling and purpose. The big point is that we are all such good friends – not only the players but the directors too.' Huddersfield went on to dominate the First Division for the rest of the decade, completing a unique treble of League titles in subsequent seasons. The penalty miss is said to have haunted Len Davies until his death from pneumonia in Liverpool some years later at the age of forty-five. Understandably concerned by his side's late-season collapse, Stewart announced his intention to rebuild by drafting in inside-forward Harold Beadles from Liverpool just before Cardiff departed on their first overseas tour to Czechoslovakia, Austria and Germany that May.

The summer of 1924 turned out to be one of the busiest the club has ever witnessed as the manager scrambled for signatures. £2,500 brought in Welsh international winger Willie Davies from Swansea, a trio of Irish imports arrived in Pat McIlvenny, Tommy Sloan and Jim McLean (who was deaf), and Joe Nicholson was signed from Orient. Alongside the recognised professionals came the customary handful of local amateurs, which this time included a young forward called Jack Nicholls, the son of a club director. There were also wider changes afoot in the game, as the offside law was revised, resulting in a glut of goals as defenders struggled to adjust to the new rules. Traditionally, British football clubs favoured what would now be called an attacking 2-3-5 formation, but this system proved far too vulnerable under the new ruling and prompted many clubs to adopt a third defender in place of an attacker.

1924–25 season

Cardiff's first two games of the season against Burnley and Sheffield United were both drawn, so they had to wait until 6 September when Leeds United visited the Welsh capital to register their first win, an emphatic 3-0 with goals by Davies (2) and Lawson. City then lost their next two, against Sheffield United and Birmingham, to set the pattern for the rest of the season. The average attendance at Ninian Park plummeted from over 30,000 to around 22,000 as the Bluebirds stuttered through the opening months. The fan-base that had held such high hopes was beginning to grow disillusioned; the team was caught out defensively far too often, and sections of the crowd began to lose patience with Stewarts's methods and ideology. Despite results not going their way and the team not playing anywhere near their best, Len Davies produced a string of dazzling one-man shows to score thirteen goals in twelve League games leading up to the New Year. City hovered around mid-table for much of the season, though positive results like the two draws against Huddersfield, the dominant force in the League, indicated to the frustrated masses that they were capable of much more.

By January 1925, the FA Cup represented a welcome distraction from the dour League programme for players and fans alike. Their first opponents, Darlington, eventual champions of the Third Division (north), put up a spirited fight but City eventually emerged victorious after two replays. Fulham were the visitors to Ninian Park in the next round, and in monsoon conditions City laboured to a narrow 1-0 win to set up a clash with League rivals Notts County at Meadow Lane. There, Gill and Nicholson did the damage to put City into the fourth round where they met Second Division champions-elect Leicester City at Ninian Park on 7 March. With the scores level at 1-1, a fervent crowd of over 50,000 erupted when Willie Davies scored at the Grangetown end direct from a corner with virtually the last kick of the match.

City returned to Meadow Lane to face Blackburn in the

semi-final, in what the press predicted would be a close contest. However, their theories were blown out of the water within 20 minutes as Nicholson, Gill and Beadles all scored to give the Bluebirds an unassailable lead (though Blackburn did manage a late consolation goal). What this meant was that Cardiff had made it to Wembley for the first time in their history. It was just as well, because by then City had been dumped out of the Welsh Cup by Swansea, their heaviest-ever defeat in the competition. With the fourth round of the FA Cup due to be played several days later, City had rested several key players for the Swansea game and were duly punished 4-0 by their arch-rivals and eventual Third Division (south) champions. At the time much was made in the local press about the Cardiff players not competing to the best of their ability, even, it was alleged, at times resorting to playing with a 'pompous swank' which angered Swansea's players and supporters.

The Vetch Field Welsh Cup storm-in-a-teacup paled into insignificance on 25 April 1925, as 92,000, the biggest crowd ever to watch a match involving Cardiff, packed into Wembley stadium, London, to see the 50th FA Cup final against Sheffield United. If reports are accurate it was a disappointing game with many City supporters begrudging the absence through injury of hotshot Len Davies. Their misery was complete when Tunstall scored to give the Blades a 1-0 win. In a carefully prepared post-match statement, a deflated Fred Keenor apologised to the supporters for his team's sorry performance and vowed a quick return to the twin towers of Wembley. It was not to be an empty promise.

Stewart recruited heavily again during the 1925 closed season. Tom Watson caught his eye during a pre-season tour of Ireland and was swiftly signed from Belfast Crusaders along with David (brother of Jimmy) Nelson, while Jack Jennings arrived from Wigan Borough, and Percy Richards from Merthyr Vale. Also, at boardroom level, 'Genial' Sid Nicholls took over the chair from Dr Nicholson.

1925–26 season

Unfortunately, it was not to be a good season for the Bluebirds, and the omens were bad from the outset when, in their very first match against Manchester City at Maine Road, Jimmy Nelson became the first Cardiff player to be sent off in the Football League. Even worse, the resultant penalty gifted the home team a 3-2 victory. This defeat heralded an awful sequence of thirteen games in which City won only three times. Decisive action was needed, and at the end of October Jimmy Gill was transferred to Blackpool for £3,200. After five years service, over 200 games for the club, and ninety-four goals, this represented a net profit of almost £2,500. The board immediately gave the nod for the money to be used to bring in inside-forward Joe Cassidy from Bolton Wanderers for a new club record of £3,800.

Despite perennially underachieving, City still had a squad bristling with international talent and a large and loyal fan-base, and were more than capable of beating anyone on their day. On Halloween 1925 they delivered a huge shock by beating Villa 2-0 at Villa Park. Then, at the beginning of November, the Bluebirds sent shock waves through the footballing world with a high-profile double-swoop, signing Motherwell's prolific striker Hughie Ferguson for £5,000 (eclipsing the transfer record they had set just a month earlier) and left-winger George McLachlan from Clyde for £2,000.

A crowd of almost 30,000 turned out on 7 November to see the Scottish duo's home debuts against League new-boys Leicester, and were treated to a 5-2 extravaganza. In true fairytale fashion, Cassidy scored a treble, while

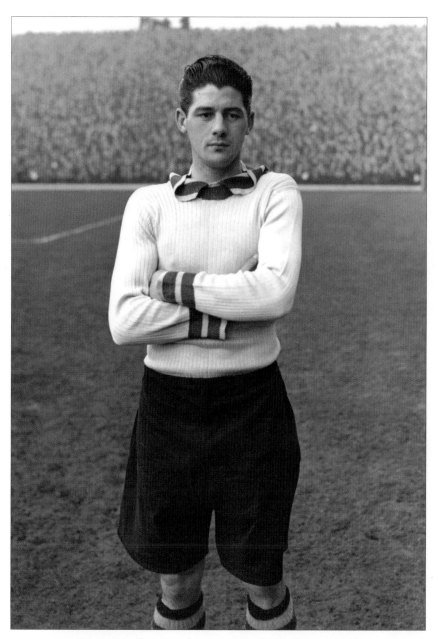

Trevor Ford pictured in his Aston Villa days, c.1947

Cardiff legends: Peter Thorne, Graham Kavanagh, Andy Legg

Lennie Lawrence and Sam Hammam

Cardiff's 1927 FA Cup-winning goal

'Gentle Giant' John Charles (player, 1963–66)

1927 FA Cup-winning team; captain Fred Keenor holding the cup

Cyril Spiers (manager 1939–46 and 1947–54)

Joe Ledley (player, 2004–10)

Michael Chopra and Jay Bothroyd

Dave Jones (manager, 2005–11)

Aaron Ramsey (player, 2006–08)

Inside the Cardiff City Stadium

Malky Mackay

Craig Bellamy

Promotion to the Premier League

Victory bus parade through the streets of Cardiff

Ferguson and crowd favourite Willie Davies also got onto the scoresheet. Later that month there was more upheaval, as both Harold Beadles and Irish international Pat McIlvenny were sold to Sheffield Wednesday, neither having made much of an impact in Wales. The team's performances improved dramatically over the crucial Christmas period, and they pulled away from the lower reaches of the League towards mid-table security with wins over Bolton, Notts County, Liverpool and West Brom. However, on New Year's Day 1926, City fell to their worst-ever League defeat when they were humiliated 11-2 by Sheffield United at Bramall Lane. The record still stands.

That season the FA Cup championship was revamped, with First and Second division clubs entering the competition in the third round, where Cardiff were drawn against fellow League strugglers Burnley. The first game failed to produce a winner, so City travelled to Burnley for a replay where a Ferguson double sealed it. The next round brought Newcastle and 42,000 fans (including a few thousand members of the Geordie Army) to Ninian Park, the biggest crowd of the season, who saw the Bluebirds tumble to a 2-0 defeat. In stark contrast, only 4000 fans were present in Merthyr Tydfil on 3 March to see the Martyrs dump the Bluebirds out of the Welsh Cup to provide the shock of the tournament.

In the aftermath of the Bramall Lane demolition, City seemed to pull together, and in nine League games played in February and March, lost only once. April began with a satisfying 1-0 win over Newcastle, with Ferguson scoring to avenge the FA Cup defeat. Successive home defeats by Sheffield United and Bolton then set up a crucial match at Notts County on 17 April, where Ferguson was the hero again with a hat-trick in a 4-2 victory that virtually condemned the home side to relegation. The season ended with a draw against Liverpool in Cardiff and away defeats at Manchester United and Burnley. During what can only be described as a troubled season, Stewart used no fewer than twenty-seven different players, a remarkable amount for the time, many of them taking on unfamiliar roles.

Attendances at Ninian Park were affected not just by the poor quality of football on show, but also by the 1926 General Strike, which saw the world coal market – 'Black Gold' to the Welsh – all but collapse. For the first time since they entered the Football League, Cardiff's 'goals against' column outweighed their 'goals for', yet unbelievably, at one stage City had a record sixteen internationals on their books: Harold Beadles, Len Davies, Willie Davies, Herbie Evans, Jack Evans, Fred Keenor, Jack Lewis, Jack Nicholls and Edgar Thomas all played for Wales; Jimmy Blair, Joe Cassidy, Dennis Lawson and Jimmy Nelson played for Scotland; Tom Farquharson, Pat McIlvenny and Tom Sloan represented Ireland.

At the end of the 1925–26 season one of these internationals, Jack Evans, Cardiff's first professional player, linked up with Joe Clennell at Bristol Rovers, having lost his place in the side to George McLachlan. For much of the preceding sixteen years he had been a virtual ever-present and would be greatly missed. Joe Nicholson departed in a swap-deal with Villa for their ex-England international George Blackburn, and one-time record signing Joe Cassidy was also shown the door after ill health restricted him to twenty-seven games that brought just seven goals. He was exchanged for utility player Sam Irving of Dundee, while local amateur Ernie Curtis was snapped up from Cardiff Corinthians, the famous amateur club. There were also significant changes at boardroom level, as Councillor W. H. Parker took over the chair from 'Genial' Sid Nicholls. Huddersfield completed their hat-trick of League titles and

Manchester City became the first club ever to reach a Cup final and be relegated in the same season.

1926–27 season

Again, on the pitch the team started the new season badly with a 4-3 reverse at Burnley. In their first nine games City registered a solitary win, a 3-1 victory over Leeds at Ninian Park. More misery was heaped upon the Bluebirds when Welsh international winger Willie Davies contracted pleurisy, an illness that was to keep him out of action for over a year. Starting on 23 October, City managed to string together three straight wins against Sunderland, Bury and Birmingham, but then, rather typically, lapsed to five defeats out of the next six games. After the club's disastrous start, Stewart decided to introduce yet more new faces. To make way he sold Scottish international fullback Jimmy Blair to Bournemouth. It was reported in the press that the south coast club paid £3,900 to secure his services: good business for a player then pushing thirty-eight!

After the reshuffle, the Bluebirds lost only one League game in ten, indicating a marked improvement in form. The run also coincided with the club's greatest-ever FA Cup campaign, beginning in January 1927 with rounds three and four, when they dispatched Villa and Darlington. Then, on 19 February, City faced high-flying Bolton before a Burnden Park crowd said to number around 50,000. A penalty from Ferguson and a late strike by Len Davies saw them through to a sixth round tie against Chelsea at Stamford Bridge where, despite the support of over 70,000, the affluent Londoners could not break City down and were forced into a replay. Back on familiar turf, goals from Sam Irving and Davies, plus a penalty from Ferguson, combined to give Cardiff a deserved 3-2 win over the Division Two title contenders. In the semi-final City faced another Division

Two team, Reading, at the neutral ground of Molineaux. Reading had already knocked out Swansea, but with confidence running high and a total of eight international players in the starting line-up, City were in no mood to take prisoners. A brace from Ferguson and a flying header from defender Harry Wake gave them an easy 3-0 win. Stewart had raided the transfer market yet again to land flying winger Billy Thirlaway from Birmingham, thus allowing Ferguson, who had been filling in on the right, to reclaim his rightful berth up front. He responded by averaging a goal a game over the next twelve matches en route to their second Wembley FA Cup final appearance in three years.

Shortly before the big day, the players adopted a lucky mascot, a black cat called Trixie. She was found by the players on the Royal Birkdale golf course in Southport, where Hughie Ferguson tracked down her owner and offered a Cup final ticket as compensation, an offer that was readily accepted. Trixie became the club's official mascot for the next twelve years, travelling to away games in her own wicker basket and becoming something of a feline media celebrity in her own right.

The greatest day in Cardiff's long and chequered history remains 23 April 1927, when they met Arsenal at Wembley Stadium in their second FA Cup final appearance in three years. Their north London opponents were also having an indifferent League season under manager Herbert Chapman, and were experimenting with different players and formations at the time. The untidy match remained goalless until the 75th minute, when McLachlan passed to Ferguson and the Scot tried his luck from the edge of the penalty area. Arsenal's Welsh international goalkeeper Dan Lewis stooped to gather the ball, was confronted with City's on-rushing forward line, and inadvertently nudged the ball over the line with his elbow for the only goal of the game.

The large Welsh contingent in the near-92,000 Wembley crowd, along with the whole of Wales (and probably large areas of Scotland) erupted. The goal was credited to Hughie Ferguson, and rightly so, but much has been written about it since. Perhaps unfairly, Dan Lewis's allegiances were called into question, while other observers campaigned for the Maerdy-born goalkeeper to be credited with an own goal as he was the last player to touch the ball. (If this logic were to be implemented, how many 'own goals' would have to be attributed to goalkeepers in any given season who manage to get a flailing hand to a ball just before it crosses the line?) The man himself blamed himself, saying that the wet wool made the ball too difficult to grip. Arsenal club folklore maintains that to this day no Arsenal goalkeeper has played in a jersey before it had been washed first. At worst it was a goalkeeping error, one of a thousand that plagues any club. The fact remains that as a result of the admittedly lucky goal, City captain Fred Keenor greedily accepted the FA Cup from King George V. On their glorious return to Cardiff over 100,000 ecstatic fans lined the main streets.

The players and directors made straight for City Hall, where they stood on the balcony to milk the rapturous applause. Trixie the cat, lovingly held by Ferguson and adorned in blue and white ribbons, lapped up the occasion. Only seven years after joining the Football League, Cardiff had defied the critics and won arguably the biggest prize in British sport, making history in the process by becoming the first and only club to date to take the FA Cup out of England.

It was also the very first match to benefit from live radio commentary, which supporters followed with the help of a numbered grid published in an early issue of the *Radio Times*. (This is where the phrase 'back to square one' is said to have originated.) Afterwards, Swansea-based newspaper

Sporting News announced 'The Cup comes to Wales' and went on to suggest that during the match, Cardiff had represented the whole of Wales in a titanic struggle against an old foe (England). The importance of the win, not just to City supporters but to the Welsh public as a whole, was immense, despite there being only three Welshmen in that historic team along with three Scots, four Irishmen and a lone Englishman.

> To the people (of Wales) it was more than a struggle between two teams; it was a struggle between two nations. This may not be exactly logical but sentiment transcends logic. So this years Cup Final will remain in consideration a Welsh victory.
>
> *South Wales News,* 25 April 1927
>
> From Wales the men and women went up to London in legions. All through the Friday night and the early hours of Saturday morning the streets of London were musical with Welsh hymns and songs. The leek and the daffodil were almost as abundant as the City's colours. It was not merely a Cardiff City occasion. It was an all-Wales occasion.
>
> *Western Mail,* 25 April 1927

Elsewhere, other reports in the Welsh press claimed that callous street-traders in London's Covent Garden trebled the price of their leeks that weekend to cash in on the Celtic invasion. Speaking about the match in a later match-day programme, goalscorer Hughie Ferguson admitted, 'We were not a great side, but we were bubbling over with determination'. The match also proved a welcome financial windfall as City netted a then-record £23,113 in gate receipts alone.

Cardiff were also in determined mood in that season's Welsh Cup, opening their account with a 0-0 away draw against holders Ebbw Vale but thrashing them 6-1 in the replay. Barry were the visitors to Ninian Park for round six, and were duly despatched to set up a mouth-watering semi-final at Wrexham. There, a Len Davies double saw off the Robins, and Cardiff progressed to meet Rhyl in the final (also at Wrexham's Racecourse Ground) on 5 May. There, goals from Len Davies and Irving ensured that Cardiff completed a unique double in being the first club to win both the English and Welsh Cups in the same season. They are likely to hold this distinction for ever! Their success would have done much to lift the gloom then settling on Wales, caused mainly by the all-encompassing General Strike and record levels of unemployment. Attendances at Ninian Park had plummeted to around 14,000, reaching new depths of 8,000 for the anti-climatic visits of West Ham and Derby. Some valley supporters had even resorted to walking to games in order to save money. In a time of such economic instability, the club decided to invest most of their FA Cup final (and Welsh Cup) earnings in ground improvements, rather than on players. The most beneficial change, for the supporters at least, was the construction of a cover over the Grangetown End of Ninian Park. At boardroom level, Mr Watkin J. Williams was appointed chairman.

1927–28 season
The controversial decision not to supplement the playing staff initially appeared to be the correct one, as the 1927-28 season brought City's best League start in years. Goals from Len Davies and George McLachlan saw off Bolton

Wanderers in the opening game on 27 August, before City fought out four battling draws. Then came back-to-back wins against Birmingham at St Andrews and Newcastle at Ninian Park. Things were going well, the club was still riding the crest of a wave after the Wembley triumph, but the euphoria was short-lived. On 1 October they played Huddersfield, and were annihilated 8-2 by the Yorkshire giants. To City's credit, they bounced back to win their next game against Spurs at Ninian Park and snatch a draw at Old Trafford.

On 12 October 1927, Cardiff City became the first non-English club to win the Charity Shield (and the last to date). It was contested not against the reigning League champions, as it is nowadays (which would have been Newcastle), but against the amateur side Corinthians at Chelsea's Stamford Bridge. The professional club was fully expected to win, and did, by the score 2-1 with Ferguson and Len Davies on target. But the fired-up amateurs, loaded with guests and representative players, made it a difficult game. City then settled into a reasonably consistent run of form, and remained in the top ten of the First Division for the entire campaign, mainly on the strength of their awesome form at Ninian Park.

On 14 January 1928, the Bluebirds began their defence of the FA Cup in the third round against Southampton at Ninian Park. The deadly duo of Ferguson and Len Davies ensured a 2-1 victory to set up another home tie in round four, this time against Liverpool. City came from behind against a spirited Anfield outfit to register another 2-1 win, thus setting up a tie at Nottingham Forest on 18 February. There, City's defence of the oldest and most coveted prize in football came to an end in a blaze of controversy, as half the spectators present vigorously disputed that the ball had crossed the line for Forest's winner. If Lady Luck had been smiling on City when Dan Lewis had allowed the ball to squirm out of his grasp ten months earlier, she turned her back on them that day.

The Bluebirds began their defence of the Welsh Cup with a 7-1 demolition of Owestry in the fifth round, then eased past Swansea and Rhyl to set up a final appointment with Bangor City. There, in the heart of north Wales, Ferguson was the match-winner once more as City ran out 2-0 winners to retain at least one of their trophies.

City recovered from their FA Cup exit by demolishing Huddersfield 4-0 at Ninian Park, atoning for the 8-2 defeat inflicted by the Yorkshiremen earlier in the season. They also won their next two games against Birmingham and Manchester United, but lost the next two at Portsmouth and Spurs. Then they beat Leicester at Ninian Park and Liverpool at Anfield before succumbing to two heavy defeats in quick succession, 5-1 to West Ham and 7-1 to Derby. The twin setbacks all but ended Cardiff's title charge, so Stewart took the opportunity to indulge in some rebuilding. Sam Irving was sold to Chelsea, Ernie Curtis left for Birmingham, and fit-again Willie Davies went to Notts County. To replace them, Stewart signed defender Bill Roberts from Flint Town and Frank Harris from Bromsgrove Rovers. Because of the questionable quality of the players coming in, this particular bout of wheeling and dealing was interpreted by many as a step backwards.

Despite conceding an average of almost two goals per game, Cardiff finished in respectable sixth spot, while Everton were crowned champions, and Huddersfield were runners-up for the second year running. The noticeable improvement in City's home form bumped up their average home attendance to around 20,000, which went some way to offsetting the losses incurred by the recession that was sweeping the country. Money was scarce, and consequently

Stewart was restricted to a bare minimum of new signings that summer. Only Welsh international inside-forward Stan Davies arrived from Birmingham and Leslie Jones, a promising amateur, was poached from Aberdare. On a historical note, it was also the season in which numbered shirts were introduced, mainly for the benefit of confused radio commentators and sports journalists.

1928–29 season

For one that was to end in such excruciating agony, the next season started encouragingly enough with old warhorse Ferguson salvaging a point from their first game away at Newcastle on 25 August. A week later the Scottish legend fired a club record-breaking five goals against a hapless Burnley side in a 7-0 romp at Ninian Park, the huge 25,000 crowd (swelled by the unveiling of the new Grangetown Stand) being treated to the Bluebirds' biggest-ever win in the First Division, a record that still stands. Over the next five matches City beat West Ham and Bury at home, but lost away trips to Derby and Sheffield United, while another Ferguson goal rescued a point at West Ham. But it was all downhill from there. In a 14-game run stretching from October until Boxing Day, Cardiff's only win came at Portsmouth on 8 December, a collapse that left them firmly entrenched in the relegation mire. Unfortunately, the Fratton Park win would be City's last on English soil in the top division for a very long time, and to make matters worse, the injuries were mounting up. Star striker Ferguson, along with Tom Watson, Jimmy Nelson and Tom Sloan, were sidelined for long spells, and an unhappy Stan Davies left the club after only fourteen games to take up a player/manager position at Rotherham United. On Boxing Day City managed a home win over Leeds, and followed it up with a barnstorming win over Newcastle, with winger Billy Thirlaway scoring in both games. But while their home form was improving, their away form continued to deteriorate as they narrowly lost at Bolton and were then humbled 3-0 by a resurgent Burnley, the team they had trounced 7-0 just a few short months earlier.

The situation was now critical, and on 12 January 1929 City suffered the indignation of their heaviest FA Cup defeat to date, going down 6-1 at Villa in a third round tie. Cardiff's goal was scored by Billy Hardy, a quality player who was constantly overlooked by the English FA selectors, allegedly because he played for a Welsh club. It was his only FA Cup goal. Coincidentally, the referee that day was Mr W. F. Bunnell, the same man who had officiated during the Bluebird's finest hour at Wembley. The only competition in which City enjoyed any success that year was the Welsh Cup, where early wins over Lovell's Athletic and Newport County pitted them against Rhyl at the semi-final stage for the second successive year. Goals from George Blackburn and Len Davies steered them to a 2-1 victory and a final appearance against Connah's Quay Nomads. The Bluebirds were heavy favourites to lift the Cup once more, but the underdogs heaped yet more misery on them by winning 3-0 to provide one of the biggest shocks the much-maligned tournament ever produced.

Between a win over Derby County on 19 January and the end of the season, City managed just one more victory, ironically (and frustratingly) against eventual League champions Sheffield Wednesday. They finished the season rock bottom of the League and were relegated for the first time in their history. It was scant consolation that the club boasted the best defensive record in the division, but tellingly, had managed only nine goals on their travels and failed to score altogether in seventeen of their matches. City's last game in their first stint in the top flight was a 1-1 draw against Blackburn on the 4 May, with Frank Harris scoring the goal. They had won only eleven matches all season, eight in the League, statistics that led to justifiable criticism of Stewart's tactics and team selection. In hindsight, it was probably the club's decision to invest in ground improvements rather than new players after their 1927 Wembley triumph, coupled with an erratic economy and fluctuating gates, that led to their demotion. Sheffield Wednesday won the title that season, while Bury joined City in the trauma of relegation.

July 1929 saw the very first World Cup tournament, a relatively low-key affair held in Uruguay contested by thirteen countries. Having left FIFA, all British countries were ineligible, and in their absence the host nation overcame deadly rivals Argentina 4-2 in the final.

Also that summer, Hughie Ferguson, perennial crowd favourite, scorer of that goal at Wembley two years earlier, and Cardiff's top scorer for the past four seasons, left the club to return to Scotland with Dundee. He had amassed a total of ninety-one goals in 138 appearances for Cardiff in all competitions. However, what should have been a happy homecoming was to have tragic repercussions sixteen months later when the very sad news came through that the legendary goalscorer had gassed himself to death after a training session at Dens Park. Since returning to Scotland he had struggled with injuries and loss of form; sections of the Dundee supporters had turned on him, and he consequently suffered from bouts of depression. He died on 9 January 1931 at just thirty-one, leaving behind a wife and two young children.

4

How the Mighty Fall
(1929–45)

On their return to the Second Division after eight bittersweet years in the top flight, Cardiff City faced Charlton Athletic in London, and went down 4-1. Again, Fred Stewart relied heavily on the old guard, but promising young talent was pushing through in the form of Walter Robbins, a forward who had been signed from Ely United the previous season. He was held in especially high regard, and cemented his growing reputation by scoring the goal against Charlton, and both goals in the 2-0 victory against Preston North End that gave the Bluebirds their first win of the season. Hull City temporarily managed to clip the Bluebirds' wings by winning at Ninian Park on 7 September, but that proved be their only home defeat before Christmas, and one of only three all season. While notching up notable victories over Notts County, Barnsley, West Bromwich Albion, Southampton, Oldham Athletic and Chelsea in Cardiff, and holding a host of others (including Swansea Town, in the great rivals' first-ever League encounter on 5 October) City struggled on their travels, losing badly at Blackpool, Nottingham Forest and Bury.

Mid season, with gates dwindling and an instant return to the First Division looking increasingly unlikely, the Cardiff board sanctioned a mass clear-out. George McLachlan was sold to Manchester United after making 154 appearances for City, and fringe players Freddie Warren, Jack Jennings and Joe Hillier all moved to Middlesbrough in an unprecedented triple deal reportedly worth a cool £8,000. Stewart immediately invested a small amount of the cash in an untried 24-year-old scoring sensation from Colwyn Bay called Ralph Williams.

On 11 January 1930, over 50,000 spectators attended Cardiff's FA Cup third round tie with Liverpool at Anfield, where Len Davies turned out to be the hero of the day, scoring twice in a famous 2-1 win. Two weeks later City travelled north to Sunderland, also of the First Division, and despite Davies scoring again, the Black Cats proved too strong and won the match 2-1. City fared better in the Welsh Cup, seeing off Llanelli in round five before exacting full revenge on Swansea for two League shut-outs by thrashing them 4-0. The Bluebirds went on to beat Wrexham 2-0 in the semi to reach a fourth successive final. Interestingly, the game against Rhyl resulted in a stalemate and the FAW made the strange decision to hold the replay over until an undecided time the following season.

City made a mockery of their poor League form by tearing apart eventual League champions Blackpool at Ninian Park on 15 February. Ralph Williams scored his first goal for the club, which was complimented by further strikes from Davies, Frank Harris and George Blackburn (his only goal in 119 appearances) as the Bluebirds ran out 4-2 winners. This kicked off a sequence of seven League games unbeaten, during which time Williams notched an impressive eight goals. But as the season ground to a halt, so did Cardiff. They failed to score in three of their last five outings, but managed to defy their many critics yet again by blasting five (including a Williams hat-trick) past Bury in the last game. The Welsh public was responding to relegation, and average attendances at Ninian Park dropped to around 12,000. On their return to the Second Division, City finished in eighth place, while bitter rivals Swansea languished in fifteenth. With both clubs now playing at roughly the same level and drawing huge crowds every time they met, there was talk of an annual Cup to be contested exclusively between the two sides, but the plan never came to fruition partly because of growing distrust amongst the respective sets of fans.

1930–1931 season

During the closed season City sold Jimmy Nelson to Newcastle for £2,000, where he went on to captain their 1932 FA Cup-winning side, and Billy Thirlaway left for Tunbridge Wells. The only signings of note were winger George Emmerson from Middlesbrough and Eddie J. J. Jenkins, a local boy who joined from Cardiff East. So it was an ageing and weakened Cardiff team that kicked off the season at the Vetch Field against Swansea Town on 30 August, and although Ralph Williams netted twice, it wasn't enough to prevent the Bluebirds slipping to defeat. The result had a demoralising effect on the team and they went on to lose their next four games, having to wait until 22 September for their first win, a 4-1 over Plymouth Argyle at Ninian Park. Tellingly, the match was witnessed by just 6,615 fans. On 8 October City contested the Welsh Cup Final replay against Rhyl that had been held over from the previous season, and Len Davies delighted the pundits by adding to his phenomenal scoring record in the competition with a hat-trick in a convincing 4-2 victory. By this time Billy Hardy, in his twentieth season at the club, had been appointed player/coach and ex-Scottish international full-back Jock Smith had been drafted in from Middlesbrough.

City managed to improve their League position by beating Barnsley, Southampton, Reading and Burnley before Christmas, but again there were problems on the road as the once solid defensive line developed an alarming habit of conceding goals. On 6 December they drew 4-4 with Millwall at Ninian Park, then lost their next game a week later at Preston 7-0. On Boxing Day they lost 5-1 at Plymouth but regained some respect by securing their first-ever League win over Swansea the very next day at Ninian Park, in front of their biggest crowd of the season.

In the New Year the sad news from Scotland of Hughie Ferguson's suicide left many in south Wales distraught. City remained rooted to the bottom of the Second Division, and they also tumbled out of the FA Cup at the hands of Third Division (south) Brentford. With the season heading towards catastrophe, Stewart tried desperately to turn things around by securing the services of Irish international forward Jim McCambridge from Everton, inside-forward Albert Keating from Blackburn, and defender Jack Galbraith from Clapton Orient, amongst others, many of whom made only a handful of appearances before moving on. These were unsettled times in the Welsh capital, and even the national Cup, so often Cardiff's saving grace, failed to offer any reprieve. After thrashing Barry Town 7-3 in round five and edging out Chester, they bowed out to non-League Shrewsbury Town in the semi-final. (The FAW had decided to open up the Welsh Cup to English 'border' clubs in an ill-advised effort to raise the profile and overall quality of the competition. The move would prove nothing short of disastrous, as the Cup left Wales no fewer than seven times during the 1930s alone.)

After their humiliating FA Cup exit, the Cardiff players managed to pick themselves up off the floor to beat Port Vale at Ninian Park on 17 January, but amazingly somehow managed to complete the rest of the League program, seventeen games in total, with only one more victory, which came against Stoke City. In those seventeen games City failed to score in twelve, finishing rock bottom of the Second Division. They were relegated to Division Three (south) well before the season ended. Alarmingly, the average attendance at Ninian Park dropped below 10,000 for the first time in two decades and a public plea from the directors for more support brought a barrage of complaints, the general consensus being that the crowds would return when the quality of football at Ninian Park improved. That season Cardiff had only two full internationals on their books: Welshmen Fred Keenor and Walter Robbins, a far cry from six years earlier when they boasted sixteen.

In the aftermath of their second relegation in three years, one of the club's greatest-ever servants, 36-year old Fred Keenor, left for Crewe Alexandra of the Third Division (north). He had made a total of 504 appearances for the club since joining in 1911, and had represented Wales thirty-one times. He eventually returned to his beloved home city in 1958 to work as a storekeeper for a building firm, staying there until his death in 1972 at the age of seventy-eight. Another great ambassador for the club, Len Davies, also left to join Thames F.C. He remains City's all-time record goal scorer, with 178 goals from 369 matches in all competitions.

1930–1932 season
To fill the gaps, Stewart brought in a cast of virtual unknowns, but obviously not of the required calibre to stop City's horrifying descent down the Leagues. They lost their first-ever match in the Third Division (south) away at Northampton on 29 August 1931, but earned a point from their next fixture against Brighton & Hove Albion at Ninian Park, to instil some much-needed confidence in an ailing team. They then romped to a 5-1 win over Reading, with Robbins scoring a hat trick and Les Jones and Jim McCambridge also on target, before slumping to another defeat at Coventry City. Cardiff then pulled together to win

three of their next five games (the highlight being a 6-1 revenge job on Coventry) before disaster struck – or, more accurately, a whole series of disasters that saw the Bluebirds win only once in their next ten League outings.

Apart from smaller gates and less attractive fixtures, another disadvantage of playing in the lower divisions was that Cardiff now had to contest the FA Cup from the very first round, where they met non-Leaguers Enfield at Ninian Park. To the delight of the disheartened City faithful, the team ran up a club record FA Cup score of 8-0, with Albert Keating becoming the first City player to score a hat-trick in the competition. They carried their form into the second round where they faced League rivals Orient, also at Ninian Park, a match they won 4-0 to set up a difficult trip to Bradford Park Avenue of Division Two. And there their short Cup run came to an end. It was a disappointing show, but not quite as disappointing as the Welsh Cup, in which City went out to Chester of Division Three (north) after notching up just one win in the competition at Llanelli.

A Boxing Day fixture against Luton Town heralded a sequence of three consecutive home wins, but the Bluebirds then succumbed to three straight defeats to drop to lowly nineteenth place. On 6 February 1932 struggling London outfit Thames FC, who dropped out of existence altogether later that year, visited Ninian Park and self-destructed to allow City to register their biggest-ever League win. In a 9-2 annihilation, Robbins scored five times, with the other goals coming from Les Jones, McCambridge, Emmerson and Keating. Poignantly, Len Davies scored for the visitors on what was to be his swansong at Ninian Park. From then until the end of the season City lost only twice, thereby achieving mid-table mediocrity. In the seven matches played between 26 March and 23 April, McCambridge hit an amazing twelve goals including hat-tricks against QPR and Orient.

Just before the end of the season, Walter Robbins was sold to West Brom in a club record-breaking deal reputedly worth over £10,000. The move angered some fans, who questioned the club's ambition and reasons for selling such a vital player. In a surreal season of broken dreams, shattered records and hopeless frustration, the Bluebirds' final tally of eighty-seven goals was their highest yet, but with a threadbare squad and their financial affairs in disarray, the club was resigned to a prolonged stay in the lower divisions.

1932–33 season

In the summer of 1932 Billy Hardy left after a wonderful twenty-one years' service, during which he made a total of 582 appearances. He took up a coaching position at Bradford Park Avenue. Coach George Latham, who had originally signed for the club on St David's Day 1911, also left, to take a staff job at Chester, and Stewart and his players agreed to accept considerable pay cuts to help the club avert a looming financial crisis. With limited funds at his disposal, despite numerous ill-fated fund-raising schemes, Stewart spent shrewdly that summer, with QPR duo Stanley Cribb and Robert Pollard being the only notable additions to the squad, along with a promising youngster called Freddie Hill. All three played in an opening day defeat at Reading on 27 August, but convincing wins over Bournemouth and Norwich City indicated that a better season was in prospect. However, those fragile hopes were obliterated every time the club played outside the Welsh capital; they went an entire season without claiming a single away League victory. This shameful run included such horror shows as an 8-1 humiliation by Luton Town, a 6-2 defeat at Swindon Town, and a 5-0 hiding at Coventry.

Despite all the away-day horror shows, there were several highlights at Ninian Park, including a 2-1 win over eventual

League champions Brentford and a 6-1 drubbing of Orient. By then, Stewart had rung the changes once more, selling Albert Keating to Bristol City for a profit after the bustling forward had scored twenty-six goals in forty-eight games. George Russell was brought in from Bristol Rovers to add some fresh blood to a faltering side, and the questionable decision was made to invest in two new strikers, Jim Henderson from St Bernards' (Edinburgh) and Tom Maidment from Workington. Many supporters were of the opinion that the money would have been better invested in resolving the team's defensive frailties, rather than bolstering an already capable attack .

Having already been dumped out of the FA Cup in the very first round by Bristol Rovers, City's involvement in the Welsh Cup began on 22 February 1933, with a home tie against Tranmere Rovers of the Third Division (north), where Les Jones and new signing, Henderson, each netted twice in a 4-2 win. The next round saw them visiting arch-rivals Swansea, where a Maidment strike forced a replay. There, Maidment was on target again as well as Jones, to record a morale-boosting 2-1 victory. For the semi-final, City travelled to Chester, and promptly lost 2-1 just as they had the season before. More bad news followed when, to help balance the books, top scorer Jim McCambridge was sold to Bristol Rovers after scoring fifty-three times in a century of League and FA Cup appearances.

On April Fool's Day, Jim Henderson, McCambridge's replacement, endeared himself to the Cardiff faithful by scoring a hat-trick at Brentford. Sadly, however, the joke was on them as the Bluebirds went down 7-3. Just three weeks later Henderson excelled himself by scoring a club record-equalling five goals against Northampton at Ninian Park in a match that ended 6-0. City finished the season in typically erratic fashion by losing 3-0 at Orient on 29 April then beating Swindon by the same score at home a week later to end their second season in Division Three (south) in a vastly disappointing nineteenth place, bizarrely, two places above neighbours Newport who had completed a League double over them. The low finish was mainly due to a slow and disorganised defence that shipped a mammoth total of 99 League goals. By the end of the season, City's average home gate had plunged to below 6,000 (compared to the divisional average of around 7,500), their lowest ever.

No sooner had the season ended than Fred Stewart resigned from the post of club secretary/manager, which he had occupied for twenty-two years. In that time he had been instrumental in securing League football in the Welsh capital, gaining promotion to the First Division, reaching the FA Cup final twice and winning it once, before being subjected to an agonising descent down the League ladder. He died on 11 February 1954 aged eighty-one, and remains to this day the most successful manager in Cardiff's history. With Stewart sadly out of the picture, club founder and assistant secretary Walter Bartley-Wilson took temporary charge of team affairs at the ripe old age of sixty-three. It was a labour of love for the old Bristolian and he, along with coach Jimmy Blair, spent the summer of 1933 scouring the country looking for fresh affordable talent. However, in an era of rising transfer fees, falling attendances and spiralling costs, encouraging new players to sign for a club on the slide wasn't an easy task. Sheer desperation led to what would later prove a critical managerial error when George Emmerson was exchanged for QPR's Ted Marcroft. The highly-rated and popular winger had made 127 appearances for the Bluebirds, scoring nineteen times. Other new arrivals included Eli Postin from Dudley Town, defender Bob Calder from Glasgow Rangers and Alex Hutchinson from Blackpool.

New man Hutchinson scored twice from the left wing in City's first game of the season at Watford to hand them a 2-1 win. They followed it up just two days later with a 2-0 home win over Reading, thanks to a brace from Henderson, and when Postin earned a creditable draw against Charlton at Ninian Park it meant that City were off to their best League start in a decade. Big things were expected; on the surface it seemed as if the club had finally stabilise. But at that stage little did anyone suspect that it would turn out to be Cardiff's worst-ever season. Over the next six games City held their own, winning three and losing three. But then they self-destructed, managing to pick up a pitiful total of two points from the next eleven matches, taking them up to 30 December when they beat Watford at Ninian Park. This disastrous run left them rooted to the bottom of the League and fighting for survival. The playing staff at Ninian Park was constantly changing, making a mockery of the consistency and stability on which the club had been founded. New arrivals now included Reg Keating (brother of Albert) who signed from Bath City, and Enoch Mort, who came from Gilfach Coch. Ex-Bluebird Ernie Curtis also returned from Birmingham, where he had spent the past six years.

On New Year's Day 1934, playing Aldershot in the very first round, City were knocked out of the Third Division (south) Cup, a new competition. Within weeks the club was forced into the sale of their prized asset, Les Jones, who moved to Coventry for a knock-down price of £1,000. The future Welsh international had scored thirty-two goals in 149 games. After being unceremoniously dumped from the FA Cup, again by League rivals Aldershot, City were also knocked out of the Welsh Cup by Bristol City after a replay at Ashton Gate leaving their season in tatters. Unable to settle into his new job and with the team faltering badly, an emotional Bartley-Wilson resigned during a meeting at Cardiff's Grand Hotel. With the club in free-fall, Ben Watts-Jones, a former Swansea chairman and committee member of the FAW, was brought in as a last resort to turn things around. He officially signed on 7 March, sparking fury amongst the Swansea supporters who, despite their team playing in a different division, were loath to lose one of their key men to their arch-enemies and local rivals.

Despite Watts-Jones' impeccable credentials, the team still struggled and won just one game after he took over, a 3-1 at Aldershot on 21 April in which Reg Keating blasted a hat-trick. Revenge can be a big motivating factor in football, and it had been Aldershot who had knocked City out of two potentially lucrative Cup competitions that season. However, Cardiff failed to capitalise on the win, losing the return match at Ninian Park four days later before a sparse crowd of only 2,500, and finished rock bottom of the League with an embarrassing return of twenty-four points from forty-two matches. Consequently, the club faced the indignity of having to be re-elected to the League for the first time in their history. Had re-election been refused, City may well have slipped out of existence altogether, but thankfully the club was re-elected with the minimum of fuss and immediately charged with the considerable task of recapturing former glories. It had been just seven years since they were joint FA and Welsh Cup holders and firmly amongst the First Division title-chasers, suggesting that somebody somewhere in a blue jersey must have broken a mirror during the mass celebrations of 1927 and got seven years' bad luck as punishment!

New secretary/manager Watts-Jones made sweeping changes in the summer of 1934, releasing all but five of Cardiff's registered players and bringing in new faces that he hoped would revitalise the club. Of the new arrivals, the most notable were left-back Jack Everest from Blackpool, Arthur Granville from Porth United, Wally Jennings from Cheltenham Town, Billy Bassett who hailed from Brithdir, Harry Riley and Eddie Lane from Notts County, and ex-Welsh internationals Fred Whitlow from Exeter City, Phil Griffiths from West Brom, and Wilf Lewis from Bath City. Among those leaving were Eli Postin, who moved to Bristol City, Tom Maidment, who went to Blyth Spartans, and Ernie Curtis who, after a bitter pay dispute, was eventually quite literally sent to Coventry. By this time, City were also looking to the future, having taken the unprecedented step of agreeing to pay Ebbw Vale FC the sum of £5 a week to act as a nursery club. Elsewhere, the second World Cup was again won by the host nation, this time Italy, who ensured that Europe staked its claim in a global footballing arena by beating Czechoslovakia in the final. Again there were no British representatives.

1934–35 season
The 'new' Cardiff team that kicked off the season at home to Charlton on 25 August was virtually unrecognisable from the one that had performed so badly the previous year. Only goalkeeper Tom Farquharson, John Gilbraith, and star striker Reg Keating had ever played for the club before, in a team that included an unparalleled eight debutants. Keating scored, along with new-man Riley, to give City a morale-boosting 2-1 victory before a rapturous crowd of 18,000. Even more fans turned up for the second home game against Luton, and saw Phil Griffiths open his account for his new club in a dramatic 1-0 win. The Bluebirds were beginning to fly, but were brought crashing back down to earth with two heavy away defeats to Crystal Palace (6-1) and Luton (4-0). Watts-Jones struggled to find a settled team, and they suffered on the pitch while the comings and goings

continued relentlessly. In October a fledgling 17-year-old right-winger called Reggie Pugh came to the club's attention whilst playing for Aberaman. Days later he was signed in time to make his debut away against Watford in an outstanding 3-1 win. He went on to make a remarkable ninety-seven consecutive appearances in Cardiff's first eleven, scoring his first goal in a 2-2 draw at Millwall on 17 November.

Barely a week later, City's stint in the FA Cup came to a premature end as Reading won their first round tie 2-1 at Ninian Park. City were already out of the Third Division (south) Cup, having lost to Crystal Palace, but started their Welsh Cup campaign encouragingly with a 3-2 win over Newport County. In the subsequent round they held Chester to a draw before losing the replay 3-0 to bow out of the competition. Having been dumped out of all the Cups, after the Watford win Cardiff began to struggle badly in the League. They claimed only one win from their next ten games until a satisfying 2-0 over Coventry at Ninian Park on 5 January 1935. Many thought the club had finally turned the corner with this win, but it was to be another two months before they picked up maximum League points again. However, City did finish strongly with three impressive wins from their last six matches, the best of which being a 5-0 demolition of Exeter at Ninian Park where Keating scored four times. The final game, a 4-0 reverse at Bristol City on the 4 May, was loyal Irishman Farquharson's last for Cardiff, having made 519 appearances between the sticks in fourteen years. On his retirement, he returned to his former trade as a painter and decorator and ran a tobacconist's shop in Cardiff's Queen Street before emigrating to join his children in Canada.

Although it represented a definite improvement on recent seasons, the Bluebirds eventually finished in disappointing nineteenth position while Charlton, the team they beat on the opening day, went on to win the championship. Rivals Newport finished rock bottom despite claiming another League double over Cardiff and faced the same uncertain fate as City had the previous year. Like Cardiff's, Newport's re-election attempt was successful.

1935–36 season
Again, during the closed season there was a mass overhaul of playing staff. New arrivals included Farquharson's replacement Jack Deighton from Everton, Cliff Godfrey from Bradford Park Avenue, Harold Smith from Notts County, and forwards Jack Diamond from Middlesbrough and Harry Roper from Tottenham Hotspur. Despite these reinforcements, City lost their opening game 3-2 at Crystal Palace on 31 August, and despite claiming several creditable draws didn't notch their first win of the new campaign until Orient visited Wales on 16 September when Roper, Riley and Hill (2) were on target in a 4-1 win. However, the win proved a rare highlight and only a narrow victory over Coventry temporarily eased the gloom. November brought convincing wins over Millwall and Bristol City, but between the Bristol game and back-to-back home wins over Newport and Gillingham in January 1936, Cardiff collected just two points.

City's overall form remained poor, and as if to emphasis the fact, non-League Dartford went to Ninian Park and thrashed the Bluebirds 3-0 in the first round of the FA Cup on what was labelled by some 'the darkest day in the club's history'. This shocker came just weeks after they had tumbled out of the Division Three (south) Cup, yet again at the first time of asking, and yet again at the hands of Crystal Palace. They fared marginally better in that season's Welsh Cup, squeezing past League rivals Bristol City and receiving a bye into the eighth round, where north Walians Rhyl knocked them out.

A key match occurred on 29 February when struggling Exeter played at Ninian Park in a crucial basement clash. City ran out comfortable 5-2 winners, and the remainder of the season saw the Bluebirds steer themselves to a shameful twentieth place in the League, just above Newport and hapless Exeter who, strangely enough, were also immediately re-elected. Coventry won the Division Three (south) championship; elsewhere Sunderland managed to wrestle the First Division from Arsenal, and original members Aston Villa and Blackburn Rovers both suffered relegation for the first time. Meanwhile in Cardiff Watts-Jones cast a critical eye over his squad and released a host of established players, subsequent new-comers including winger James Prescott from Everton, centre-forward Cecil Smith from Burnley, Les Talbot and Albert Pinxton from Blackburn, and goalkeeper Bill Fielding. At this time Cardiff were in such dire financial straits that the spending spree was funded, at least in part, by a generous club director who wished to remain anonymous. Rather unfairly, the board of directors came under fire throughout the 1930s from fans who accused them of not really wanting the club to succeed because (theoretically) a struggling club in a high division would make less money than a successful club in a lower division.

1936–37 season
In keeping with the recent tradition, there were seven debutants in the team that took the field at Walsall on 29 August and, not surprisingly, they lost. But then City embarked on a thrilling run of six wins and two draws that saw them stride to the top of the table. As predicted, the Welsh public returned to the fold in droves, and 28 September saw over 30,000 packed into Ninian Park for the visit of Southend United. The team was playing good,

flowing football and was further boosted by the arrival of experienced striker George Walton from Bolton Wanderers. For a while it looked as though the glory days were rolling around again, but then the bubble burst spectacularly. On 14 November the Bluebirds beat Northampton at Ninian Park, but inexplicably, that proved to be their last League win for over three months. During that time they suffered some of the most humiliating defeats in their history, including 8-1 drubbings at Luton and Southend, a 6-0 at QPR, and a 7-2 by Watford at Ninian Park.

Throughout this frenetic period, yet more new players arrived at Cardiff as Watts-Jones looked to a succession of journeymen to help stem the tide. Full-back John Mellor came in from Manchester United, along with Plymouth striker Eugene Melaniphy and ex-Scottish international Bob MacAulay. The fact that MacAulay played only four games before being off-loaded to Sligo Rovers speaks volumes. By the time the team got back to winning ways with a League victory over Bournemouth on 13 March 1937, they had tumbled out of every Cup they had been involved in. After despatching of Southall and Swindon in the FA Cup, City lost out to Grimsby Town in round three. They made their customary early exit from the Division Three (south) Cup at the hands of Exeter, and Barry Town accounted for them with embarrassing ease in the Welsh Cup.

Amidst all his chopping-and-changing, Watts-Jones eventually found a winning formula and Cardiff won three out of their last four League matches to ensure their League status for another year, but after so much early promise to finish in eighteenth place was a real kick in the teeth. Watts-Jones officially resigned on 1 April (funny, that) and moved 'upstairs' as a director leaving trainer and ex-Welsh international Bill Jennings to be appointed secretary/manager.

1937–38 season

Jennings brought his own vision to the club, and immediately set about remedying matters by exploiting his contacts within the game to strengthen the squad as cheaply and effectively as possible. Right-half Cecil McCaughey was recruited from Coventry, outside-left Albert Turner from Doncaster Rovers, goalkeeper Bob Jones from Bolton and centre-forward Jimmy Collins from Liverpool. New man Collins, who would quickly become a firm fan favourite, grabbed a debut goal to earn a draw at Orient in the first game of the season, then went into overdrive and blasted a hat-trick in a 5-2 victory over Torquay United. City kept up the good work and went on to notch up convincing wins over Southend, Northampton, Brighton and Walsall in the early exchanges. Home games were regularly attended by 20,000-plus. When playing in front of their own fans, the team had a solid, determined look that had been sadly lacking from previous seasons, and a front trio of Collins, Bert Turner and George Walton that struck fear into the hearts of opposing defenders.

For once, Cardiff's good form threatened to transmit through to the Cup competitions, and they finally broke their jinx by progressing to the second round of the Division Three (south) Cup at the expense of Northampton, only to be undone by Bristol City. After seeing off Northampton again, City had their revenge over the Robins in round two of the FA Cup, when a Collins brace settled a replayed tie and booked a third round clash at First Division Charlton Athletic, which they went on to lose 5-0. Non-League Cheltenham accounted for them in the latest in a string of Welsh Cup upsets.

That November, City secured the services of the ex-England captain Ernie Blenkinsop from Sheffield Wednesday as player-coach, and his steadying influence ensured that the Bluebirds run of form continued over the Christmas period and beyond with free-flowing, goal-laden wins over Gillingham, champions-elect Millwall, Crystal Palace, Mansfield Town and Bournemouth. By February 1938 however, they began to lose momentum and fell into a steady decline that saw them drop from potential title contenders to mid-table mediocrity. They scored twenty-six goals in the first eleven League games and by way of contrast, managed only seven from their last eleven, with four of those coming in a 4-1 mauling of Reading. Probably the only other matches of note were a 1-0 victory over League runners-up Bristol City at Ashton Gate on 5 March where a record attendance for a Division Three (south) game of 38,066 saw Collins nick the points, and a 3-1 friendly win over European giants RC Lens in France.

By the end of a much-improved season, Cardiff were able to announce record profits, primarily by curbing their spending. Public support also played a significant role in the financial turnaround as the average gate at Ninian Park swelled to almost 20,000 compared to a divisional average of just 11,000. Interestingly, although local unemployment stood at around 20.1 per cent, a marketing survey published in 1937 named Cardiff as being among Britain's most prosperous cities. Around this time, the ever-loyal fan-base began to wonder where all the money the club was making was going, and made their feelings known via the local media. International tensions were also rising, and several prominent England players voiced their concerns at being made to give Nazi salutes before slamming Germany 6-3 at Berlin's Olympic Stadium. The match was watched by Hitler's henchmen Goering and Goebbels, barely two years before the start of World War II.

1938–39 season

The summer of 1938 saw Italy retain the World Cup in France, while in Cardiff Jennings endeavoured to strengthen his playing staff by recruiting forward Ted 'Tex' Rickards from his former club Notts County, highly-rated left-back Jimmy Kelso from Newport, Welsh-born right-back George Ballsom from Gillingham, and outside-left Ritchie Smith from Aberdeen. Encouraged by the previous season, a bumper crowd of around 25,000 flocked to Ninian Park on 27 August to witness the opening game against Exeter, which City disappointingly lost 2-1. Despite all the pre-season optimism City made an indifferent start, winning five of their first fifteen League games and losing six. On the plus side, Jimmy Collins continued to show his class as he bagged eleven goals in those games, including a hat-trick in a 5-3 triumph over Watford. To bolster their attack City invested in Aldershot's Harry Egan, who scored on his debut in a 1-1 draw at Exeter on Christmas Eve.

While they struggled for consistency in the League, City enjoyed their best season of Cup competition for years. (That is, if you discount the 6-0 hammering dished out by Bristol City at Ashton Gate in the first round of the Division Three (south) Cup!) Shortly afterwards, the FA Cup got under way with City disposing of non-League Cheltenham and then Crewe Alexandra to set up a mouth-watering clash with First Division Charlton on 7 January 1939, to whom they had lost heavily at the same stage of the competition almost exactly a year earlier. Inevitably, the game was to be used as a yardstick to gauge just how far the club had progressed in that time, and nobody was more ecstatic than Bill Jennings when George Walton scored the only goal to settle it Cardiff's way. FA Cup fever hit south Wales when the next draw pitted them at home against mighty Newcastle United. Over 42,000 turned out on 21 January to see the spectacle, and although the Bluebirds played above their station they were unable to make the breakthrough and the game finished goalless. In the replay four days later, the Welsh side were completely out-gunned and lost 4-1.

The 1938-39 FAW annual report stated in no uncertain terms that from then on all clubs involved in the Welsh Cup were obliged to field their strongest available sides. Cardiff had long since been criticised for not taking the competition seriously enough, often using it to give youth and reserve players rare run-outs. That year they entered in round five, where Swansea held them to a draw at Ninian Park. The Swans were well and truly vanquished in the replay however, as the Bluebirds won 4-1. That season's Division Three (south) champions Newport awaited in round six and put up little defence as City rampaged to a 5-1 victory to avenge the latest League double they had suffered at the hands of their Monmouthshire opponents. They faced Owestry in the semi-final, eventually overcoming their non-League opponents at the third attempt to set up a meeting with South Liverpool to contend the crown. Despite the best efforts of Collins who scored for the bookie's favourites, City succumbed to a shock 2-1 defeat and the unknowns ran off with the trophy.

Back to League matters, and try as they might, City could just not find the consistency needed for a sustained promotion push. After back-to-back wins over Brighton and Bournemouth, a disastrous run of only one win in nine condemned them to more mid-table obscurity. This anti-climactic period prompted action behind the scenes as after a long business flirtation Herbert H. Merrett was elected to the board of directors and quickly became chairman. One of the first things he did was to replace secretary/manager Bill Jennings with former Villa and Spurs goalkeeper Cyril Spiers, handing him full control of team affairs.

One of Spiers' first acts was to sign up a young winger from Troedyrhiw called Billy Baker, who broke into the first team late in the season and would go on to make a huge contribution at the club. City ended the season with a flourish, winning three and drawing two of the last six, though the very last match was a 6-3 hammering at Walsall. While storm clouds gathered around Europe and the countdown to World War II commenced, Spiers busied himself shaping his new team. Out went Bill Bassett, Les Talbot and George Nicholson (each of whom had made over 100 appearances for Cardiff) and in came a flood of new players, none of whom had much of a chance to make any impact, except Trevor Morris, who would later return as manager, and Wilf Wooler, the archetypal all-round sportsman who later became captain of Cardiff rugby club, a Welsh rugby international, and a Glamorgan County cricketer.

The ill-fated 1939-40 season began with two consecutive away wins, at Norwich and Swindon on 26 and 30 August respectively. The irrepressible Jimmy Collins scored in both games, and notched two more against Notts County at Ninian Park on 2 September, despite being on the losing side. The next morning, with Blackpool sitting proudly atop Division One, it was announced that Britain was going to war and that the Football League was to be suspended.

Most contracted players left their clubs for one reason or another, and Cardiff immediately lost Collins, George Nicholson and Billy Bassett. Spiers, left with only a handful of recognised professionals, was charged with the unenviable task of recruiting a stream of young local lads and guest players (including the late, great Bill Shankly in the 1942-43 'season') to contest the friendly and local League fixtures the club were encouraged to arrange to boost public morale. These fixtures soon descended into chaos often reaching farcical proportions, with most sides content just to be able to field a full team. To illustrate how precarious the situation was, on Christmas morning 1940 Brighton were forced to travel to Norwich with only five players. They managed to field a team only after borrowing some Norwich reserves and recruiting a few off-duty soldiers from the crowd, but still lost 18-0!

The international scene was also badly affected, to such an extent that England agreed to let their 'spare man' Stan Mortensen play against them for Wales in a match at Wembley in September 1943. It's doubtful that he tried too hard on behalf of his new team-mates, as England galloped to an 8-3 victory. Records show that during World War II Cardiff called upon over 200 players, some of whom made only a solitary appearance for the club. Nevertheless, during this time Cyril Spiers made some astute signings that would grace Ninian Park for years to come.

When the war was declared over in the summer of 1945, the FA decided to virtually write off the coming season in order to give the clubs time to re-organise their financial affairs and acquire something approaching a workable playing staff. The local Leagues remained in place for the time being, but the FA Cup was reinstated in an altered format whereby from round three (where Cardiff would enter) matches would be played over two legs. On 17 November, after exchanging miniature miners' lamps for bouquets of flowers in a pre-match ceremony, City engaged the marauding Russians Dynamo Moscow in a friendly at Ninian Park, where around 31,000 spectators were struck dumb by the visitors' awesome display of attacking flair as they crushed the home side 10-1.

Cardiff City's involvement in the first FA Cup for seven years began on 5 January 1946, when West Brom visited Ninian Park and were held to a 1-1 draw with Bryn Allen, a lively forward newly signed from Swansea, scoring the goal in front of a football-starved crowd of 33,000. In the replay four days later the Midlanders ran out convincing winners by the score 4-0, despite being cheered on by a comparatively paltry 18,000. Among Spiers' most significant discoveries during the lost war years were flying wingers Beriah Moore and Roy Clarke, centre-half Fred Stansfield, right-back Arthur 'Buller' Lever, outside-right Colin Gibson, inside-forward Billy Rees (an ex- coal miner who scored an incredible 74 goals in 83 games during the war years), and legends-to-be Ken Hollyman and Alf Sherwood.

During the hostilities, Cardiff lost their reserve goalkeeper Jackie Pritchard, who was drowned at sea in 1943, and several other players were unable to resume their careers due to injuries sustained in battle. On the bright side, dazzling young winger Billy Baker, amongst others, returned to join forces with those newly assembled to spark a new and exciting era in the club's history that would soon eclipse the awful 1930s.

However, all was not yet wine and roses, and a huge shock was in store on 7 June 1946 when Cyril Spiers suddenly resigned from his position as caretaker/manager. It later transpired that he left in protest, having agreed to take a considerable pay cut during the war years to stay with the club on the understanding that his original contract would be honoured and his wage increased accordingly once the war was over. Apparently, his demands were not met, and Spiers reluctantly packed his bags and headed off to take charge of Norwich. In his place the board appointed ex-Newport manager Billy McCandless, an Irishman who had bossed the Monmouthshire club to the Second Division title before the war. With him, he brought wing-half Glyn Williams from Caerau to supplement the exciting team of emerging talent so painstakingly and effectively assembled by his predecessor.

5

On The Up
(1946–57)

1946–47 season

In an ironic twist of fate, the FA decreed that when the Football League finally recommenced on 31 August 1946, it would do so by fulfilling the fixtures from the abandoned 1939-40 season. This meant that Cardiff City were immediately faced with a trip to Norwich City, new home of the fired-up and recently departed Cyril Spears. The Cardiff team that took to the field consisted of George Poland, Arthur Lever, Alf Sherwood, Ken Hollyman, Fred Stansfield, Ernie Marshall, Colin Gibson, Billy Rees, Stan Richards, Bryn Allen and Roy Clarke. Spiers' inside knowledge of the Bluebirds paid handsome dividends as the Canaries won 2-1. The second game also ended in defeat at Swindon Town but then, ominously for the rest of the division, the young team began to gel. Notts County were the first visitors to Ninian Park that season, quickly followed by Bournemouth. City won both games with Billy James scoring in each, but sadly the war had taken its toll on James, who had been a Japanese POW, and he was quickly forced out of the side to accommodate Richards who had been dropped despite scoring in the first two games. The other change of note was between the sticks where Pontypridd-born Danny Canning replaced the 46-year-old Poland.

The team never looked back, and remained unbeaten for an astonishing 21 matches, a run that sent them flying to the top of the Third Division (south) by Christmas. Some clubs were still in a state of disarray after the war and City showed them no mercy, inflicting heavy defeats on Swindon, Brighton & Hove Albion, Exeter City, Port Vale and Bristol Rovers, all of whom they beat by four goals or more. The crowning achievement came on 28 December, the last game of 1946, when Cyril Spiers took Norwich to Ninian Park in search of a League double. A partisan and vociferous crowd of 36, 285 turned out to watch the Bluebirds thrash the Canaries 6-1, with Richards' stunning hat-trick supplemented by strikes from Rees, Allen and Clarke. Tough defender Ken Hollyman later remembered that the team around that time was a 'Young and very fit side built on good defence. We would stop the opposition playing and then give the ball to our forwards who had a field day.'

The war had caused the demise of the Division Three (south) Cup (cue widespread sighs of relief!) but both the FA and Welsh Cups returned unchanged. City were knocked out of the former at the first time of asking at Brentford, and met the same fate in the latter at Merthyr Tydfil, the team formed from the ashes of the pre-war Merthyr Town, who were taking the Southern League by storm. No matter; by the time League football resumed at Ninian Park with the visit of Southend United on St David's Day 1947, after atrocious weather had forced an impromptu winter break, the Bluebirds had the League championship firmly in their sights. Throughout the season, the crowds had been flocking to Ninian Park to worship the silky skills and attacking flair of a team regularly containing no fewer than ten proud Welshmen (the odd man out being Englishman Colin Gibson). This was exactly what the Cardiff supporters had been crying out for, and to prove it 51,626 crammed into the ground on Easter Monday to watch their heroes face high-flying Bristol City. The match ended in a draw, but it signified the end of City's worst spell of the season – four draws and a defeat – which, pre-war, might well have qualified as their best spell! They ended the season in fine form, winning their last six games on the bounce to finish champions, a clear nine points above second-placed QPR. They had lost only eight games all season, including both Cup exits, and fulfilled the entire League programme undefeated at home.

This team, which has been hailed by some older supporters as the best ever, also set a new club record of eight consecutive away victories during their march to their first-ever Football League title. They were only outdone by Doncaster Rovers of Division Three (north) who set no fewer than four separate records in winning their League: most points, most wins, most away points, and most away wins. A combined Great Britain side celebrated the return to FIFA of the four home nations with a resounding 6-1 defeat of a 'Rest of Europe XI' in an exhibition match at Hampden Park, Scotland before 135,000 baying fans.

After winning promotion to Division Two in such impressive fashion, McCandless didn't have much tinkering to do with his inherited side. Only winger George Wardle came in from Exeter to replace Welsh international Roy Clarke, who left in a money-spinning deal taking him to Manchester City. That great servant of the war years, Beriah Moore, was re-signed from Bangor, and Dougie Blair, son of the 1920s full-back Jimmy, arrived from Blackpool. He would go on to make even more appearances for the Bluebirds than his legendary father.

1947–48 season

City's first season in Division Two for sixteen years began with a flourish; after a goalless home draw with Chesterfield on 23 August, City met record-breaking Doncaster, Third Division (north) champions, in a clash that attracted an estimated crowd of 47,000. Cardiff roared to a 3-0 win courtesy of Stan Richard's first goal of another prolific season and a brace by new-signing Wardle, who endeared himself to the Cardiff faithful by adding to his tally in each of the next two matches. An early highlight came when City thrashed Southampton 5-1 at Ninian Park on 6 September, and followed it up with impressive home wins over Plymouth Argyle, Bradford PA and Luton Town, as they gradually began to acclimatize to life in the higher division. But changes were afoot: Newport County swooped for Bryn Allen and Billy Lewis. Then, on 14 November, Billy McCandless suddenly resigned. He had accepted an offer from rivals Swansea Town, where two years later he would secure a unique treble by steering them to the Division Three (south) title, just as he had with both Newport and Cardiff.

On 3 December, ripples of excitement began to emanate from Ninian Park when it was announced that Cyril Spiers would be returning as secretary/manager – this time with a significantly improved contract. Spiers' reappointment coincided with the Bluebirds' best run of the season, which culminated on 3 January 1948 when they hit Millwall for six at Ninian Park to edge closer to the promotion places. However, this wasn't to be another fairytale season. By the time the Bluebirds played their next League match, which they lost at Tottenham Hotspur a fortnight later, they had tumbled out of both Cups with barely a whimper, Sheffield Wednesday progressing in the FA Cup and lowly Lovell's Athletic winning a Welsh Cup shocker at Ninian Park.

Concerns over the long-term fitness of Stan Richards prompted Spiers to sign centre-forward Bill Hullett from Merthyr, who made an immediate impact by hitting seven goals in his first six games. But then City began conceding goals and dropping points all over the place, and had to wait until the last game of the season for another win, a trip to Barnsley, where strikes from Rees and Moore were enough to ensure a highly creditable fifth spot. Like many other Football League clubs in the euphoric post- World War II era, Cardiff reaped the rewards of elevated attendance figures and regularly attracted crowds of 40,000-plus, even when they were playing badly, while Blackpool's Stanley Matthews deservedly won the inaugural 'Player of the Year' award.

At the end of the season, Stan Richards left Ninian Park to link up once more with Billy McCandless at Swansea, having scored thirty-nine goals in fifty-seven League games for the Bluebirds. Goalkeeper Phil Joslin arrived from Torquay and immediately displaced Danny Canning, sparking a seven-year agreement between the two clubs during which players were exchanged freely. In a surprise move, Spiers exchanged City's reserve centre-forward Reg Parker for Bryn Allen, who had been at Newport for only seven months.

1948–49 season
Despite the fine-tuning, Cardiff made a poor start to the season, losing the first match 3-0 at Bradford PA and claiming just one win from the opening six games. The team's indifferent form prompted Spiers into action. He sold Bill Hullett to Nottingham Forest and signed Tommy Best (Cardiff's first black player) from Chester, before paying a club record £10,000 to Wolverhampton Wanderers for inside-forward Ernie Stevenson. City's biggest problem seemed to be a lack of speed and creativity on the left wing, where a string of players were tried in the early stages of the season. In a 1-1 home draw with Sheffield Wednesday on 20 November the spot was filled by Albert Stitfall, with his brother Ron playing down the opposite flank. It was the first time a pair of brothers had represented Cardiff in a League game. In December, Spiers made a bid to rectify the

situation once and for all by signing Birmingham City's Welsh international George Edwards for £6,000. It proved to be one of his better investments, as Edwards scored after just four minutes of his home debut against Bradford along with Allen, Stevenson (2), Lever and Hollyman, to inflict a crushing 6-1 defeat on the highly-fancied visitors.

City also managed to make some small progress in the Cups that term. In the FA Cup, they brushed off the challenge of Oldham Athletic to set up an epic tie at Aston Villa on 29 January 1949, where an astonishing crowd of 70,718 saw Hollyman and Rees score the goals in a thrilling 2-1 victory. Unfortunately, City were unable to repeat the feat and went out to Derby County in the next round. In the Welsh Cup, City saw off Troedyrhiw and Milford United before Merthyr put them out under 'glue pot' conditions in the semi-final.

In a home defeat to Barnsley, Welsh international centre-half Fred Stansfield sustained an injury that all but finished his career but his replacement, Stan Montgomery, stepped effortlessly into his boots, scoring on his debut in a 2-2 draw at Grimsby Town the following week. Shortly afterwards another centre-half was purchased, Alf Rowland from Aldershot, for a fee said to at least equal the record £10,000 paid to Wolves for Stevenson. However, while Rowland failed to make much of an impact, the acquisition of the powerful Montgomery proved a master-stroke. Montgomery had initially arrived on the recommendation of his father-in-law, the great full-back of the 1920's Jimmy Nelson, as Cardiff went on to lose just two more League matches that season.

In the final standings, that shaky start had cost the club dear and they eventually settled in fourth place, one position and four points better off than the previous season. Fulham were crowned champions. At a time when match-fixing allegations were rife, a huge talking point arose in the very last match of the season at home to Leicester on 7 May. By that stage City had nothing much to play for, but the midlanders needed at least a point to secure their Second Division status. The match was labelled a fiasco, as both sets of players seemed overly reluctant to attack, and the general feeling was that the result had been contrived. The game ended in a questionable draw.

All this was overshadowed by a horrific air crash three days earlier that claimed the cream of Italian football in an eerie precursor to the tragedy that would later befall Manchester United's Busby Babes. The Italian episode claimed the lives of thirty-one people, virtually wiping out the Torino team that stood on the brink of a historic fifth consecutive Serie A title and had provided the bulk of the national side.

After such a hectic period in the transfer market, City was content to have a quiet summer for once with Elfed Evans, a former Welsh League player with Treharris, being the only significant signing. Notable departures included Billy Rees, who joined Spurs for £11,000, and Bryn Allen, who this time left for Reading. Just before the new season started in earnest, chairman Herbert Merrett audaciously informed the board that he was sending promising right-sided defender/winger Ken Hollyman to Blackpool to receive special coaching from the great Stanley Matthews, a privilege for which he was allegedly prepared to pay ten guineas.

1949–50 season
For the first time in quite a while, City kicked off the new campaign, at Blackburn Rovers on 20 August, with no debutants in their line up, and promptly lost 1-0. They redressed the balance two days later by beating Sheffield

Wednesday at Ninian Park, then it was the turn of Billy McCandless' Division Three (south) champs Swansea. A record crowd of 57,510 (this figure refers to the number of tickets sold – the actual number of spectators could be considerably higher) swamped Ninian Park, the vast majority of which were sent home happy as Best scored the only goal of a tight game to give Cardiff temporary bragging rights. Again, though, they struggled to find any consistency, with a lack of goals being a particular worry. In the six games played between 8 October and 26 November they scored just once (in a defeat at Coventry). After this barren spell Spiers juggled his players around, eventually gambling on winger Ron Stitfall up front. The gamble paid off and Stitfall came up with the goods, scoring in each of the wins over Grimsby, QPR, Preston North End and Blackburn. He also scored in the next game at Swansea on Christmas Eve: not bad for a player who scored only eight goals for the club in his entire career (which stretched to an incredible 454 matches). But unfortunately there was little seasonal cheer for the Bluebirds, as McCandless masterminded a 5-1 triumph for the Swans.

On 7 January 1950, City embarked on another famous FA Cup run. First out of the hat was a home tie with West Bromwich Albion, where they were held to a draw before nicking the replay with a George Edwards goal. They met Division One outfit Charlton Athletic in the next round and eventually triumphed over the Londoners, which left them quietly optimistic about defeating Leeds. It wasn't to be, however, and they ended the game well beaten. In the Welsh Cup the third Stitfall brother on Cardiff's books, goalkeeper Bob, made his one and only appearance for the first team as they beat Ebbw Vale 3-0 at home. Swansea awaited at the Vetch Field in the next phase, where a hapless Cardiff side was dismantled 3-0.

After the departure of Tommy Best to QPR in December, young Elfed Evans emerged as a real threat up front, scoring his first goal for Cardiff in a narrow win over Plymouth and managing to keep his place in the team ahead of stiff competition. In March, record signing Ernie Stevenson, who was in the middle of a severe goal drought, was exchanged for Southampton winger Wilf Grant in time for City's best win of the season, a 4-0 demolition of struggling QPR at Ninian Park. While the defence coped admirably for most of the season, goal scoring remained problematic; consequently City languished in tenth place in the final standings. Evans finished as top scorer despite not breaking into the team until the New Year, and even then notching only eight League goals, making him the lowest top-placed marksman in City's history.

In an attempt to address the lack of fire-power, during the closed season Spiers paid Wrexham £5,000 for their forward Bobby McLaughlin. He also signed goalkeeper Ron Howells from Barry Town and promoted several reserve players to the first team. The sports pages for much of that summer were bereft of transfer news, focusing instead on the latest World Cup competition in Brazil. The hosts and England were jointly installed as favourites before the tournament started, but even as Brazil lost to Uruguay in the final, the headlines were made by England for all the wrong reasons. Captained by Eddie McIlvenny, a Glasgow-born centre-half who had been free-transferred by Wrexham three years earlier, the English were beaten 1-0 by the USA in one of the biggest shocks ever in international football. Britain had originally been awarded two places in the competition, but Scotland refused to go to their first World Cup out of principle, having grudgingly lost out in the previous years' International Championship to England. The Scots insisted that they would go only as British champions.

1950–51 season

Cardiff kicked off the new season with a point at Grimsby on 20 August, and went on to make a decent enough start to the campaign, losing just twice in the first ten games, though a frustrating habit of drawing rather than winning games was beginning to develop. Arthur 'Buller' Lever, a virtual ever-present since the war years, was sold to Leicester for £10,000, and in November Spiers recruited right-winger Mike Tiddy from Torquay in the transfer agreement that still existed between the two clubs. The arrival of the lively Tiddy, instantly distinguishable because of a grey streak in his otherwise dark hair, enabled Spiers to move Wilf Grant into the problem centre-forward berth in a switch that revitalized the entire team. Before the change City had drawn half of their twenty games, but after it they discovered a new killer instinct, perfectly illustrated by a 5-2 home victory over Grimsby on 16 December, where Grant grabbed a hat-trick and strike-partner Roley Williams hit the other two. A week later they registered their first away win of the season at Notts County where both Grant and Williams scored again in a 2-1 win. Slowly but surely, City began climbing the table.

They began their latest quest for Cup silverware in the worst possible manner, going out of the FA Cup in the third round at West Ham on 6 January 1951. However, by the time the Welsh Cup began the following month City were playing much better and romped to landslide victories over Barry and Bangor City (8-0 and 7-1 respectively) in the opening rounds. Wrexham awaited in the semi-final, where Edwards' goal was enough to separate the sides and set up a final meeting with Merthyr. After a 1-1 draw at the neutral ground of Swansea's Vetch Field forced a replay, City fielded their strongest available team in an effort to win their first post-war trophy. It made no difference, as the valley town managed to record one of their greatest results, running out 3-2 winners.

For a time City looked a good bet for promotion, and to add some steel to their attack invested in Milford Haven-born Marwood Marchant, who scored on his debut in a 3-0 win at Chesterfield on 3 February. Later that month they reached the lofty heights of second in the League, but they could not maintain the momentum and were eventually overtaken by Manchester City who finished five points behind League winners Preston North End and two points ahead of City. Since the resumption of the Football League after World War II City had made steady progress, and there was a genuine feeling amongst the Ninian Park faithful that their club was on the verge of much greater things.

1951–52 season
Given past histories, the 1951 closed season was another remarkably quiet affair in the Welsh capital. Goalkeeper Phil Joslin broke his leg in a training match the week before the new season started (an injury that ultimately finished his career). Only then did Spiers dip into the transfer market to secure the services of Iorwerth Hughes, Luton's Welsh international shot-stopper, for a record fee of £15,000. Hughes, who would spend the season vying with Ron Howells for the Number 1 jersey, was the only new face in the team that beat Leicester 4-0 at Ninian Park with goals by Edwards, Grant (2) and Williams. It was the first time City had won on the opening day of the season since 1934. The early games were the usual lottery, with City winning three and losing four of the first seven, but then they began to discover the one thing they had been lacking since their 1920s heyday: consistency.

In the thirteen games played between 15 September and 8 December, City lost just once (at Barnsley on 27 October) and over the course of the first twenty matches, the skilful Grant averaged almost a goal a game. On Christmas Day Cardiff made the short journey to Swansea, where a bad-tempered draw was the result. The return fixture was scheduled for the very next day, when 46,003 crammed in to Ninian Park to see the Swans demolished 3-0 with goals from Baker, Grant and Tiddy. On 5 January 1952, City beat Doncaster Rovers 2-1 at Ninian Park with a brace from Sherwood to climb to the top of the League, where they were engaged in a three-way battle with Sheffield Wednesday and Birmingham for the title. This was just as well, because by the beginning of February the League was all City had to play for, having made early exits from both the FA and the Welsh Cups, the former after a third round replay at Swindon and the latter at the hands of Merthyr (again) having disposed of Milford Haven.

The Welsh Cup débâcle coincided with City's worst League run of the season, as they tumbled to defeat at Sheffield Wednesday and Coventry and scraped a draw with West Ham, before suffering the indignation of going down 6-1 at Sheffield United. The poor run prompted Spiers to delve into the transfer market once more, this time emerging with Ken Chisholm, Coventry's powerful front man. The Scot immediately set about justifying his weighty £12,000 fee by scoring twice on his debut in a 3-0 win over Barnsley at Ninian Park on 15 March. A long succession of dismal away performances blighted the club's progress (they won only two all season) and even the arrival of Chisholm couldn't stop the rot as a run of three away games saw the Bluebirds return to Wales with a haul of just two points.

However, all was not lost. City had games in hand over their promotion rivals and as luck would have it, five of their last six were at home, where they had lost only once all season. Chisholm scored the only goal in the match against Notts County to make up some ground, and followed it up with a brace in a 3-1 victory against Birmingham on Easter Monday. A trip to Luton followed, where City were held to another draw, meaning that they had to win each of their last three games to pip Birmingham to runners-up spot behind Sheffield Wednesday, for whom Derek Dooley had scored a phenomenal forty-six goals in just thirty League games. Tragically, less than a year later the young centre-forward contracted gangrene after receiving treatment on a broken leg sustained in a match and there was no alternative but to amputate.

Blackburn visited Cardiff in a re-arranged match on 21 April, and were soundly beaten 3-1 and five days later, two goals from Dougie Blair and another from Wilf Grant was enough to send Bury home pointless. So at a rain-soaked Ninian Park, on the final day of the season, a frenetic crowd of 45,925 witnessed one of the greatest days in City's history as Grant (2) and Chisholm scored the goals in a 3-1 win over Leeds that secured runner-up spot and promotion back to the First Division after an absence of more than twenty years. In fact, there was cause for a triple celebration in Welsh football as the national team celebrated winning the International Championship (jointly) for the first time post-war, in the FAW's centenary season.

1952–53 season
Strangely, Spiers again chose not to make any significant signings that summer and the only additions of note were Keith Thomas (of Sheffield Wednesday) and George Hazlett (Bury) who were 'invited' to join the playing staff after impressing in a trial match. The long-awaited return to First Division football came at Wolves on 23 August 1952, where the Bluebirds succumbed to a 1-0 defeat. They

suffered another away-day horror show and lost 3-0 at Middlesbrough four days later before finding their feet. Second Division champs Sheffield Wednesday must have fancied their chances when they visited Ninian Park on Saturday 30 August, but they left demoralised after goals from new-signing Hazlett, Grant, and a double from Chisolm-led City to a triumphant 4-0 victory. However, the glory was short-lived as Cardiff went through another period of readjustment and had to wait almost a month before their next win, which came away at Preston North End. A week later they won again, a Roley Williams double being enough to see off Stoke in Cardiff, and at last City began to string together some good results. Over the next two months they enjoyed some incredible moments, among them beating Chelsea 2-0 at Stamford Bridge, and crushing Sunderland 4-1 at Ninian Park. Though suffering the cumulative effects of fatigue, and injuries to several key players, they invariably looked solid at the back, creative and decisive in midfield, and productive and dangerous up front.

But then, mid-season, the goals inexplicably dried up. Unbelievably, what followed now stands as the most barren spell in the club's entire history as they went eight matches, 720 minutes in total, without scoring a single League goal. That run was halted in style on 21 February 1953 when Manchester City left Ninian Park on the wrong end of a humiliating 6-0 scoreline thanks to goals from Roley Williams, Keith Thomas (2), Wilf Grant (2) and the ever-dependable George Edwards. On 7 March Cardiff stunned eventual League champions Arsenal by winning at Highbury, but quite possibly City's best results of the season occurred within two days of each other over the Easter period. First they travelled north to Old Trafford where they trounced the mighty Manchester United 4-1, then they crushed Liverpool at Ninian Park 4-0. Unfortunately, the latter proved to be their last win of the season, and they finished the season in a respectable twelfth place.

At the height of their barren spell, City played at Halifax Town in the third round of the FA Cup and though they managed a goal through veteran Billy Baker, City were powerless to curtail the march of the Division Three (north) side. In their first outing in the Welsh Cup, City settled some old scores by thrashing Merthyr 5-2 at Penydarren Park, and went on to edge out Barry in the subsequent round before losing a semi-final 1-0 at Rhyl.

1953–54 season

All things considered, City acquitted themselves well back in Division One, but there was much to do if the club was ever going to seriously challenge for silverware again. That summer, Cyril Spiers frustrated the fans by yet again refraining from signing any big-name players. In his defence, this was mainly because the club was still consolidating after the lean war years. Cardiff began the season with a goalless draw at Middlesbrough and followed it up with a 2-1 home win over Villa, when both ex- Crystal Palace forward Johnny Rainford and home-grown winger Peter Thomas scored their first and only goals for the club. After away defeats at Huddersfield and Wolves, City began to find some consistency and put together a run of ten games in which they lost only once (at Arsenal), taking them up to seventh place. On Halloween they put Charlton through the horrors by thrashing them 5-0 at Ninian Park with Chisholm grabbing a hat-trick, but then the wheels spectacularly came off. The Bluebirds suffered three heavy losses in a row in which they conceded a worrying sixteen goals, the worst performance being a 6-1 demolition job by Manchester United. After these stinging defeats, City raised their game enough to register an impressive 3-1 win over Liverpool, then shook the football world by paying Sunderland £30,000 for Welsh international striker Trevor Ford. For the time, the fee was astronomical, and only one British player had ever cost more (Jackie Sewell, who had moved from Notts County to Sheffield Wednesday).

Several departures paved the way for Ford's arrival, who it was hoped would hold the key to ongoing scoring success for City. Jack Mansell was sold to Portsmouth and Ken Hollyman, the player who had once received private tuition from Stanley Matthews, left for Newport after making 202 appearances. Chairman Sir Herbert Merrett, who had recently taken over from Tudor Steer, believed Ford would be a disruptive influence in the dressing room and publicly objected to his arrival so strongly that he later claimed that the cheque that paid for his services was the only one he didn't personally sign. The difference of opinion would not be forgotten. After Ford's controversial arrival, Chisholm lost his place in the team and was soon packing his bags for Sunderland who, in another twist, saw him as a replacement for Ninian Park's new hero.

On his home debut against Middlesbrough on 12 December, Ford scored the only goal. It is estimated that his presence alone swelled the gate by more than 10,000. Tommy Northcott, a young forward, signed the year before in the agreement Cardiff had with Torquay, scored twice the following week as the Bluebirds won at Villa. But then, due in part to a catastrophic injury crisis, the team fell into a slump and didn't win another League game for two months. During that time they were forced to reclaim defender Harry Parfitt, in a premature return from Torquay where he had been loaned, sparking a bitter row which led to the 'agreement' between the clubs being terminated.

Predictably, Cardiff's latest FA Cup campaign was less than spectacular. Ford and Northcott gave them passage through to round four at the expense of non-League Peterborough United, where they were again the victims of a giant-killing act as Division Three (north) Port Vale beat them 2-0. In the Welsh Cup City made it to the semi-final stage by scraping past Barry and Merthyr Tydfil (who they met for the fourth consecutive season), but they lost out to minnows Flint Town.

After Ford's dramatic equalizer rescued a point against Arsenal at Highbury on 13 February 1954, City put together a run which saw them win six matches from their next eight. The sequence included victories over Spurs, Newcastle, Manchester United and League-leaders West Brom, where Ford was again amongst the goals. In an extraordinary match against Liverpool at Anfield just before the end of the season, City lost keeper Ron Howells through injury. Alf Sherwood took over in goal and performed heroics, including saving a penalty, as City won 1-0, famously relegating the Merseysiders. Cardiff finished in tenth place, while Wolves won the championship ahead of Midlands rivals West Brom.

1954 was an eventful year off the field, too, for Cardiff City. In May, Cyril Spiers walked out on the club for the second (and last) time to go to alternative employment at Crystal Palace; two of the club's most loved patrons, Fred Stewart and Bartley Wilson, both died, and there were widespread directorial and staff disputes and changes. It was rumoured that Spiers left because of repercussions arising from the Trevor Ford saga. The upshot of the matter was that club secretary, Caerphilly-born Trevor Morris, who had had his own footballing career wrecked when he broke a leg whilst guesting for the Bluebirds during the war, was appointed secretary/manager.

Meanwhile, stubborn Scotland relented and travelled to Switzerland to contest the World Cup as International

Championship runners-up to England, but must have wished they hadn't bothered as they lost every match, including a 7-0 thrashing by Uruguay, who then knocked England out of the quarter-final of a competition eventually won by West Germany.

1954–55 season

Back in the UK, Cardiff was a club in turmoil. It showed, when the new season began, with defeat away to Burnley on 21 August. An expectant crowd of 39,448 crammed into Ninian Park four days later to see the Bluebirds routinely dismantled by a rampaging Preston North End side. Tellingly, the crowd was significantly lower when Northcott and Ford scored against Leicester to give Cardiff their first points of the season. The next match saw City travel to Preston, where they fell to their heaviest post-war defeat, 7-1. After that match City scraped together a run of three wins and four draws, during which time Morris made his first major signing by paying Wolves £12,000 for inside-forward Ron Stockin. Morris also invested in the services of Coventry winger Gordon Nutt, who made his debut in a 3-0 home defeat by Burnley on 18 December. Seven days later, in the last professional football match staged in Cardiff on Christmas Day, City beat West Brom 3-2, with two goals from Ford and a rare strike by Stan Montgomery to lift flagging spirits.

City went out of the FA Cup at the hands of Arsenal in a third round clash at Highbury, and fared only marginally better in the Welsh version of the competition where, despite being the leading club in Wales, Cardiff had underachieved badly in recent years. Ford notched four goals in a 7-1 thumping of Pembroke in round five and scored again in a subsequent 3-1 win over Newport, but missed the semi-final at Wrexham where City were soundly beaten by Chester.

After the West Brom Christmas cracker, City didn't win

another League game until Everton visited Ninian Park on 12 February 1955, when Ford and Stockin both scored twice in a 4-3 victory. They outplayed Manchester United in the next game, winning 3-0, and after drawing at Sunderland beat Charlton 4-3 at Ninian Park to secure their First Division status. Afterwards however, it was downhill all the way, and City didn't win again until the penultimate match of the season against reigning champions Wolves at Ninian Park. Chelsea won their very first League title that year, thereby qualifying for an embryonic version of the European Cup, though they were quick to withdraw from that tournament on the advice of the Football League, who feared the effects of simmering political tensions.

At the end of the season, there were several notable departures from Ninian Park. Billy Baker, a Bluebird since 1938, left for Ipswich Town; Stan Montgomery moved to Worcester City; and George Edwards retired at the age of thirty-five, only to return a few years later as a director. It was as if the backbone of the team had been ripped out, and in an effort to replace it Morris quickly signed Sunderland trio Harry Kirtley, Howard Sheppard and Johnny McSeveney. There was some friction developing between the club and star striker Trevor Ford who was, perhaps, beginning to live up to Merrett's assessment of him by refusing to sign a new contract. Although the dispute was eventually resolved, Ford lost many admirers who had, until then, tolerated his perceived arrogance and general questionable attitude.

On a historical note, 1955 was also the year that Cardiff was formally made a City, having polled 90 per cent of local council delegates' votes.

1955–56 season
City began the next season reasonably enough, with McSeveney scoring twice on his debut and Ford also on

target in a 3-1 home win over Sunderland. Then they lost at both Arsenal and Villa before beating Bolton at Ninian Park to settle the early-season nerves. The next match in the Welsh capital, on 3 September, before 42,546 fans, was a historic one for all the wrong reasons as the Bluebirds were humiliated 9-1 by Wolves, who equalled the divisional record away win. The Welsh public were horrified, especially when Cardiff also lost their next two games heavily at Bolton and Manchester City. A home win over Sheffield United restored some confidence in the shattered team, but their erratic form and tendency to ship goals was a major worry.

With their season already in tatters, City yielded to temptation and accepted an offer from Arsenal of £20,000 plus outside-right Brian Walsh, for wingers Mike Tiddy and Gordon Nutt. Happily, Walsh's debut coincided with Cardiff's first away win of the season at Preston on 8 October, when Ford and Stockin scored in a 2-1 win. The following month, the talismanic Ford was suspended and placed on the transfer list after a row that resulted from his refusal to play out of position. Though commonplace in today's game, back then such petulant behaviour was almost unheard of. Weeks later, Morris paid Dundee £17,000 for pivot Danny Molloy in a bid to solve the team's defensive crisis, and gave a start to outside-left Neil O'Halloran, a part-time boilermaker who had risen through the youth ranks. Both made their first appearances for Cardiff at home against Charlton on 10 December, when O'Halloran made history by becoming the first City player to score a hat-trick on his League debut. Despite such early promise, however, O'Halloran didn't quite make the grade and played only nine more games before moving to Newport a year later; while Molloy went on to be a commanding presence in City's back four for the next five years. With him in the team

City were a different prospect, and picked up some good results, including a famous 2-0 revenge attack at Molineux where they beat Wolves 2-0 on the last day of 1955 with goals from Gerry Hitchens and the reinstated and revitalized Trevor Ford.

City's next match was a third round FA Cup tie at Leeds on 7 January 1956, where Hitchens and McSeveney scored to inflict a first home defeat on the Elland Road club for thirty-two games and secure a meeting with West Ham at Upton Park. Unfortunately, despite another timely strike from Ford, City went down to the Second Division side 2-1. However, at last City appeared to have begun taking the Welsh Cup seriously when they won a fifth round replay against Pembroke at Ninian Park 9-0 with a four-goal salvo from Ford, a treble from Hitchens, and further strikes from McSeveney and Colin Baker. Hitchens scored another hat-trick in round six in a 5-3 win over Wrexham, and bagged a remarkable five in the semi-final against Owestry, with Ford bagging the other two goals in a resounding 7-0 victory. City met old adversaries Swansea in the final at Ninian Park, where a crowd of over 37,000, easily the best the competition had ever produced, saw City power to a 3-2 win despite losing Kirtley in the first half with a badly broken leg. The injury meant that City played the remainder of the match with only ten men, but still managed to win the Cup for the first time since 1930.

The Welsh Cup run and ultimate triumph served as a welcome distraction to the drudgery of the League. While Ford's continued presence saw the Bluebirds coast through February on the back of four consecutive wins, with the mercurial striker scoring in every game to underline his value to the team and guide them to mid-table security, this didn't last. From a position of relative promise the League season soon deteriorated into what can only be described as a farce, as City somehow contrived to fulfill their entire remaining fixture list, eleven games in total, collecting just one more win (a home tie with Luton). This late slump combined with the usual crippling injury list and patchy form throughout, meant that City finished in lowly seventeenth place. Manchester United's 'Busby Babes' won the title by a record-equalling margin of eleven points while fallen champions Chelsea ended up with the same points total as Cardiff (thirty-nine). Where the Londoners had given in to politically-motivated pressure from above and agreed not to contest the European Cup, Manchester United ignored Football League directives and announced their imminent involvement in the competition, taking the first step in a European odyssey.

1956–57 season
In the summer of 1956, skipper Alf Sherwood moved to Newport after representing Cardiff 372 times in all competitions since joining in 1941. His loss would have catastrophic repercussions for the club. The only new player to join in the closed season was inside-forward Brayley Reynolds, who joined from Lovell's. City began the new campaign with a scoreless draw at Arsenal on 18 August and followed it up with an exhilarating 5-2 win over Newcastle at Ninian Park where McSeveney, Ford (2) and utility forward Cliff Nugent (2) were the scorers.

City drew their next game 3-3 with Burnley, then lost the return match with Newcastle, before being hit for six by Preston at Deepdale. Strangely enough, this embarrassing result occurred on the same date that they had lost 7-1 to the same opponents at the same venue two years previously. Alarm bells were ringing in their ears, and their form dipped. A 4-1 home win over Leeds on 6 October represented City's only win in ten games. Hitchens scored twice in that match along with McSeveney and Ford, who had taken over the captain's role with relish. Little did anyone know at the time that that was the volatile striker's last goal for City. He made his final appearance for the club in a 1-1 home draw with Manchester City on 3 November. Soon after the match, extracts from his then-unpublished autobiography appeared in a Sunday newspaper and caused a storm of controversy, mainly surrounding the subject of illegal payments in the football world. As a result of his revelations, Ford was originally banned from playing football for life, but had the ban cut to three years on appeal, after which time he briefly joined PSV Eindhoven in Holland.

It was another strange season all round for Cardiff. On 4 January 1957 they met Leeds in the third round of the FA Cup at Elland Road and triumphed 2-1, just as they had the previous campaign. Their Cup run was short-lived, however: they met Second Division Barnsley at Ninian Park in round four and lost to a late goal. In their defence of the Welsh Cup they met Haverfordwest in round five, who held the Bluebirds to a draw before being swept aside 8-1 in the replay. Encouraging as this was, City surrendered possession of the trophy seemingly without a fight in the next phase, losing to Third Division (north) side Chester.

After a 2-1 win at West Brom on 9 February, City fell into another late-season slump from which this time there was to be no escape. An Easter double over the Bluebirds by Portsmouth, which saved the South Coast club from relegation, all-but condemned Cardiff to the drop, and they won only once in the last fourteen games. They failed to score in five of their last six and ended up second bottom, seven points above Charlton and three points behind Sunderland. The Busby Babes retained the championship (this time by an even bigger margin) as City tumbled out of the top flight a second time.

6

Punching Above Your Weight
(1957-62)

In the summer of 1957, Trevor Morris, faced with the considerable task of getting Cardiff City back into the First Division, secured the services of forward Ron Hewitt from Wrexham and influential winger Colin 'Rock' Hudson from Newport County, with Johnny McSeveney and Neil O'Halloran moving the opposite way. There were many other departures, most notably ex-Welsh international goalkeeper Ron Howells, who moved to Worcester City.

1957–58 season
City's first game back in the Second Division was a baptism of fire; Swansea Town, a team then full of Welsh internationals, at Ninian Park on 24 August. The Cardiff team that faced their most bitter rivals that Saturday afternoon was: Graham Vearncombe, Charlie Rutter, Ron Stitfall, Alan Harrington, Danny Molloy, Derrick Sullivan, Hudson, Hewitt, Gerry Hitchens, Nicholls and Ken Tucker. Despite City unveiling their much-touted new strike force in front of 42,482 fervent supporters, the match ended goalless.

Whichever way you look at it, the Bluebirds made a dismal start to the season, with 1-0s over Huddersfield and Doncaster Rovers being their only wins in the first eleven games. On both occasions the goal was scored by fullback Ron Davies, who was often played up front to bolster a shot-shy attack. In October the faltering team registered three wins on the bounce courtesy of Derby County, Bristol Rovers and Lincoln City, but were then heavily beaten at both Notts County and Stoke. Joe Bunson joined from Wolves and scored on his debut to earn his new team a home draw against Ipswich Town on 9 November, but he had to wait almost a month before finding himself on the winning side. The wait eventually came to an end on 7 December with the visit of Barnsley. To everyone's surprise City completely outplayed their opponents and notched their biggest win of the season, a storming 7-0 with Cliff Nugent (3), Hewitt (2), Bonson and Hudson doing the damage.

For the Bluebirds 21 December was a landmark day, as they registered their first-ever League win over Swansea, 1-0 at the Vetch Field with the goal attributed to winger 'Rock' Hudson. On Boxing Day they thrashed Stoke City 5-2 at Ninian Park then, two days later, humbled the mighty Liverpool who left Ninian Park on the wrong end of a 6-1 hammering. However, all was far from being well at Cardiff. The club had accepted an offer of £22,500 from Aston Villa for star striker Hitchens, whose departure would outrage many supporters. Hitchens, who scored forty-one goals for City in ninetey-nine appearances, went on to become an England international and enjoyed a lucrative career plying his trade in Italy while his old City team-mates laboured on in the lower divisions. Somewhat bizarrely for a proud Englishman, he always spoke of his love of Wales, and returned there for a brief spell with Merthyr Tydfil before retiring. Sadly, he died in 1983 at the age of forty-eight whilst playing in a charity match in north Wales.

In an amazing coincidence unparalleled in the FA Cup, City were drawn to face Leeds United at Elland Road in the third round of the competition for the third year running. The match was played on 4 January 1958 and unbelievably, City again won 2-1 to confound the statisticians. They went on to beat Leyton Orient at Ninian Park before losing a fifth round replay at League rivals Blackburn Rovers. In the Welsh Cup they didn't even get under starter's orders, as Hereford United of the Southern League won 2-0 at Ninian Park to end Cardiff's challenge in the formative stages.

On 6 February the football world was stunned when the aircraft carrying the Manchester United 'Busby Babes', along with club officials and various journalists, crashed on take-off at Munich airport while en route from a European Cup quarter-final match against Red Star Belgrade. More than half the forty passengers on board were killed, manager Matt Busby was critically injured. The legendary Bobby Charlton amazingly managed to escape serious injury after being thrown clear of the plane still strapped in his seat.

The Munich air disaster put Cardiff's comparatively inconsequential plight into context as they languished in the lower reaches of the League, during which time they were forced to sell Ron Davies to Southampton and Ken Tucker to Shrewsbury Town to offset lost revenue caused by falling gate receipts. There were few highlights, though a thrilling 4-3 win over promotion-chasing Blackburn Rovers at Ninian Park on 29 March must surely count as one. There was also an impressive win at Derby and a 3-0 humbling of Fulham in their last home game of the season, in which Welsh international defensive pairing Baker and Sullivan both scored their first goals of the season. Sullivan, having never scored for City before in twenty-one appearances, added a second shortly after. City's final game saw them travel to Lincoln City for a rearranged match that had originally been abandoned due to a blizzard, with City 3-0 up! Lincoln, fighting to save their Second Division skins against a Cardiff side with nothing left to play for, won the rearranged fixture 3-1.

City finished the season in lowly fifteenth position, four places and six points above Swansea, while attendances

slumped to around 16,000. In that summer's 1958 World
Cup Finals held in Sweden, Cardiff representatives Colin
Baker, Derek Sullivan and Ron Hewitt all played for Wales
in their first major tournament as they stormed through to
the quarter-finals, where Pele's first-ever World Cup goal for
Brazil put them out. Wales were initially eliminated in the
qualifiers but won a reprieve after several nations withdrew
rather than face political outcasts Israel. Tension was
building in the Middle East around the Lebanon crisis, and
was compounded when President Eisenhower sent in
troops to stave off the threat of international communism.

Inspired by John Charles, Wales played, and beat Israel
twice, to win the right to travel to Sweden along with every
other home nation where they performed admirably until
coming up against Pele. Weeks after their triumphant return
to the Principality, the Cardiff City Welsh international
contingent learned that Trevor Morris had accepted a
caretaker/manager job at Swansea, and the comparatively
inexperienced coach Bill Jones had been appointed manager
in his place. There has rarely been a dull moment in the lives
of Cardiff City supporters or playing staff!

1958–59 season

Jones' first course of action as acting manager was to find
cover for goalkeeper Graham Vearncombe, who at the time
was serving in the merchant navy. He eventually settled for
multi-talented Bristol Rovers stopper Ron Nicholls, who
was also a county cricketer with Gloucestershire. Despite
the new acquisition, the new season started disastrously as
City lost their first three games without so much as scoring
a goal. They had to wait until Huddersfield Town visited the
Welsh capital on 3 September before picking up their first
points, which they did with a 3-2 victory courtesy of goals by
Baker, Brian Walsh and Cliff Nugent. Two weeks later Jones

made one of the most inspired signings in Cardiff's history by paying Arsenal £10,000 for striker Derek Tapscott, who had developed into a key member of the Welsh national side during his time at Highbury. Tapscott's first game for the Bluebirds was Grimsby Town at home, and although Ninian Park's newest hero didn't score, his mere presence proved instrumental as the visitors were swept away on a blue tide. The 4-1 result kick-started City's season, and they went on to win seven out of their next ten as Jones fine-tuned his team by introducing gifted youngsters Graham Moore and Steve Gammon to the set-up. Jones also brought former ex-Bluebird Wilf Grant back to Ninian Park as trainer/coach, and sold forward Cliff Nugent to Mansfield Town after he had made 122 appearances for the club, scoring twenty goals. This winning run was broken by successive away defeats at Scunthorpe and Barnsley, but Christmas brought welcome cheer in the form of a double over neighbours Bristol City. The good form continued into the New Year with home wins over Rotherham and Brighton & Hove Albion on 3 and 31 January 1959.

The impact of the tigerish Tapscott was plain to see as Cardiff climbed effortlessly into the upper echelons of the division. There was little love shown in Cardiff on St Valentine's Day as city beat Liverpool 3-0 with Tapscott scoring twice, and Brayley Reynolds, a young forward signed from Lovell's Athletic two years earlier, also on target. However, City lacked the resilience needed for a sustained promotion push, and, after the Liverpool game, won only three more League matches that season, the most satisfying of which was a 3-1 over Swansea at the Vetch Field on 15 April. Despite their shortcomings, City had made a significant improvement on the previous season's showing and finished in ninth position, their progress reflected by an average increase of 2,000 on their home gates.

Just for a change, City hadn't beaten Leeds 2-1 at Elland Road in the third round of that season's FA Cup; instead they beat Third Division Plymouth Argyle 3-0 away before going down 3-2 at Norwich. The Canaries had already put out a weakened post-Munich Manchester United, and were going all the way to the semi-finals. City fared considerably better in the Welsh Cup where, after overcoming Gloucester and Rhyl, they crushed Wrexham 6-0 in the semi-final at Shrewsbury to set up a final meeting with Lovell's Athletic. Their Southern League opponents pushed City all the way, but eventually the gulf in class showed and Cardiff won the Cup with goals from Bonson and Hudson.

1959–60 season
At the season's conclusion, Swansea moved in to sign Reynolds for a nominal fee and Hewitt, who had scored thirty goals in seventy-one games for Cardiff and had won five Welsh caps while with the club, returned to Wrexham. To replace them Jones signed South African international forward Steve Mokone from Dutch club Heracles, and experienced Bristol City left-winger Johnny Watkins. Both lined up in the City team to play Liverpool in the opening game of their Jubilee season at Ninian Park on 22 August. In a memorable match, Mokone took only five minutes to open the scoring, but the Bluebirds had fallen behind by half time thanks to a pair of own goals by Molloy. Young Moore equalized just after the break but the glory fell to Walker, who scored the winner on his debut to break the hearts of the Merseysiders.

Moore and Watkins were the scorers again when City beat Middlesbrough midweek, but Mokone's stay was short-lived He failed to settle, and after only three games lost his place in the team and was replaced by Bonson. He would soon be on his way to Barnsley. After tasting defeat at

Charlton in the third game, City put together an amazing run that saw them lose only twice in the next twenty. In the midst of this run the club was rocked by the death of its president, Sir Herbert Merrett, who was largely responsible for keeping the club afloat during the war years. The team honoured his memory in the best possible fashion by thumping Leyton Orient 5-1 at Ninian Park in their next match, with Moore (2), Tapscott (2) and Sullivan the scorers.

On 19 December, City heaped more misery on Liverpool by thrashing them 4-0 on the hallowed turf of Anfield, with Tapscott again scoring a brace. Then, on 27 February 1960, the match in which talented youngster Barry Hole made his debut, City won 4-3 at Leyton Orient to go three points clear at the top of the League. The following week at Ninian Park, goals from Moore and Watkins sealed another win against Huddersfield.

Sadly, the Bluebirds could not transfer their League form to the FA Cup, where they were unceremoniously dumped out of the competition in the third round by Port Vale. In the Welsh Cup they beat Lovell's Athletic 5-0 to set up a sixth round grudge match with Swansea Town. In a match of three dismissals and a mud fight, City managed to win by the odd goal in three. Despite the victory, they incurred the wrath of the authorities once more for fielding an under strength XI because of impending League fixtures. Following an FAW inquiry, they were fined and told in no uncertain terms that if they failed to play their strongest available side again they would face expulsion. City needed a replay to edge past Bangor City to meet Wrexham in the final. A draw at Ninian Park meant another replay, this time in north Wales, where a jaded Cardiff lost 1-0.

For the last third of the season, City were engaged in a thrilling title race with Aston Villa, a race they ultimately lost by inexplicably belying their outstanding home form and suffering defeats by Portsmouth, Brighton & Hove Albion, and Plymouth. They also dropped points against Sunderland, Bristol Rovers and Swansea (where at one stage the Bluebirds had a comfortable 3-0 lead) to hand the championship to the Villans, who won it by a single point. Though City missed out on the League title, nobody could take the second prize away from them – finishing an impressive eight points clear of third-placed Rotherham United, they were promoted back to the First Division in second place.

Thankfully, the new man at the helm didn't make the same mistakes as his predecessors and no sooner had the season ended than Jones was busying himself strengthening his squad. Joe Bonson was exchanged for Scunthorpe United's Peter Donnelly, Welsh international fullback Trevor Edwards arrived from Charlton, and forward Brian Edgley was lured into the fold from Shrewsbury Town. Also, in what was probably Jones' best bit of business, reserve forward Harry Knowles was exchanged for Worcester City's Peter King, though it would be over a year before that starlet made his debut.

1960–61 season

Cardiff City FC resumed its First Division career after a three-year break with a visit to Fulham on 20 August 1960 where they drew 2-2 thanks to goals from Walsh and Moore. After losing their first home game to Sheffield Wednesday, it was left to Tapscott to secure the Bluebirds' first win of the season, which he did by scoring both goals against Preston North End in a 2-0 success. On 3 September, City sent minor shockwaves through the footballing world when they beat reigning First Division champions Burnley 2-1 at Turf Moor, with Watkins scoring a dramatic winner after

Tapscott had netted. Tapscott found the net yet again on 24 September at home to Arsenal to give the Bluebirds a narrow victory before a crowd of almost 35,000, but the team were losing more games than they were winning, and drawing far too many.

The 1960–61 season saw the introduction of the Football League Cup, though it was shrouded in controversy as many of the country's leading clubs, including Arsenal, Sheffield Wed and Spurs, declined to enter. Cardiff played their first-ever match in the new competition at Middlesbrough on 3 October when they ran out 4-3 winners over the Second Division club. The second round paired them with high-flying Burnley, who trounced the Bluebirds 4-0 on their own patch three weeks later. In City's next match, a home League game with Leicester, Jones unveiled his latest signing, winger Derek Hogg who had cost £12,000 from West Brom. Hogg made an immediate impact by scoring in a much-needed 2-1 win. City's best run of the season began with a 2-1 victory against Chelsea at Ninian Park. They lost only one game out of the next ten, including the completion of a League double over Burnley and three consecutive 3-2 wins during February to hoist themselves towards their modest target of maintaining First Division status.

The FA Cup pitted Cardiff against League rivals Manchester City, who showed remarkable resilience in taking the tie to a second replay, which Cardiff eventually lost 2-0 at Highbury. An extraordinary match was played at Ninian Park in the Welsh Cup on 28 January 1961, when Knighton of the mid-Wales League were the visitors. Under normal circumstances City would have fielded their reserve side, but in light of the punishment dished out by the FAW the previous season they were forced to play their strongest XI. City showed no mercy and eventually won the game 16-

0 with Tapscott setting a new club record of six goals in a single game. The other goals came from Moore (4), Donnelly (2), Hogg and Malloy. The score remains City's highest-ever total in a competitive match, and even in hindsight it's difficult to see what good the FAW's directives did anybody, least of all poor Knighton. City went on to beat Newport County in the next round to set up a semi-final meeting with Swansea, who were still smarting from the unfortunate sequence of events that had occurred during and after their last encounter. The match was a predictably tight affair, eventually being extended to a replay, with the Swans emerging as 1-0 winners.

On 11 March City came up against the so-called 'team of the century', Spurs, at Ninian Park. In one of the club's greatest-ever performances, they came from behind twice to beat the affluent Londoners 3-2 with goals from Hogg, Walsh and, of course, Tapscott, who, along with Malloy in the centre of defence, was at the heart of everything that was good about the Cardiff City team. The match, unusually for the period, kicked off at 7:00pm because of a Wales-Ireland rugby international played that afternoon at Cardiff Arms Park. Unfortunately, after that historic encounter, City's season evaporated and they could pick up only three points from the remaining nine games, with a 6-1 hammering at Chelsea on April Fool's Day being their lowest ebb. Despite a few blushes, in their first season back in the First Division City finished in fifteenth position, which seemed to please the supporters as the average attendance at Ninian Park surpassed the 23,000 mark. Despite their blip at Ninian Park, Spurs went on to win a Division One and FA Cup double, dominating the League with a record thirty-one wins.

The season had been disrupted around the mid-way point and the football world thrown into chaos when, under threat of strike action by the players, the Football League agreed to abolish the £20 maximum wage for footballers. While this was obviously good news for the players, many smaller clubs were faced with the prospect of being unable to compete with the 'big boys' when it came to offering contracts to prospective employees. As a result, a larger gulf began to develop between 'rich' and 'poor' clubs.

Cardiff made only one major signing that summer, centre forward Johnny King, who cost £11,500 from Stoke City. In addition, a clutch of youngsters signed professional forms with the club, most notably wingers Alan McIntosh and Gareth Williams, and goalkeeper Dilwyn John, who went straight into a head-to-head battle with Vearncombe for the number one jersey following Ron Nicholl's departure to Bristol City. Hengoed native Williams would take time to settle, but would eventually become club captain and a virtual ever-present. Cardiff's First Division survival hopes were dealt a savage blow when captain and defensive lynch-pin Danny Malloy suddenly left after making almost 250 appearances for the Bluebirds, during which time he managed to score an incredible fourteen own goals. When Jimmy Hill and the Players Union had the wage cap lifted, City were keen to have all their players on the same pay scale to avoid complications. Malloy, however, wanted higher wages than everybody else and when the club refused to bow to his demands, he left to take up a player/coach role at Doncaster Rovers. Reserve Frank Rankmore stepped up to take his place and performed admirably, but the influential Malloy was sorely missed.

1961–62 season

City drew their first two games of the new season and had to wait until 26 August and the visit of Blackpool before collecting maximum points. Several defeats followed before

City completed a League double over Chelsea to boost their flagging confidence. The home victory, on 6 September, was a spectacular affair with Welsh international forward Dai Ward scoring twice and Tapscott and Moore notching their first goals of the season as the Bluebirds won 5-2. It was to be their biggest win of a long and trying season. When City beat Sheffield Wednesday on 11 November at Ninian Park with a brace from Tapscott, they lay in seventh place in the League. Nobody, least of all the fans, could have expected that from then on, City would embark on a truly horrific run of twenty-one games that saw them win only once, a narrow 1-0 win over Aston Villa on Boxing Day at Ninian Park in which Tapscott again grabbed the all-important goal.

Bill Jones' systematic dismantling of the team didn't help matters one iota. Welsh international Derrick Sullivan, who had played in no fewer than nine different positions and had made 285 appearances for the club over a 13-year span, moved to Exeter City, Peter Donnelly was sold to Swansea, and Brian Walsh was transferred to Newport County after playing 224 matches for the Bluebirds. He would make only twenty-seven appearances for his new club before retiring from the game.

The biggest disappointment of all came when Welsh international striker prodigy Graham Moore, who had begun his career with Bargoed YMCA, was sold to Chelsea. The fact that City received a then record fee of £35,000 for him did little to ease the frustration and resentment simmering amongst the Ninian Park faithful. Chelsea manager Tommy Docherty later sold Moore to Manchester United for a huge profit. Jones tinkered with the team relentlessly, chopping and changing for almost every game. Even the purchase of Welsh international forward Mel Charles from Arsenal for £28,000 could neither appease the fans nor halt the club's alarming slide into the relegation zone.

By the time City's League form began to pick up again, they had been dumped out of all three Cup competitions. After seeing off Wrexham in the first round of the Football League Cup they needed a replay to edge out Mansfield Town, after which they travelled to Bournemouth for a third round tie which they lost 3-0. Cardiff received a bye to the equivalent stage in the FA Cup, but that's where the dream ended as Middlesbrough beat them 1-0 at Ayresome Park on 10 January 1962. In the Welsh Cup they managed to beat struggling Newport County and Bristol City (the distant possibility of European football had enticed several of the larger English clubs into the competition) before losing a semi-final 2-0 at part-timers Bangor City despite fielding a side that included six full Welsh internationals.

City finally managed a League win against Birmingham City at Ninian Park on 21 April (ten days after Mel Charles had scored all the goals as Wales beat Northern Ireland 4-0), where a Tapscott hat trick secured a 3-2 win before fewer than 9,000 spectators. Tapscott scored again in the next game along with Ward (twice) as the Bluebirds beat West Ham 3-0, but by then it was a case of too little too late and an emphatic 8-3 Everton victory at Goodison Park in the penultimate game only reiterated the point. They eventually finished in twenty-first place and, after only two seasons in the top flight, were relegated back to the Second Division along with Chelsea. Ipswich Town won the championship in their first season up under the guidance of the legendary Alf Ramsay, while Spurs retained the FA Cup.

The sale of Moore to Chelsea (ironically, the only team to finish below City that year) was interpreted by many as a sure-fire sign that the club lacked ambition – a charge that has been repeatedly levelled at them over the years. City's uninspired form throughout led to a drastic decline in attendances, which eventually plummeted to an average of just below 20,000, despite heartfelt pleas by the club for public support (the plight made even more poignant by the 61,566 record gate that turned up at Ninian Park on 14 October to watch a Wales v England international). The bubble had well and truly burst, and a long stint out of the First Division looked a certainty.

1962–63 season
During the summer of 1962, in which Brazil managed to retain the World Cup, two more first-team regulars left Ninian Park: Dai Ward was sold to Oxford and Johnny King returned to his first club Crewe Alexandra. The Cardiff City faithful were rapidly losing patience with manager Bill Jones, but were temporarily appeased when he splashed out £18,000 on Newcastle United's 32-year old Welsh international Ivor Allchurch and a further £7,000 on Bristol Rovers winger Peter Hooper. Both went straight into the team to play Allchurch's old club Newcastle at Ninian Park on 18 August, and their presence helped swell the gate to over 28,000. The thrilling match ended in a 4-4 draw, with Hooper, Charles and Hole (2) scoring the goals. City drew their next match at Norwich, then travelled to Derby County where a Hooper penalty and Allchurch's first goal for the club handed them victory. It was a decent enough start, with Allchurch in outstanding form, but then City capitulated and lost four matches in a row, including a demoralising 2-1 defeat at Swansea. On 10 of September, for the first time in the club's history, manager Bill Jones (along with trainer/coach Wilf Grant) was dismissed. There were also changes in the boardroom as Fred Dewey, an ex-Welsh international footballer before becoming a prominent figure in the shipping world, took over the chair from Ron Beecher, a local butcher, who had passed away.

Under the short-term guidance of coach Ernie Curtis

and his side-kick Ron Stitfall, Cardiff City then shrugged off the cloak of uncertainty surrounding Ninian Park and embarked on a short but awesome run of results that saw them avenge the Vetch Field defeat in spectacular style by beating the Swans 5-2 in Cardiff, notch an impressive League double over Grimsby, and break a long-standing club record by beating Preston North End 6-2 away. Amazingly however, in their very next game the run was brought to a shuddering halt when Chelsea beat them 6-0 at Stamford Bridge. City then recovered to beat Luton Town and Scunthorpe United at home before travelling to Southampton on 31 October and winning 5-3 with goals from Hole, Allchurch (2), McIntosh and Durban. The next day the mounting speculation over the vacant manager's job at Cardiff City was finally put to rest, and the board of directors announced that ex-Norwich City manager George Swindin would be taking over the post. But before Swindin and his trainer/coach ex-Bluebird Stan Montgomery could get to grips with their new charges and the task at hand, the 'big freeze' enveloped the country, meaning that it would be two months before City took to the field again.

Cardiff City were technically still manager-less when they came from a 1-0 half-time deficit to thrash Reading 5-1 at Ninian Park in the second round of the Football League Cup (where they now entered the restructured competition), only to bow out at the next stage to plucky Bristol Rovers. After a delayed start, Cardiff City's annual FA Cup challenge started on 18 February 1963 at League rivals Charlton Athletic. Unfortunately, that was also where it ended as the Londoners won 1-0. City didn't perform much better in the Welsh Cup; after a thumping 7-1 win over Welsh Leaguers Abergavenny Thursdays, Swansea beat them 2-0 at the Vetch Field to send Cardiff out in the most disappointing fashion.

League football recommenced at Ninian Park on 23 February with a 1-0 victory over title-challengers Chelsea, given to them via a rare Harrington strike. Over the coming weeks City recorded impressive wins over Southampton, Bury, Sunderland and Plymouth Argyle, but this was not enough to impress new manager Swindin, who was livid at his side's lack of consistency, perfectly illustrated by the two League fixtures against Chelsea. To force the players to shape up, at the end of the season thirteen of them were transfer-listed, including no fewer than six internationals. By way of explanation, Swindin claimed that due to the club's precarious financial position, he was being obliged to 'sell in order to buy', while some speculated that it was all an act of kidology by the new boss designed to demonstrate a hard-line approach.

He had a lot to disapprove of, as Cardiff ended a turbulent season in tenth position while Stoke City, featuring 48-year old maestro Stanley Matthews who had recently moved there from Blackpool, won the Second Division championship. Chelsea also returned to the First Division and their London rivals Spurs, inspired by Jimmy Greaves, made history by becoming the first British club to win a European trophy, thrashing Atletico Madrid 5-1 in the Cup Winners' Cup final held in Rotterdam, Holland.

Player dissatisfaction at the wages on offer, coupled with the 'up for grabs' approach to the transfer market by the disillusioned Swindin, made for a hectic summer at Ninian Park. Top scorer Hooper left for Bristol City after scoring twenty-three goals in forty-three games for Cardiff; in-form Durban was sold to Derby County; and centre-half Rankmore moved to Peterborough after making over seventy appearances. The departures paved the way for the signing of the summer, ex-Leeds and Juventus striker (and brother of Mel) John Charles from Roma at a cost somewhere in the region of £25,000. The signing of Welsh hero John Charles, dubbed 'the Gentle Giant' for his gentlemanly ways and the fact that he was never booked or dismissed from the field in his entire glittering career, was a major coup for the Ninian Park club. Almost unnoticed in the media furore surrounding Charles' arrival was the purchase of utility player Dick Scott from Swindin's old club Norwich.

1963–64 season
As fate would have it, the opening League match was at home to the Canaries on 24 August, where both Scott and John Charles made their competitive debuts for the Bluebirds. The match went down in Bluebird folklore as the Gentle Giant scored with an indirect free kick from an amazing 75 yards that found its way into the net off goalkeeper Kevin Keelan, to help Cardiff on their way to a 3-1 victory. Peter King and Allchurch scored the other less memorable, but no less important goals. Allchurch and John Charles each scored in a 2-2 draw with Manchester City at Ninian Park four days later, and goals from young Gareth Williams and the fading centre-forward Derrick Tapscott ensured a 2-1 win at Scunthorpe in their first away game. It was an encouraging enough start, but the injuries were mounting up and Swindin often struggled to fill unwanted gaps as the threadbare side won only twice in the next twelve League games.

At the height of their injury problems Cardiff played Wrexham in the second round of the Football League Cup. At that stage in the season the last thing City wanted was for the tie to go to a replay, never mind two replays, but that was exactly what happened. The north Wales side eventually won the third match 3-0 at the Racecourse Ground. On 4 January 1964, City faced old adversaries Leeds United in the third round of the FA Cup at Ninian Park. After only eight minutes of the match highly-rated winger McIntosh suffered a double fracture of his left leg, prematurely ending his career. While he recuperated at St David's hospital, Cardiff, he found himself lying in the next bed to Leeds defender Freddie Goodwin, who had also suffered a broken leg in the same match. As per the rules of the day, both teams had to finish the game with ten men and to compound City's misery still further, Billy Bremner scored a winner for Don Revie's Leeds United.

That same day it was announced that Ron Beecher, the Cardiff City chairman for the past seven years, had died in hospital following a long illness.

A 3-0 trouncing at Swansea on 28 March seemed to spur City into action and to lift the gloom they reeled off three more home wins against Swindon Town, Derby County and Scunthorpe to allay any lingering fears of relegation. The club settled into fifteenth place which, disappointing as it was, was still four places above Swansea.

As they were struggling in the League for most of the season and had made quick exits from both main Cup competitions, by the time City's involvement in the Welsh Cup began it represented their only realistic chance of silverware. In the early rounds City easily saw off the challenge of Ebbw Vale and Chester, winning the matches 6-1 and 3-1 respectively. In the semi-final Newport County held them to a draw before being edged out of the competition by a Mel Charles goal. The final against giant-killers Bangor City was a two-leg affair decided on a points system rather than goal aggregate, and after all the mathematics it amounted to yet another replay (or 'play-off'), to be held at Wrexham's Racecourse Ground on 4 May. On the eve of the big day the club 'dispensed with the services' of Swindin after he refused to resign during a stormy board meeting, leaving his charges to go on and win the Welsh Cup without him. Peter King scored both goals in a sweet 2-0 victory that led Cardiff City into the glorious arena of competitive European football, which had now been expanded to three separate tournaments, for the very first time.

To replace Swindin, the club appointed Jimmy Scoular as manager.

7

Stuck in Second
(1964-73)

Jimmy Scoular, aka 'The Iron Man', was ex-Royal Navy and a strict disciplinarian who had won the First Division twice as a player with Portsmouth, and the FA Cup with Newcastle United. It was hoped that his confrontational, no-nonsense approach would lick the dispirited Cardiff team into shape. But first he had to assess his new team and make the necessary changes.

Goalkeeper Graham Vearncombe was among the first out of the door after making 216 appearances, and was closely followed by Trevor Edwards, who emigrated to Australia. Aston Villa's Bob Wilson was bought as Vearncombe's short-term replacement and went straight into the team to kick off the season with a 0-0 draw against Ipswich Town on 22 August.

Sadly, the arrival of Scoular did not have an instant effect as City were forced to wait another eleven games before picking up their first League win under his guidance. By the time that win came, a 2-1 defeat of Derby County at Ninian Park where Peter King and Derek Tapscott were the scorers, Dick Scott had been exchanged for Scunthorpe United striker Keith Ellis. After the Derby win City's form improved dramatically, and further home wins came over Portsmouth, Charlton Athletic, Bury and Plymouth Argyle, along with their first away win which came at the expense of Leyton Orient. Slowly but surely, City began to pull clear of the relegation zone. A painful Boxing Day defeat at Swansea Town was followed by an incredible 6-1 home win over

Middlesbrough, with King, now converted into a handy inside-forward, blasting a hat-trick.

All the excitement that season was provided by Cardiff's first excursion into Europe (as Welsh Cup holders), the success of which owed much to the continental experience of John Charles. Their first-ever European Cup Winners' Cup tie, the first for any Welsh club, was a 0-0 draw away at Danish club Esbjerg on 9 September 1964, which was followed on 13 October by the home leg, when a King strike gave City safe passage to round two. There, they were drawn against Sporting Lisbon of Portugal, the Cup holders. Hardly anyone expected City to progress past these giants of European football, but goals from Greg Farrell and Tapscott gave them a deserved 2-1 lead going into the second leg at Ninian Park on 23 December. There, a 0-0 draw was enough to ensure a quarter-final against Spain's Real Zaragoza to the delight of the Welsh public. The first leg was played in Spain on 20 January 1965, where City fought back from two goals down to salvage a draw. In the return match, City battled hard but lost 1-0, and the overall tie 3-2.

By the time their European dream ended, City had already been dumped out of the Football League Cup at Southampton and lost an FA Cup third round match at home to Charlton. It followed that retaining the Welsh Cup represented City's only chance of silverware that season, as well as the added incentive of another crack at the European odyssey. Cardiff breezed past Merthyr Tydfil and Hereford United in the early rounds on their way to a semi-final showdown with Swansea, which was settled by a Farrell penalty. In the final City faced Wrexham, and swamped their opponents 5-1. In any other competition the margin of victory would have been enough to virtually guarantee winning the tie, but the FAW still insisted on a points system so, amazingly, Wrexham's 1-0 win at the Racecourse was enough to warrant a replay. In the ensuing play-off in Shrewsbury (another bizarre decision) on 5 May, Allchurch scored twice in a convincing 3-0 win that ensured a quick return to Europe.

Animated by their success in the Welsh Cup, City finished the League on a high, helping to relegate Swansea by trouncing them 5-0 at Ninian Park, with Allchurch scoring a hat-trick (and John Charles the other two), and winning three of their last four to finish in thirteenth place.

The summer of 1965 was, in many ways, the end of an era for the club as it waved goodbye to several good servants. The sublimely talented Ivor Allchurch went 'home' to Swansea; local boy Ron Stitfall, then aged thirty-nine, retired after making over 400 appearances; and goal machine Derrick Tapscott moved on to Newport County after seven years' service. Additionally, Steve Gammon, Alec Milne and Alan McIntosh were all forced to leave the club through injury and, finding his age catching up with him, Mel Charles dropped into the non-League quagmire with Portmadoc. Scoular knew he couldn't hope to replace so many prominent figures, so he didn't even try, making just one significant signing in the form of Crewe Alexandra forward Terry Harkin, and choosing instead to put his faith in a host of young prospects he planned to integrate into the first team.

1965–66 season

On a historical note, the 1965–66 season saw the introduction of substitutes, initially only for injured players. Previously, if a player was injured during the course of a match and unable to continue, his team-mates were expected to play out the game a man down. Cardiff's first registered substitute was local youngster David Summerhayes, who replaced injured veteran Colin Baker towards the end of the first match of the season at home to Bury on 21 August, which was settled by a John Charles header. Charles also scored in the next game along in a 2-1 victory over Derby. Defeat at Norwich City followed, before the return game with Derby at the Baseball Ground, which City won 5-1. However, their makeshift defence soon began leaking goals at an alarming rate as they first lost 4-1 to Wolverhampton Wanderers at home, then went on the road to lose 6-4 at Rotherham United and 5-2 at Charlton, before regrouping to beat Manchester City 4-3. By October young centre forward George Andrews had broken into the team and was soon grabbing the headlines with his goalscoring exploits, but most of the hype was reserved for a local apprentice by the name of John Toshack, who in time would become one of Cardiff's most famous sons.

Toshack made his first appearance as a substitute against Orient at Ninian Park on 13 November, aged just sixteen years and 236 days, making him the youngest ever to play a first team game for City. Skilful, quick and adept, he scored the third goal in a 3-1 win and made his full debut at Middlesbrough a week later where he bagged two in a 4-3 win (the other goals being scored by another teenage prodigy, George Johnston). In his 1982 autobiography *Tosh*, he says that on signing professional forms with the club, 'I felt I had made it. Cardiff City were my team and I was so proud to be pulling on their shirt'. Toshack certainly was a different class, but for all their attacking flair Cardiff had severe problems at the back, and didn't register another League win that calendar year.

In round one of the European Cup Winners' Cup, City were paired with Standard Liege of Belgium. Sadly, there was to be no repeat of the previous season's exploits as they lost 3-1 on aggregate. Surprisingly enough given their past record, City's redemption that season came by way of an extended run in the Football League Cup. They saw off Crewe (after a replay) and Portsmouth in rounds two and three, then thrashed Reading 5-1 at Ninian Park, with Johnston scoring a hat trick and Harkin a brace. In the fifth round (quarter-final) they entertained Ipswich and beat the Tractor Boys 2-1 to progress to a two-leg semi-final with First Division West Ham United. City proved no match for the Hammers, losing the first game 5-2 at Upton Park and the second 5-1 to bow out of the competition on the wrong end of a hammering, but with their heads held high. The Londoners went on to lose the final to WBA.

Cardiff also scraped past Port Vale to reach round four of the FA Cup and a trip to no-hopers Southport where, in true Cup fashion, the minnows completely outplayed their Second Division opponents to win 2-0 and send Cardiff out. A similar fate awaited in the Welsh Cup where sworn enemy Swansea stood in their way. When a 2-2 draw at the Vetch called for a replay at Ninian Park, City must have had high hopes for the competition they had dominated for the past two years, especially when they roared into a 3-0 lead. However, the Swans had other ideas, and took full advantage of Don Murray's sending-off for a head-butt, eventually winning a truly amazing match 5-3 after extra time.

In December City accepted a £45,000 offer from Leicester City for their Welsh international full-back Peter Rodrigues. After a stint at Sheffield Wednesday, the cultured defender went on to captain Southampton to an unforgettable FA Cup triumph over Manchester United in 1976. After the sale, Cardiff immediately splashed out £5000 on Derby's Bobby Ferguson, who slotted straight into the team to play Plymouth at Ninian Park on New Year's Day 1966, where City put in one of their best performances of the season to register an impressive 5-1 win. However, this victory didn't fire the struggling Bluebirds as had been hoped, and they soon fell into the old habit of drawing too many games. Right-back Alan Harrington, who had made a total of 381 appearances for the club, was another victim of a career-ending injury, and Scoular swiftly looked to the transfer market to boost his floundering squad. New arrivals included fullback David Carver and left-winger Ronnie Bird, who was drafted in from Bury for a bargain £5000 to assist in the increasingly desperate situation at Ninian Park.

City were not assured of Second Division safety until 4 May when Middlesbrough were the visitors to Ninian Park. It was Boro's last game and if they lost they would be relegated, while Cardiff also had to win to stay up. In another enthralling match, Boro centre-half Dickie Rooks scored an unlikely hat-trick but goals by Hole, Greg Farrell, Andrews (2) and King saw City through. Incredibly they lost their next game 9-0 at Preston North End and went on to lose the final match 2-0 at home to Norwich, but by that point had already done just enough to stay up. They finished in twentieth place, a single point above the doomed Boro who were relegated along with Orient, while Manchester City and Southampton won promotion.

Much has been written about the events of the summer of 1966, but while Alf Ramsey's England were making history, it was business as usual at Ninian Park. The expected upheaval came when City accepted an offer of £42,000 from Blackburn Rovers for want-away star Barrie Hole. This battling Welsh international had become frustrated at the club's lack of progress since their relegation from the First Division, and saw his future elsewhere. John Charles also left for Hereford after notching eighteen goals in seventy-nine appearances, and mainstay Colin Baker joined the coaching staff. With attendances in steep decline and funds generally sparse, Scoular resisted the urge to spend, preferring to tackle the new season with the players already at his disposal.

1966–67 season

Without any star attractions to entice them, only 7,735 turned up to watch City lose their opening game to Ipswich, although almost twice that number (no doubt encouraged by a 2-1 win at Bristol City) attended the next home game to see the Bluebirds thrashed 3-0 by a rampant Wolves team. City's first home win of the season came against Carlisle United where a double from King and further goals by Andrews and Toshack gave them a 4-2 victory. It soon became obvious that another difficult season was in prospect, and it was another eleven games before City tasted victory again in the League, a run that included heavy defeats at Wolves (7-1), Charlton (5-0) and Plymouth (also 7-1). During this disastrous spell, Scoular finally decided to put his hand in his pocket to land centre-forward Bobby Brown from Northampton Town and experienced half-back Brian Harris from Everton, who had won the FA Cup with the Toffees just six months earlier.

The tide began to turn in Cardiff's favour after a 3-0 home win over Bury on 19 November when Toshack scored a brace and Brown his first for the club. Two weeks later City beat Norwich at Ninian Park and then travelled to Birmingham City, where they won with a last-minute Brown strike. On 14 December they beat Northampton 4-2 to claw themselves off the foot of the table, but just when the team was beginning to gel it was dealt another heavy blow when young hotshot George Johnston was sold to Arsenal. As if that wasn't enough, it wasn't long before Greg Farrell joined Bury and George Andrews went to Southport. To his credit, Scoular used the money wisely, recruiting Welsh international winger Barrie Jones from Plymouth and forward Norman Dean from Southampton. With the League season drawing ominously to a close City again lapsed into the relegation mire, and only a 3-0 win over Birmingham at Ninian Park in the penultimate game saved them from the drop. Again they finished in twentieth position, with an even lower points total than they had accumulated the season before.

In that season's Football League Cup a Toshack goal was enough to beat Bristol Rovers in the first round, and the subsequent draw seemed kind, handing the Bluebirds a home tie against Exeter City. However, they failed to capitalize and lost 1-0. In the FA Cup, a third round tie with Fourth Division Barnsley needed a replay to decide the winner, with Cardiff eventually going through and assuming home advantage over Manchester City in the next round. That game also required a replay, which Cardiff lost 3-1.

The primary aim that season must surely have been to bring European football back to Ninian Park via the Welsh Cup, and City started the competition in determined mood by hammering Swansea 4-0 on their own patch and then beating John Charles' new club Hereford 6-3 in Cardiff. They eased past semi-final opponents Newport County to enter a two-legged final with Wrexham. The first game at the Racecourse Ground ended 2-2, but a goal from new-signing Dean and an own goal sealed a 2-1 victory, and the trophy, at Ninian Park on 3 May. While the comparatively irrelevant Welsh Cup was being played out, the other trophy in the news, the cherished World Cup that temporarily resided at FA headquarters, was stolen and later recovered in a north London suburb by a black and white mongrel called Pickles.

1967–68 season

The summer of 1967 was another relatively quiet period at Ninian Park with Scoular making just one notable signing, that of Leicester wing-half Malcolm Clarke. A crowd of over 17,000 (more than double that of the first match the previous season) were at Ninian Park on 19 August to welcome the visit of Plymouth, who left with a share of the spoils. City also drew their next game at Bolton, then beat Crystal Palace 4-2 at home with goals by Barrie Jones, Bobby Brown, Ronnie Bird and the incomparable Peter King, before tasting defeat for the first time at Portsmouth. Again, Cardiff's notorious inconsistencies were a source of frustration for all. This was never more apparent than at Ninian Park on 23 September when, after a 5-1 mauling by Derby, Scoular and the then Derby chief Brian Clough had to be restrained from coming to blows in the tunnel.

Mid-season, when it became obvious that City were not going to challenge for promotion, they accepted a club record fee of £45,000 from Bolton for Gareth Williams, sparking more fans' fury. This time though, after leaving Ninian Park the classy winger's career nosedived. Suffering from loss of form and disciplinary problems he failed to shine for Bolton, and after a brief spell at Bury left the game entirely to open a bar in Gran Canaria. Shortly after Williams' departure, Scoular paid Blackpool £15,000 for replacement winger Les Lea; yet another young upstart, defender Steve Derrett, began forcing his way into the team.

One of City's best-ever campaigns in the European Cup Winners Cup began on 20 September, a run that would dominate their entire season and capture the imagination of a success-starved Welsh public. The epic excursion began in Ireland where City drew 1-1 with Shamrock Rovers; goals from Brown and Toshack completed the job two weeks later. Their second round opponents were Dutch side NAC Breda, and City produced a solid away draw before putting on a breathtaking performance to win the return leg 4-1. The quarter-finals pitted Cardiff against Torpedo Moscow, and in the first leg at Ninian Park on 6 March 1968, they beat the Russians by virtue of a Barrie Jones strike. However, City lost the return match in Tashkent by the same score, thereby instigating the need for a play-off at a neutral ground (Augsberg, West Germany) which City won 1-0 with the winning goal coming from Dean. Dean scored again in the fourth minute of the semi-final first leg away against crack West German side SV Hamburg, after which it was one way traffic but again City stubbornly held out for a draw. Amazingly, Dean put the Bluebirds in front at Ninian Park to put a debut European final appearance firmly within their sights but the opposition, brimming with international talent, soon swept into a 2-1 lead but then in the eighty-eighth minute Brian Harris scored his one and only goal for Cardiff (in 181 matches) to pull them level and send Ninian Park into delirium. Cruelly, however, just two minutes later the Germans scored a third to send the Welsh club out 4-3 on aggregate.

To illustrate the gravity of City's unlikely nine-month run in the Cup Winners Cup, the first tie at Ninian Park against Shamrock Rovers attracted a crowd of around 14,000, while their final game there against Hamburg drew almost four times that number. City were often forced to field weakened teams in Europe partly because of the 'foreigner' rule that severely restricted the amount of non-Welsh players that could be used, and partly because in 1968 new signings had to wait three months before they could be considered eligible for Europe. However, this didn't seem to hamper Manchester United's efforts that season as they became the first English club to win Europe's premier competition, Matt Busby's Red Devils finally clinching the European Cup by beating Benfica in the final a decade after the Munich air disaster. (Celtic had become the first British winners of the trophy when they beat Inter

Milan the year before, and Tottenham the first UK-based winners of any continental competition when they won the Cup Winners' Cup in 1963.)

The domestic Cup competitions paled in comparison to City's triumphant Cup Winners' Cup campaign, and City's lacklustre performances reflected this. In the Football League Cup they beat Aldershot only to bow out at First Division Burnley in round two, and their FA Cup challenge was even shorter as they lost 4-1 at Stoke in the very first round. The Welsh Cup, City's tour-de-force, kicked off with an 8-0 thrashing of Ebbw Vale, and Wrexham and Chester also fell by the wayside as Cardiff marched into a final meeting with Hereford United. There City easily retained the trophy with a 6-1 aggregate win to storm into Europe for the fourth time in five years.

An amazing League match took place at Ninian Park on Boxing Day 1967, where City faced Villa and won 3-0 despite playing much of the game with only nine men after being hit by injuries to Brown and Carver. Although often touted as an excuse around this time Cardiff's injury list really was devastating to the team, the latest tragedy to befall them being the enforced retirement of promising striker Bobby Brown, who had scored twenty-seven goals in just fifty-nine appearances. Consequently, Scoular was forced into shelling out £8,000 on Huddersfield Town striker Brian Clark, and recruited highly-rated goalkeeper Fred Davies from Wolves. The former made a spectacular debut at Derby on 3 February 1968 where he scored twice in a thrilling 4-3 win, and though he was ineligible for the European games, settled into the team well scoring six goals in six games. City ended the season well, and despite scoring only three more goals, were beaten just once in the last seven to finish in a respectable thirteenth place.

By way of strict training regimes, shrewd tactical

changes, attention to detail and inspired dealings in the transfer market, the signs were there that Scoular was finally beginning to change the club's fortunes. As part of a major fitness and team-building exercise, at the end of the season Cardiff jetted off for a mammoth six-week tour of New Zealand and Australia, playing fourteen matches and losing just once.

Meanwhile, new World Champions England contested the first European Championship in Italy, completely failed to live up to expectations and lost a semi-final to Yugoslavia. In the other semi-final, eventual winners Italy progressed past the USSR by virtue of a toss of a coin after the two sides finished level.

1968–69 season

Back in Cardiff, the 1968–69 season started disastrously with three straight defeats and City had to wait until a visit to Bury on 21 August brought a 3-3 draw and their first point of the campaign. Three days later a King strike was enough to give them their first victory of the season at home to Preston. From there their season really began and they lost just once in the next seven. Unable to hold down a first team place, Euro hero Norman Dean was transferred to Barnsley, and after a little tinkering, the team began to take on a new, more disciplined approach. The result was astonishing. Between the end of October and the New Year, City played eleven games, of which they won eight and drew two to rocket up Division Two. The best win in this spell was a 5-1 at Fulham on 7 December when Clark, Jones (2), Toshack and Lea did the damage.

John Toshack was beginning to turn heads, and turned a few more by scoring in both games against Porto of Portugal in round one of the Cup Winners Cup. However, his efforts were not enough and there was no repeat of the previous season's exploits as City exited the competition 4-3 on aggregate. Disappointingly, City also went out of the Football League and the FA Cups at the same stage, the former at the gleeful hands of Carlisle, and the latter after a draw at Ninian Park on 4 January 1969 (watched by 55,136) forced a replay at Arsenal which they lost 2-0. Thankfully however, the Bluebirds encountered little resistance in the Welsh Cup, where they convincingly beat Aberystwyth Town and Bethesda Athletic to book a semi-final meeting at Chester, where a Toshack brace won the game. Old enemy Swansea awaited in the two-legged final, and City won both games to emerge 5-1 aggregate winners, retaining the Cup with the minimum of fuss.

City's best League result of the season was a 5-0 win over Oxford United at Ninian Park on 8 February, where Bird put the Bluebirds ahead before making way for the blossoming strike partnership of Toshack and Clark, who each scored twice. Over the coming weeks, Cardiff also defeated Blackpool and Norwich at home, but their dismal away form, coupled with that atrocious start, ensured that they never really threatened runaway leaders Derby at the top of the table. As the League wound up, City let things slip, winning just once in the last seven games, but still did enough to finish in a slightly flattering fifth place. Scoular's tireless work in moulding a solid, efficient and often exciting team had restored some confidence at the club. People responded, and gradually attendance figures began to creep up. Many fringe supporters flocked to the ground just to see the boy-hero Toshack play, and he rarely disappointed becoming the first Cardiff player to top the divisional scoring charts with twenty-two goals.

In some quarters the drastic upturn in City's fortunes midway through the season was attributed to Scoular's tactical awareness and willingness to experiment.

Traditionally, British teams played with what would now be considered a 3-3-4 formation with three defenders, three midfielders, two advanced wingers and two centre-forwards. But like anything else, the formations favoured by managers were susceptible to various fads and trends. For example, the dazzling success of the Brazilians at the 1958 World Cup prompted many clubs to adopt a 4-2-4, while Italian clubs famously pioneered the more defensive 'sweeper' system. England won the 1966 World Cup with a 4-3-3 formation, so no prizes for guessing what the next trend that swept British football was. Whether by accident or design, Scoular took elements of all these styles and blended them together, putting his own unique spin on things to always keep the opposition guessing.

1969–70 season
Toshack was in the headlines again on 9 August, when he scored the fastest goal of the season after just 28 seconds of the first match at Carlisle which City went on to win 3-2. Amazingly, it was Cardiff's first away win on the opening day since 1933. City then drew two home games and lost at Swindon before rattling off consecutive wins against Bristol City, Middlesbrough and Bolton. A mammoth crowd of over 30,000, their biggest in eight years, flocked to Ninian Park on 27 September to see Toshack's first-ever hat-trick in a 4-2 win over Queen's Park Rangers. In their next home game they thrashed Villa 4-0, but kept their best for the visit of Hull City on 1 November, who were sent home on the wrong end of a 6-0 hiding. Towards the end of the month City began producing some of their best League form in years to record seven straight wins, the pick of which being an outstanding 3-0 win over Sheffield United on 10 January 1970 when Clark (2) and Bird were the scorers. This run, that climaxed with the Bluebirds perched proudly on top of

the League, coincided with the introduction of Palace utility player Bobby Woodruff, for whom Scoular had paid £25,000 when it emerged that Barrie Jones was the latest victim of the club's injury jinx. Jones' career was effectively finished when he sustained a double leg fracture in a defeat at Blackpool in October.

City were in blistering form in round one of the Cup Winners' Cup, where they registered a club record 12-2 aggregate win over Norwegian Cup winners Mjondalen IF. However, the second round proved a bridge too far as they tumbled out 3-1 on aggregate to Turkish outfit Goztepe Izmar, despite winning the home leg 1-0. City made their customary early exit from the Football League Cup, losing 3-1 at Palace, and were then the unwitting victims of another famous FA Cup giant-killing act when Fourth Division York City knocked them out of the third round after two replays. To their credit, Cardiff managed to put their other Cup disappointments behind them to reinforce their dominance in the Welsh Cup by sweeping aside Barmouth & Dyffryn 6-1 and Wrexham 3-0 in rounds five and six. Both ties were played at Ninian Park and Clark scored seven of the nine goals. They faced Swansea in the semi-final, and beat them 2-0 at the Vetch Field to reach yet another final. As their opponents Chester were an English club and therefore ineligible to represent Wales, City were guaranteed a place in the next season's European Cup Winners' Cup draw whether they won or lost. Nevertheless, City proved that they would be there on merit after recording an impressive 5-0 aggregate win over Chester.

Cardiff were top of Division Two for about a week, then they lapsed into a dreadful sequence of results that produced just one win from the next eight games stretching into March. They recovered to end the season with one defeat in six, but eventually had to settle for seventh place, a vastly disappointing return on a season that at the mid-way point had promised so much more. Toshack was undoubtedly the brightest spark in the team, boasting a stunning strike rate of thirty-one goals from fifty-one appearances in all competitions.

1970–71 season

The 1970–71 campaign is undoubtedly one of the most memorable and dramatic in Cardiff's illustrious history. They signalled their intent before a ball had even been kicked by splashing out £15,000 on Palace goalkeeper Frank Parsons and £35,000 (a new club record) on Coventry City's midfield maestro Ian Gibson, a large chunk of the outlay being instantly recouped when Les Lea was sold to Barnsley. As expected, both Gibson and Parsons were drafted into the side to face Leicester City at Filbert Street on the opening day, 15 August. The home team that day had England legend Peter Shilton between the sticks and were among the hot favourites for promotion, but Clark headed the only goal of the game to the delight of the travelling support. A week later, in Cardiff's first home game, Toshack and King scored in a 2-2 draw with Millwall. Then they put on another impressive performance to beat Sheffield Wednesday at Hillsborough before coming unstuck for the first time that season at Bristol City. On 5 September, Toshack underlined his star quality by notching a brace against Birmingham, for whom a 16- year-old Trevor Francis was making his League debut. He would go on to become Britain's first million-pound footballer.

By the time Middlesbrough visited the Welsh capital on 3 October, new keeper Parsons was under fire, having made some costly errors. The axe was waiting to fall, and despite saving a penalty in the match, Parsons was again found wanting as the Bluebirds slumped to a 4-3 defeat. He was banished to the reserves. Later that month, Toshack notched a stunning hat-trick in a 5-1 home win over Hull, thereby cementing his position as one of the best forwards in Britain. It could only be a matter of time before he left his beloved Wales for pastures new, and soon after, Bill Shankly's Liverpool came in with an offer of £110,000 that City simply couldn't refuse. By 8 November Toshack had signed for the Anfield outfit and soon began terrorizing defences with legendary Kop strike-partner Kenny Dalglish. For the record, Toshack had notched a century of goals in 203 appearances for Cardiff, and went on to score 95 in 245 appearances for Liverpool before leaving in 1977 to join Swansea as player/manager. There he masterminded an unprecedented turn of fortune for City's biggest rivals as they rose swiftly through the Leagues to the First Division. But the fairytale didn't last. The Swans failed to attract large enough crowds and soon plummeted gracelessly back down the Leagues. Toshack then left to begin a lucrative and highly successful managerial career in continental Europe, the pinnacle being a trophy-laden stint in charge of Real Madrid.

The Toshack transfer caused uproar amongst the City faithful, the ripples of which can still be felt today. It was interpreted by some as the latest in a string of dubious managerial decisions by Scoular that had included dropping top-scorer Clark, and playing various players in unfamiliar roles. Sections of the press even hinted (perhaps unfairly) that Cardiff were actually deliberately avoiding winning promotion, the logic being that they were quite happy to plod along in Division Two and win the Welsh Cup every season guaranteeing European football year after year, something most First Division clubs could only dream about. Who knows if the press was right? I like to think not, but this is Cardiff City we are talking about! Nothing can ever be proved, the claims being based on speculation and circumstantial evidence.

Following Toshack's departure, Clark was reinstated and announced his arrival by scoring twice in a 4-1 mauling of Blackburn. But then City began to stutter, losing to Charlton, Oxford United and Millwall before Christmas. Scoular responded by breaking the club's transfer record for the second time in six months, paying a somewhat inflated £42,000 for Sheffield Wednesday striker Alan Warboys. The exact opposite of Toshack, Warboys was big and powerful, as opposed to skilful and sublime. The signing of Warboys proved a master-stroke as the new boy responded by scoring a brace in an emphatic 4-1 win against his former employers. The following Saturday he notched two more at Portsmouth to shoot City back to the top of the League. 'Warbs', as he became known, quickly won the affection of the crowd and his team-mates, who saw him as something of a maverick wind-up merchant.

Cardiff City travelled to QPR in the second round of the Football League Cup ... and promptly lost 4-0. Just eight days later they faced Cypriot part-timers P.O. Lanarca in the Cup Winners' Cup first round, first leg tie at Ninian Park, and so began City's best-ever excursion into European football. City were at the top of their game that night, and ruthlessly dispatched their inexperienced opponents 8-0, the result remaining City's biggest single-leg victory in European football. A 0-0 draw two weeks later completed the job. In round two they met Nantes, and beat the French aristocrats home and away, the first leg at Ninian Park being especially memorable as Toshack (2), Gibson, King and Phillips all scored in a runaway 5-1 victory.

The hype surrounding Real Madrid's visit to Ninian Park for the quarter-final first leg clash on 10 March 1971 was immense. Hotshot Warboys was ineligible for the competition having signed too late, so a home-grown youngster called Nigel Rees was pulled out of the Wales youth squad to take his place against the Spanish giants, who turned out before a crowd of 47,500 in a red kit instead of their famous all-white. In true fairytale fashion, it was Rees' cross that picked out the trusty head of Clark to give City one of their most-famous-ever wins. A draw would have been enough to see them through to the semi-finals for the first time, but the Bernabéu was, as it is now, a formidable stage on which to perform. Though they battled well, City ended up losing 2-0 to go out 2-1 on aggregate. Although by their own high standards, Real Madrid 1971–72 was generally regarded as a poor team, nothing could be taken away from Cardiff, who came so close to causing a major upset.

The triumph at Ninian Park in the home leg is still one of the highlights in their history, but kit man Harry Parsons later revealed that the win wasn't down to superior footballing ability, or even good luck! In later interviews he recalled how, at the instructions of Scoular, he turned off the heating in the away dressing room at Ninian Park that night making it, in his own words, 'Like a bloody iceberg in there!' in an effort to throw the sun-kissed Spaniards off their stride. Such skulduggery was not uncommon in those days, and undoubtedly still goes on behind the scenes today. Whatever your views on the subject, it can never be said that such spoiling tactics don't work!

By the time they exited European football that season, Cardiff had also been on the receiving end of yet another FA Cup shock. After seeing off Brighton & Hove Albion in round three, Fourth Division Brentford beat them 2-0 at Ninian Park.

The City carried on their good form into February, and against Carlisle at Ninian Park on 6 March Warboys wrote his name into the history books. In a top-of-the-table clash he scored a brilliant hat trick inside ten minutes, and added to his tally in the second half to complete a 4-0 rout. City remained in the promotion places until 17 April, when a home defeat by Watford knocked them down to third behind Leicester and Sheffield United. By the end of the month, City were a point behind Sheffield with a game in hand. It was do-or-die for both clubs. On a muggy evening, 42,963 packed into Bramall Lane to watch the Blades slice the Bluebirds apart with a ferocious display of attacking football. City lost 5-1 to leave their promotion hopes in tatters and Sheffield went on to claim the runner-up spot behind Leicester leaving City in third. All that remained in that barnstorming season was the comparatively low-key Welsh Cup, where Cardiff reinforced their reputation as Wales' leading club by beating Newport County, Bangor and Chester on their way to a final meeting with Wrexham. After the first leg they held a slim lead going into the Ninian Park game, when the mercurial Gibson stole the show with a well taken double to help them to a resounding 4-1 aggregate win that saw them qualify for Europe for a fifth consecutive season. That season, City's fledgling Bluebirds also excelled in reaching the FA Youth Cup final, where they were beaten by Arsenal.

1971–72 season
Bird's goal in the Welsh Cup final was his first and only of the season. It was also his last in a Cardiff shirt because in the summer of 1971, he and Brian Harris, two rocks of the late 1960s, moved on. On the eve of the new season, Scoular drafted in Newcastle winger Alan Foggon, who took his place in the team to play Burnley at Ninian Park on 14 August where a Clark double gave City their first point before a crowd of over 23,000. After the previous season's heroics the Cardiff public had high hopes for their team, but

From The Ashes: The REAL Story of Cardiff City Football Club

their optimism diminished as they were forced to wait until the seventh game for a win, a 3-2 home success over Sheffield Wednesday. In October goalkeeper Bill Irwin was bought from Bangor City (N. Ireland), and made his debut in a 2-1 home defeat by Millwall. The defeat seemed to sting the team into action as they won their next game in the Welsh capital 6-1, inflicting their biggest win of the season over a hapless Charlton side. It could and should have been a turning point, but sadly it wasn't, and the Bluebirds lost four of the next five to languish in the lower reaches.

Given their growing pedigree in the competition, many expected Cardiff to progress past Dynamo Berlin in round one of the Cup Winners' Cup, especially when they returned from East Germany with a draw and an away goal under their belts. But the Germans had other ideas, and won a penalty shoot-out at Ninian Park to send the Bluebirds out. First Division West Ham accounted for them early in the Football League Cup, so by January 1972 it was then left to the FA Cup to instil some hope into an ailing season. The team duly obliged, beating Sheffield United 3-1 at Bramall Lane (the ground where their promotion hopes had been so cruelly dashed the year before) and progressing to an epic fourth round tie with Sunderland. Both the original game and the replay ended 1-1, so the match had to be settled with a second replay at Manchester's Maine Road with City eventually taking it 3-1 with goals from Clark, Woodruff and a first for the club from Billy Kellock, a new signing from Villa. The visit of First Division leaders Leeds United in the next round certainly grabbed the attention of the public as an official figure of 49,180 (even more than attended the visit of Real Madrid eleven months earlier) crammed in to see Johnny Giles score twice as the Yorkshire club coasted to a 2-0 win. They went on to win the Cup, but lost out on a double to Brian Clough's Derby.

162

After that FA Cup mini-excursion, it was back to the bread and butter of League business. After a 4-3 home defeat by Blackpool, a draw at Charlton on 12 February sparked a much-improved run during which City lost just once in 12 games, with a 5-2 home win over Preston in which Warboys scored a hat-trick, all-but eliminating any lingering relegation worries. With their safety assured, City grew complacent and lost three of their last four to eventually finish in nineteenth place, just a point above Charlton, who were relegated with Watford. After being promotion contenders for two of the past three seasons, Cardiff's final League position was a huge disappointment. As in the year before, City's last games of the 1971–72 season were a two-legged Welsh Cup final with Wrexham, having knocked out Swansea, Llanelli and Rhyl en route. There, in a final insult, City's relinquished their grip on the Cup after five years and Wrexham gleefully snatched it back, winning 3-2 on aggregate.

1972–73 season
That summer, Mel Sutton departed Ninian Park for Wrexham and Scoular used the proceeds to buy defender Albert Larmour from Linfield. The Irishman went straight into the team to play Luton Town at Ninian Park on 12 August where, despite utilizing some experimental tactics to the bemusement and derision of the 16,000-plus crowd, City won with a Bell penalty and a timely winner from Warboys. But those who expected a promotion challenge were again sorely disappointed, as after their opening day victory City went on to lose seven of their next eight. This awful run prompted Scoular to part with Warboys in an exchange deal with Sheffield United for their pair of Welsh internationals Gil Reece (who had been released by Cardiff in the early 1960's) and David Powell. Days after the duo's

arrival, Scoular invoked the wrath of the fans once more by accepting a £100,000 offer from Bournemouth for Clark and Gibson, and allowing right-back Carver, who had lost his place in the team to a blossoming Phil Dwyer, to go to Swansea on loan. Clark later said that in an age where most footballers outside the First Division were only paid around 25 per cent more than the average working man, a double-your-money offer from Bournemouth manager John Bond was simply too good to refuse. Without him his old Cardiff team-mates laboured to a draw at Orient, where Alan Foggon was sent off and subsequently sold to Middlesbrough, meaning that Scoular had to move fast to restructure his decimated team.

That October, David Goldstone, a wealthy London property developer, paid £110,000 to take charge of the club from chairman Fred Dewey. Goldstone promised 'First Division football within five years', and signalled his intent by allowing Scoular to make two substantial signings, midfield general Johnny Vincent from Boro and prolific striker Andy McCulloch, from QPR, who cost a new club record of £45,000. Fittingly, both scored on their debuts, the former in a 2-0 home win over his old club and the latter in a 3-0 home whitewash of Preston. But while City were irresistible at home yet again they struggled on the road, and would end up the only team in the division to finish the entire campaign without notching a single away victory.

With a worryingly low League position, no Cup Winners' Cup, and another early Football League Cup exit (to Bristol Rovers), January 1973 saw the start of the FA and the Welsh Cups, which represented City's only hopes of success. In the English competition they beat Scunthorpe in the third round only to suffer a demoralising defeat at the hands of Third Division Bolton. Having lost out the year before, the Welsh Cup was high on Cardiff's list of priorities, and that showed when they walloped Aberystwyth 7-1 in round four. Newport and Chester also fell by the wayside as City booked a final place against Bangor City. A rule change in the competition meant that when City lost the first leg 1-0 in they would have to score twice at Ninian Park on 11 April to take the Cup on goal aggregate. They duly obliged and then some, winning the game 5-0 and the overall tie 5-1.

In February, new Chairman David Goldstone gave Scoular the red light to break the club transfer record for the second time in four months to bring Villa winger Willie Anderson to Ninian Park in a £60,000 deal. Unfortunately, his arrival did not have the desired effect, as in his first ten League outings City won only once and failed to score in seven. The visit of Huddersfield on 21 April was an all-out relegation scrap, with both teams in serious trouble, but on this occasion Cardiff rose to the challenge and thumped their Yorkshire rivals 4-1. A draw at Millwall then meant that City only needed a point from their home match with Sunderland to maintain their Second Division status. The Black Cats were fresh from an epic FA Cup Final win over Leeds, but City did just enough to get the required draw. They ended the season in lowly twentieth place, and it was clear to all that the club's flirtations with relegation were becoming increasingly desperate. This time around, they had only managed to finish above Huddersfield on goal difference, after both clubs collected thirty-three points. Cardiff's total of forty-three goals from forty-two games was their lowest since 1929.

1973–74 season

The summer of 1973 saw the introduction of the three-up/three-down promotion/relegation format, and a new Grandstand at Ninian Park housing 3,300 seats, unveiled at cost of almost £250,000. Personnel-wise, David Carver severed his ties with the club and moved to Hereford after 243 appearances, and misfit Billy Kellock was sold to Norwich. The big signing was powerful wing-half George Smith, who was bought from Birmingham for £45,000. In addition, local boys Brian Attley and Peter Sayer signed professional contracts with the Bluebirds, both going on to have big futures at Ninian Park. Of their first six League games of the 1973–74 season, City drew five and won one, a 5-0 drubbing of Oxford where McCulloch notched a hat-trick. Then, from the lofty heights of fifth in the table, City spluttered dramatically, their luck deserted them, and they plunged downwards. A narrow 1-0 home win over Blackpool on 13 October was their only win in the next ten outings.

City's Cup form was also less than spectacular. Only 13,300 turned up to see them draw 0-0 with Sporting Lisbon at Ninian Park on 19 September in the Cup Winners Cup, and the Portuguese side finished the job by winning the away leg 2-1. The first round of the Football League Cup brought Hereford United to Ninian Park, where a McCulloch double put them out. In the next round City faced First Division opposition in Burnley and acquitted themselves well, forcing a replay at Turf Moor which they narrowly lost 3-2.

On 9 November Scoular was given his marching orders after nine years in the Ninian Park hot seat, his last match in charge being a 1-0 home defeat by West Bromwich Albion. In that time he had taken the club from the Second Division doldrums to the brink of promotion and, unfortunately, back again. Whatever his shortcomings, the man definitely left a lasting impression. Everybody who came into contact with him has a story to tell, and not all are pleasant. By all accounts the tough-talking disciplinarian thoroughly enjoyed living up to his nickname 'Iron Man', and his confrontational style often put him at loggerheads with rival managers, notably the equally volatile Brian Clough. Legend has it that the two crossed swords repeatedly after Clough, when he was Derby manager in 1968, made derogatory comments about the City squad. The simmering feud eventually came to a head years later with Scoular gripping his adversary by the neck and apparently trying to strangle him!

Scoular's immediate replacement was trainer Lew Clayton, who was officially installed at the helm for a 2-0 defeat at Millwall, but watching the game from the stand that day was ex-Leicester and Manchester United manager Frank O'Farrell. Within days the Irishman was appointed Cardiff's new manager, apparently heralding the start of a new era at Ninian Park.

8

Trapdoor Learning
(1973–82)

1973–74 season (continued)

Frank O'Farrell was a big-name manager who had been forced out of Manchester United after failing to solve the infamous George Best disciplinary problems, and his first unenviable task as manager of Cardiff City FC was to watch them lose 3-0 at Middlesbrough on 17 November 1973. Therefore, his next meaningful action was to shatter the club's transfer record by spending £62,000 on Leicester City winger John Farrington, who made his debut in a 1-0 home win over Bolton Wanderers. The following week at Leyton Orient, Woodruff and McCulloch scored the goals as City claimed maximum points away from Ninian Park for the first time since October 1971. For once, the club enjoyed a fruitful Christmas period, drawing at Hull City and beating both Swindon Town and Sunderland at home. In the latter match, Farrington scored a hat-trick and Willie Anderson a 30-yard wonder goal as they came from behind to thrash the reigning FA Cup champions 4-1.

However, the New Year proved anything but prosperous as they went down 1-0 at Portsmouth's Fratton Park in the first match of 1974. City persevered gamely through February and March, notching wins against Fulham, Notts County and Preston North End (a game in which Phil Dwyer scored his first goal in eighty-one consecutive appearances). But then all form deserted them, and they lost to Sheffield Wednesday and Millwall, forcing O'Farrell to take more decisive action. He raided Manchester City for goalkeeper Ron Healey and West Ham United for defender Clive Charles, but neither did much to help the club's fortunes and City went the rest of the season picking up only one more League win. Ironically enough, that win came over leaders and eventual champions Middlesbrough. Despite that result, the Boro match was O'Farrell's last. A statement released shortly afterwards said that he was leaving to take a job, reputedly worth £20,000 a year, on the coaching staff of the Iranian national team. He had been in the Cardiff job for only 158 days. To his credit Jimmy Andrews, the first team coach employed by O'Farrell, refused the offer to join him in the Middle East and agreed instead to take over as new City manager. The softly-spoken Scot, once described by Mike England as 'the best coach in the game', was officially appointed City's third manager of the season on 1 May. Though it offered a slight improvement to the previous season, Cardiff's final League position of seventeenth did little to inspire anyone and O'Farrell's sudden, undignified departure angered many. Initially, it was thought that the Irishman would spark big things at Ninian Park, but sadly the task proved too much for him and he disappeared into the sunset.

When Birmingham dumped them out of the FA Cup a few days after the Portsmouth defeat back in January, everything rested, as usual, on the Welsh Cup. City duly obliged by beating Ton Pentre, whose visit to Ninian Park on 9 January attracted only 856 supporters – Cardiff City's lowest-ever attendance for a competitive first team match. City also beat Owestry and Shrewsbury Town on their way to yet another final. City were overwhelming favourites to beat Southern League side Stourbridge over two legs, but eventually did so with little room for error, winning both games 1-0 either side of Andrews' appointment to retain the trophy and secure another eventful foray into Europe.

1974–75 season

Elsewhere, Denis Law's famous back-heel goal for Manchester City against his former club Manchester United ensured that the fallen giants would be plying their trade in the same division as Cardiff, outside the top flight for the first time. By then, the extended stay in Division Two was taking its toll on Cardiff financially so again there were no funds for Andrews to strengthen the lop-sided squad he had inherited. Already in an impossible position, his plight was made worse by the loss of first-team regulars Bobby Woodruff and Gary Bell who both left on free transfers, and the sale of Andy McCulloch who joined Oxford United for £73,000. McCulloch was back at Ninian Park sooner then he probably imagined, as the two clubs met on the opening day of the new season when new Cardiff captain Clive Charles scored the equalizer in a 1-1 draw. That was as good as it got for a while, because out of the next ten games City lost eight and failed to score in seven, an awful run that deservedly saw them propping up the division. To balance the books Welsh international Leighton Phillips was sold to Aston Villa for £80,000, and seasoned defender Don Murray left on a free transfer to Swansea Town. And still there was no money to spend.

Cardiff were sent reeling out of the Football League Cup, the first competition the season, at Bristol City as early as 19 August. A month later they lost 2-0 at home to Ferencvaros in the European Cup Winners Cup, and went on to lose the return match in Hungary 4-1. In round three of the FA Cup, City resumed their sporadic duel with Leeds United, on this occasion losing 4-1 at Elland Road. That season, even the Welsh Cup could not spare the Bluebirds' blushes. After seeing off Hereford United, Owestry and Newport County, they lost a two-leg final 5-2 to Wrexham.

The situation at Ninian Park was so desperate that

Andrews was forced into exchanging Farrington, City's record signing only a year earlier, for Northampton Town midfielder John Buchanan. Although a few eyebrows were raised after that swap, Buchanan was pure quality and it is probably no accident that his introduction to the team coincided with their best form of the season, beginning with a 3-2 defeat of York City on 16 October. Buchanan scored his first goal for the club in the next game, a 2-1 defeat at Bolton, but the team recovered well to put together a run that included just one defeat from the next twelve outings, highlights being home wins over Oldham Athletic, Sunderland, Aston Villa and Norwich City. Gradually, City began to climb the table towards safety but the run came to an abrupt end in Cardiff's 1,000th League match, a 5-1 drubbing at Millwall on 25 January 1975. Sadly, it was all downhill from there, and all the hard work and good results of the past few months were laid waste as City slipped back into the dreaded relegation zone with barely a whimper. Most agreed that the problem stemmed from a lack of goals, but with no money to spend, how was Andrews supposed to address that issue?

Defeat followed defeat, and though they managed a sequence of three draws and two wins in the last third of the season, it was not enough to save them. City finally succumbed after a long flirtation with the drop. The 5-1 loss at Millwall proved critical, as the Londoners stayed up at City's expense simply on goal difference. Tellingly, Cardiff had scored only thirty-six League goals in forty-two games, compared to champions Manchester United's tally of sixty-six.

The prospect of Third Division football was too much for chairman David Goldstone to even contemplate, and within weeks he sold his holdings in the club to a consortium of businessmen headed by local man Clive

Griffiths. By way of explanation, Goldstone later said, 'Whatever the fans may think or say, you are in the hands of the players and manager… Ultimately, it's down to those 90 minutes on the pitch when those guys either do the business or they don't'.

1975–76 season

Under the new regime, Stefan Terleski was elected as the new chairman, while from the playing staff George Smith left for Swansea, Peter Vincent joined Atherstone Town, and David Powell left to join the South Wales Police Force. With City's uncertain future and precarious financial situation there was still no money for the luckless Andrews to spend on new players, so again he was forced to negotiate a series of free transfers and loan deals, which he did with aplomb. To address the goal-scoring crisis, Tony Evans was obtained from Blackpool and old crowd favourite Brian Clark was re-signed from Millwall, but the major coup that summer was the acquisition of ex-Wales and Spurs defender Mike England, whom Andrews persuaded to postpone retirement for a season. After an eye-opening defeat at Grimsby Town in the first game, the board realized the need for a quality midfielder and released the £18,000 necessary to purchase Doug Livermore from Norwich. Evans, England, and Livermore all made their League debuts in a 1-1 draw with Bury on 23 August, and together they went on to form the backbone of a very capable team in what would be a much-improved season, though the early stages brought mixed results.

City suffered a first home League defeat at the hands of Crystal Palace, and lost at Port Vale and Preston, but picked up good wins over Brighton and Mansfield before beating Wrexham at Ninian Park on 4 October in what was, remarkably, the two sides' first-ever League meeting. In a comfortable 3-0 win, Phil Dwyer scored a rare double and went on to miss the penalty that would have given him the only hat-trick of his career. Later that month a welcome surprise boost was provided when Andrews was allowed to sign former Australian World Cup star Adrian Alston from Luton for £20,000, and it was then that City's season really took off. Alston marked his debut at home to Chesterfield on 31 October with a blistering double inside the first quarter of a 4-3 victory, and formed a lethal strike partnership with summer-signing Evans. Over the coming weeks the duo scored eleven goals in seven games, and had both media and fans eating out of the palms of their hands as City breezed into the top six. As his reward for his hard work Andrews received the Divisional Manager of the Month award for December.

Having lost out in a restructured League Cup to Bristol Rovers, the fruits of the blossoming new strike partnership were never more apparent than in that year's FA Cup. For the first time in twenty-nine years, Cardiff entered at the first round stage, where Alston scored a hat-trick and Evans a double in a 6-2 demolition job of Exeter City. Evans scored the only goal in a subsequent home tie against Wycombe Wanderers, and Alston hit the winner at Orient in the third round. Their best FA Cup run since 1972 came to a controversial end at Southend United on 24 January 1976 where, despite yet another Evans goal, City went out to an injury time winner from Stuart Parker.

Two weeks after crashing out of the FA Cup, City lost 4-1 at League leaders Hereford, but travelled to Walsall three days later and came from behind to win 3-2 with Alston again claiming a double. The following week, City entertained Gillingham and won 4-1 with goals from Livermore, Buchanan and, as expected, one each from Alston and Evans. City were now in a promotion fight, and though their form dipped slightly in March, they remained on course, especially when tenacious midfielder Alan Campbell, signed from Birmingham City for a bargain £20,000, began to stamp his authority on games. The Scot scored his first goal for Cardiff in the pivotal game of the season, a home tie against League leaders Hereford on 14 April which drew a crowd of 35,501, City's biggest home gate since they had graced the First Division more than a decade earlier. Livermore also scored in a 2-0 win that came hot on the heels of consecutive victories over Southend, Grimsby, Preston and Palace. An Alston goal in the last game of the season at Bury was enough to grind out another victory that ensured runner-up spot and instant promotion back to Division Two.

Wrestling the Welsh Cup back from Wrexham would have put the icing on the cake of a good season, and the Bluebirds started the competition in determined mood by beating Sully and Swansea en route to a semi-final against Chester, which they eventually won at the second time of asking with a lucky own goal. Controversy reigned when the first game of the two-legged final against League rivals Hereford, which ended in a 2-2 draw, was declared void when it was revealed that Peter Spiring (who had scored both Hereford goals) was ineligible for the competition. On 18 May the two sides met at Edgar Street and played out another draw, meaning that the trophy depended on the re-play of the original void match at Ninian Park, which was played the day after the Edgar Street game. Though the corresponding League fixture drew that phenomenal 35,000+ crowd, disappointingly, the Welsh Cup game was witnessed by less than a tenth of that number. Those die-hards that did attend were treated to an entertaining match and witnessed Freddie Pethard, a young defender signed from Celtic, score his first senior goal. Clark also scored in what was for him an emotional last appearance, and trigger-happy Evans rounded off the scoring in a thrilling 3-2 win that sent the Bluebirds soaring back into the Cup Winners' Cup.

Before the Welsh Cup final, City were rocked by the news that Mike England would be leaving the club for an American side with the unlikely name of the New England Teamen with immediate effect. It was later suggested that he had been offered and then refused a position on the coaching staff at Ninian Park, and was unhappy at his treatment over the affair. England was closely followed out of the club by fellow ex-Welsh internationals Gil Reece and Tony Villars. Losing such influential players was not the best preparation for life in a higher division, and Andrews did little to lift sinking spirits when he announced that he was 'happy' with his remaining playing staff and would not be making any significant signings that summer, thereby neatly side-stepping any awkward questions about the ongoing cash crisis. He also had other things on his mind.

Sporadic outbreaks of violence had been creeping into the game for years, but the 1975–76 season is perceived by many as being the one when football violence exploded into the mainstream. Trouble erupted at several City games, but was low-key in comparison to a Division Two match between Chelsea and Luton Town that resulted in over 100 arrests. Elsewhere, fifty Manchester United supporters were apprehended after a game in Stoke, and there were disturbances on a huge scale at Ibrox in the Old Firm clash between Glasgow Rangers and Celtic. Football hooliganism, the so-called 'English Disease' was such a growing concern that the government held an investigation into crowd behaviour and published their findings in guidelines that were later issued to clubs. The bad press and safety concerns were contributing factors in a widespread decline in attendance figures at League grounds, and the situation wasn't helped by the fact that within a few years almost every professional club in the country would be forced to keep its supporters behind fences.

1976–77 season

Wales went to the 1976 European Championship in Czechoslovakia, only their second major tournament qualification, largely due to a general lack of interest from other nations, and somehow entered a depleted competition at the quarter-final stage, where Yugoslavia knocked them out. Cardiff's season started early that year, on 4 August with a 1-0 home win over Swiss club Servette in the first leg of the Cup Winners' Cup first round. Though they lost the return leg 2-1, resulting in a scoreline tied on aggregate, they progressed to the second round on the 'away goals' rule, where Russian side Dynamo Tblisi awaited. Despite being outplayed, City won the first leg at Ninian Park with an Alston screamer, but lost the away game in Tblisi 3-0 before a reported crowd in excess of 100,000.

That season, the League Cup also started early, and City were on fire in the two-legged first round tie against Bristol Rovers, who had knocked them out of the competition in two of the last four years. City won the first game 2-1 at Ninian Park with a goal each from Alston (a penalty) and Evans, who excelled himself in the second game by scoring all City's goals in a remarkable 4-4 draw. The second round saw Cardiff visit Queens Park Rangers where they lost 3-1, Evans predictably scoring City's consolation.

The League season kicked off on 21 August with a comfortable 2-0 win at Charlton Athletic thanks to a double from popular Merthyr Tydfil native Derek Showers, whose only drawback seemed to be a poor goals-to-games ratio. An extended run in the coveted number nine shirt in the 1974–75 season brought a return of only five goals in thirty-five appearances, though his commitment and work rate were to be admired. Showers was on target, along with the fading Alston, when City registered their first home points of the season at the expense of Blackburn Rovers a week later. Just when the disillusioned Cardiff public were beginning to show a little faith, the team started losing, and one bad result followed another. Inevitably, Andrews was drawn back into the transfer market and took full advantage of a financial crisis sweeping Portsmouth, which was evidently even worse than the one sweeping City, to land defender Paul Went, who made his debut in a 3-2 home win over Bolton. However, City's form remained erratic and important victories over Fulham and Southampton were over-shadowed by crushing home defeats to Sheffield United and Nottingham Forest.

Before Christmas, Alston joined the exodus of UK-based footballers heading for the bright lights of the USA by joining the Tampa Bay Rowdies, and Andrews wasted no time in using that transfer fee to sign winger Steve Grapes from Norwich and striker Robin Friday from Reading. Friday was an interesting character who gained cult hero status and has since become popularly known as 'the greatest footballer you never saw'. It was common knowledge within the game that he was fond of indulging in LSD and other mind-altering substances, and some of his fellow pros later admitted to being terrified of his simmering temper and notorious unpredictability, two traits that seemed to blight every aspect of his life. Team-mate Phil Dwyer remembered that Friday was 'very volatile' and used to 'terrorise the opposition'.

On 27 December City beat Hereford 3-1 at Ninian Park, and followed it up with a storming 3-0 home win over Fulham on New Year's Day 1977, a match in which Friday showed off his precocious talent by scoring twice in the absence of Fulham's own flawed genius, George Best. But then City let their form slip and plunged back down the table into the danger zone, winning only twice in fourteen games.

City's latest FA Cup campaign kicked off with the visit of First Division Spurs on 8 January. Peter Sayer scored the only goal, and in the process propelled himself to stardom via the opening sequence of the BBC's flagship football programme Match of the Day. The irrepressible Sayer was on target again in round four, along with Giles and Buchanan, as they beat Wrexham 3-2 in front of 29,000 ecstatic fans at Ninian Park. City also landed a home tie in the next round against Everton, but slumped to a 2-1 defeat. In the Welsh Cup they beat Stourbridge and Bangor City on their way to a semi-final appointment with Bridgend Town, which they won 2-1 to progress to a final against Shrewsbury. Goals from Freddie Pethard and Robin Friday ensured that City carried a lead into the away leg, but there they were overrun and went down 3-0. The result itself mattered little as Cardiff were still granted a place in the following season's Cup Winners' Cup, because Shrewsbury is an English club.

City left it late in the League, and retention of their Division Two status was not secured until the very last game. On 16 April they had beaten Luton 4-2 at Ninian Park and provided a shock a week later when a Sayer goal was enough to beat Division One-bound Forest on their own ground. A few mixed results followed, until the situation arose that required City to earn a point from their final game at home to Carlisle United, who were also fighting for their lives to stay up. The Bluebirds did just enough to secure the result, and at the same time condemned Carlisle to the drop. It wasn't a great season by any means, but City's two main objectives, to avoid relegation and to secure a place in the lucrative Cup Winners' Cup, had been achieved. Just.

Encouragingly, after contesting the 1976 European Championship the Welsh national squad drew more plaudits at the end of May by beating England in the Home Championship to claim a first-ever win at Wembley. The same venue, for so long the fortress of English football, was also the scene of an ugly Scotland victory that saw rampaging Scottish supporters celebrate the win that clinched the Championship by ripping up the hallowed Wembley turf.

It was business as usual during another quiet closed season at Ninian Park, the only activity of note being the transfer of Derek Showers to Bournemouth for a 'small fee' after almost a decade with the Bluebirds. Off the pitch, the government-sanctioned Safety of Sports Grounds Act was implemented. Consequently, the capacity of the ground was reduced. Just before the new season kicked off, it was revealed that striker Robin Friday was suffering from a 'mystery illness' that would cause him to miss the start of the season. It was the beginning of the end for the wayward star, whose disciplinary problems and annoying habit of going AWOL for days on end was causing great concern. Andrews later conceded that, 'He was brilliant, there was no two ways about it – the boy could play. At the time I didn't know what his major problem was so I bought him ... For a period I handled it but I'm afraid Robin was a hopeless case. He was lost and by the end he was uncontrollable, you could never depend on him'.

1977–78 season

The team's lack of fire-power was underlined once again in a tame opening day draw with Bristol Rovers at Ninian Park, and Andrews quickly signed Ray Bishop from Cheltenham Town and forward Keith Robson from West Ham. However, neither made much impact and Cardiff ground out just two wins from the first 12 League games. During this awful spell the club were also knocked out of the Cup Winners' Cup in the first round by Austria Vienna and, after seeing off Torquay United, humbled 5-1 by Swindon Town in the second round of the League Cup. The club was in turmoil, plagued by disciplinary problems on the pitch and power struggles off it, which culminated in Bob Grogan replacing Stefan Terleski as chairman. With regards to the constantly revolving (and steadily diminishing) playing staff, Robin Friday went AWOL at the most inconvenient time, the influential Doug Livermore was sold to Chester, and Welsh international full-back Rod Thomas was drafted in from Derby County to help in what was fast becoming a relegation dog fight. At the beginning of December the Bluebirds were soundly beaten 6-1 at home by Sheffield United and lost 6-3 at Bolton a week later.

That game proved to be Friday's last hoorah for the club, and when he left his career nosedived. Still plagued by drink and drug demons he died in Ealing, West London, in 1990, aged just thirty-eight. He had such an impact on Welsh popular culture that the band Super Furry Animals dedicated their 1996 single 'The man Don't Give a Fuck' to his memory, and in a BBC poll in 2004 he was voted 'All Time Cult Hero' by both Reading and Cardiff supporters, despite making only twenty-one appearances for the Bluebirds.

Friday wasn't the only volatile and unpredictable character at Ninian Park at the time. After a goalless home draw with Hull, striker Keith Robson was involved in a much-publicized skirmish with coach Alan Sealey in the staff car park that just about epitomized the state of affairs at the club. After Christmas Cardiff powered to a 4-1 home win over Millwall with goals from Bishop, Buchanan (2) and Robson, and followed it up with a 1-0 over Charlton. But just as it seemed that City were turning the corner, their hopes were dealt a massive blow when Robson was sold to Norwich for £18,000, probably as a result of the infamous car park episode.

That year's Welsh Cup was nothing short of a fiasco. In the early rounds, City struggled to overcome non-Leaguers Worcester City and Kidderminster Harriers before losing to the first Welsh club they met, Wrexham. In February 1978, weeks after the club's early FA Cup exit at the hands of Ipswich Town, Andrews sparked more controversy when he issued a statement to the press declaring that he was putting his entire squad up for sale. Not surprisingly, given the way the team were performing at the time, only Welsh international forward Sayer attracted any significant interest, eventually moving to Brighton & Hove Albion for a lavish £100,000. In the absence of their two most prolific forwards, a Buchanan penalty brought a much-needed win over Sayer's new employers, and Bishop rescued a point at Millwall the next day. The makeshift striker was on target again to gift the Bluebirds a victory in the next game, a home tie against Southampton, but defeats at Stoke City and Burnley quickly followed. City then picked up useful points against Charlton Athletic and Palace, and beat Bolton and Sheffield United to give themselves the smallest glimmer of hope. The pivotal game came on 3 May when Notts County visited Ninian Park. For once City rose to the occasion, coming from behind to win 2-1. City lost their final League game to Orient, but by then their safety had been assured. For long periods Cardiff had looked odds-on for relegation and most agree that they did well to finish such a traumatic season so strongly, but it was clear that wholesale changes had to be made if the club was to survive another trying season in Division Two.

Thankfully, the holder of the purse-strings

acknowledged the fact and despite the sharp decline in attendance figures at Ninian Park (partly due to the enforced ground modifications) in the summer of 1978, those purse-strings were loosened enough for Andrews to spend more money than any other Cardiff manager before him. Like a deprived kid in a sweet shop, he gleefully established a new club record by splashing out £75,000 on Newcastle United's Mickey Burns. Burns was a player of undoubted class, but his best years were behind him and he soon found himself installed as a (rather expensive) coach after injury restricted him to just a handful of first-team appearances. In addition to Burns, Andrew's paid a hefty £70,000 for Hull's Welsh international defender Dave Roberts, but by far their best signing that summer was striker Gary Stevens, a former chicken factory worker who cost a paltry £3,000 from non-League Evesham. Finding himself surplus to requirements, Paul Went was sold to Orient for £20,000. Before the new season started proper City participated in a new, high-profile competition called the Anglo-Scottish Cup, which pitted English and Scottish League clubs against each other. Curiously enough, their group didn't contain a single Scottish representative, consisting instead of Fulham and both Bristol clubs. Though they managed to beat Fulham, elsewhere Cardiff performed poorly and lost their other two matches. They also exited the League Cup in the very first round, losing 4-2 on aggregate to Oxford. Early indications were that despite all the money that had been spent, there was much hard work still to be done if the Bluebirds were to avoid another relegation scrap.

1978–79 season
The League programme began on 19 August with a 2-2 home draw against Preston, but then the Bluebirds

collapsed and suffered three defeats on the bounce. They recovered enough to notch their first win of the season against Cambridge United, courtesy of a Buchanan strike, but then slumped to one of their worst post-war defeats, a 7-1 drubbing at Luton. In the next game, Stevens scored on his belated home debut to help Cardiff to a 2-0 win over Blackburn, and a Buchanan double secured the points at Wrexham the week after. Inexplicably, the Bluebird's form then nosedived again, and they managed just one win from the next 11. During that time Mickey Burns, City's record signing just months earlier, was transferred to Middlesbrough after a disastrous stint in the Welsh capital.

On 6 November, days after a 4-1 home defeat by Charlton, the news that many had been expecting finally broke; Jimmy Andrews was to be relieved of his duties half way through his five-year contract. Richie Morgan was appointed temporary caretaker/manager, and showed such enthusiasm for the job that he was given the post permanently a month later. At thirty-four he was the youngest manager in the club's history, but he was made to wait until 23 December for his first win when goals from Roberts and Tony Evans handed Cardiff a home win over Fulham. City's last League point of 1978, a 0-0 draw at Burnley, was sandwiched between abysmal 5-0 thrashings at Brighton and Cambridge.

On 30 January 1979, City lost 3-0 at Swindon in the FA Cup third round, and their misery was complete just weeks later when they went out of the Welsh Cup to a fired-up Worcester City after edging out Merthyr Tydfil. Hence, by the time the winter finally broke at the end of February, the League was the only competition City were still involved in, and suddenly they began to appreciate the fact. It was a much-changed team that resumed League action, as Morgan had strengthened the squad by paying Norwich

£70,000 for left-back Colin Sullivan before proceeding to smash City's transfer record by forking out £100,000 for Tranmere Rovers' in-demand centre-forward Ronnie Moore. Also, Linden Jones, a trainee from New Tredegar, a small valley town in the Rhymney valley, began to emerge as a useful full-back.

To make way for the new arrivals, David Giles was sold to Wrexham and Brian Attley moved to Swansea. A sequence of four straight wins against Orient, Blackburn, Leicester and the mighty Newcastle soon followed and after a brief patchy spell in March, City ended the season unbeaten in eleven. The highlights were storming home wins over Brighton and Sheffield United (when Buchanan scored a hat-trick) and a 2-1 win at Sunderland that denied the Black Cats a place in Division One. In the first half of the season, City had looked like firm relegation candidates, but they recovered so well under Morgan's guidance that they finished ninth, their highest position since 1971. At the end of the season Tony Evans, who boasted a record of fifty-eight goals from 145 matches, was sold to Birmingham for a slightly inflated £120,000, giving Morgan the means to eclipse the existing transfer record for a second time by paying Blackpool £130,000 for midfield marvel Billy Ronson.

1979–80 season
The 1979–80 season brought the three top Welsh clubs (Cardiff, Swansea and Wrexham) together in the same division of the Football League for the first time in history, and Cardiff set the standard by shrugging off a 4-1 opening day defeat at Notts County to win three of their next four. Stevens scored the winning goal in every game, and also scored in the one they lost when Tony Evans scored twice for Birmingham on his return to Ninian Park. As Moore

struggled to settle in, Bishop emerged as a competent strike partner for Stevens and scored twice as City avenged that opening day defeat by beating Notts County 3-2 in Cardiff. Morgan then caused a stir by paying American club Tulsa Roughnecks £70,000 for Wayne Hughes who was, in fact, a Welshman originally hailing from Port Talbot. He also signed Lincoln City goalkeeper Peter Grotier, who had previously had a loan spell at Cardiff in 1973, when Ron Healey succumbed to injury. Already flirting with relegation, the club suffered a disastrous dawn to the new decade, beginning in the worst possible manner on New Year's Day 1980 when they lost 2-1 to Swansea before a riotous Vetch crowd of 21,306. City old-boy David Giles delivered the killer blow by scoring the winner in injury time.

Then it was FA Cup time again and, though City were held to a draw at Ninian Park, old foes Arsenal saw off City's plucky challenge by winning 2-1 in north London. Given the gulf in class between the two sides, there was no shame in going out to the Cup-holders, especially as the two games were witnessed by a total of almost 60,000. City had already bombed out of the League Cup at the first hurdle to Everton, so the Welsh Cup again represented their only distraction from the drudgery of the League. Cardiff met Newport at Somerton Park and lost 2-0 to their south-Wales rivals and eventual tournament winners, to complete a miserable month.

As far as League matters were concerned, things improved slightly when Ronnie Moore's second goal in twenty-nine appearances was enough to beat Wrexham, and he was on target again at Shrewsbury a week later as the Bluebirds won 2-1. Sadly, that was his last goal in City's colours. His quest for form ultimately proved fruitless, he lost his place in the team and started the next season in the

Third Division at Rotherham. John Lewis snatched a few headlines by scoring the winner against Watford in early February, but City kept their best form for the spring when they beat Charlton, Luton, and Swansea to hoist themselves clear of the relegation zone. Their last win came by virtue of a 3-0 drubbing of Oldham on 12 April meaning that in the final standings Cardiff finished second in the unofficial Battle of Wales in overall fifteenth position, one place above Wrexham and three places behind Swansea. At the end of the season Ron Jones, a former Olympic athlete, was appointed General Manager to work alongside Richie Morgan. The arrangement was that while Jones saw to the day-to-day running of the club and various commercial enterprises, Morgan took charge of team affairs.

1980–81 season
The first hurdle for the new set up to negotiate was the League Cup, where they scraped past Torquay United 2-1 on aggregate to enter the second round, by which time striker Peter Kitchen had arrived from Fulham. The new signing scored his first Cardiff goal in a 1-1 draw at Chelsea in round two on 3 September after Bishop had given the Bluebirds a slender first leg lead to blast them into the third round of the competition for the first time since their semi-final appearance of 1965–66. Sadly though, there was to be no repeat of past heroics as Barnsley beat them 3-2. City went on to make their customary early exits from the other two Cup competitions, going down 3-0 at Leicester in round three of the FA Cup and losing by the same score at Wrexham in the Welsh version of the trophy. They had earlier beaten Cardiff Corinthians 6-0, with Kitchen netting five against the famous amateur club.

In the early exchanges, City's League form was patchy. An opening day defeat by Blackburn and an unconvincing win over Wrexham set the pattern, and their best run of form was heralded on 12 November by a 1-0 home win over Wrexham courtesy of a Kitchen penalty. This was followed by City's first away win, a 3-2 at Blackburn, and Buchanan made it three from three when he scored against Luton. The Bluebirds were then held to six consecutive draws, including a memorable 3-3 with Swansea when Buchanan scored, in his own words, 'the best goal of my life' – a last-minute 35-yard tap free kick to square the match, before losing their proud nine-match unbeaten record to Oldham on 31 January 1981. That defeat was the first of four in quick succession. New signing Tim Gilbert played at left-back in City's first League win of the year which came courtesy of another Kitchen goal against Newcastle on 25 February, and Steve Grapes scored at Bristol Rovers to claim the points three days later. But then Cardiff had to wait until April for another win, a 1-0 at Chelsea. Despite often proving hard to beat, as the season progressed, City continued to hover around the relegation zone and were still faced with the same problems, the most pressing of which seemed to be disharmony amongst the players. This particular issue came to a head with a nightclub fracas between Ray Bishop and John Lewis, which almost cost Lewis the sight of an eye. It certainly cost Bishop his Cardiff career, because he was off-loaded to Newport before the next transfer deadline. With just three matches left, City's fate still hung in the balance, until a Stevens goal earned them a vital win at Grimsby and home draws against Derby and West Ham saved their bacon. City finished in nineteenth position, staying up only on goal difference whilst unlucky Preston were relegated (with the same points total as City) along with both Bristol clubs. Wrexham finished in sixteenth place, while Swansea, now managed by Cardiff's one-time teenage prodigy John Toshack, were about to get their first taste of First Division football. The Cardiff public showed their displeasure by staying away from Ninian Park in their droves, the average home gate that season slumping to just 6,500, and there was a feeling that even this modest number had been swelled by the visits of clubs with large travelling support.

Instead of rebuilding the team, that summer the club amazed and confused all by ploughing all their money into launching the Cardiff City Blue Dragons Rugby League Club, who were to play their home matches at Ninian Park. The decision can best be described as 'questionable', as the Cardiff supporters, already disillusioned at the state of affairs at the club, had precious little time for Rugby League. In fact, as it was played almost exclusively in the north of England, the sport was so overlooked in Wales that many potential fans couldn't even distinguish it from Rugby Union, and the mere concept of setting up a Rugby League outfit at a football club in the middle of a Rugby Union heartland even now seems preposterous. The ill-fated venture meant that the funds Morgan so badly needed were simply not available, while elsewhere a lack of funds was given as the reason for the club's withdrawal from the Welsh League, and they also failed to be re-elected into the Football Combination. This put them in the unthinkable position of having no competitive football for their reserves and youngsters to play, except the first team. It would go on to become a recurring problem.

1981–82 season
For the new season, the Football League decided to introduce three points for a League win instead of two in an effort to promote attacking play, and the decision certainly seemed to produce more goals. With the new season only minutes old, City found themselves 2-0 down at Oldham, yet rediscovered some of the resolve that had won them so

many points the previous campaign and came back to snatch a draw. That comeback proved a rare highlight as City then lost three on the trot. The awful start to the season belatedly convinced the club to make more transfer funds available, leading to the purchase of Manchester City winger Dave Bennett for £120,000 and a succession of new arrivals on trial and short-term loan deals, including a second spell at Ninian Park for Peter Sayer. In the case of Gary (older brother of Dave) Bennett, the trial would lead to a permanent role in City's defence. Through the 'out' door went Billy Ronson, who moved to Wrexham, and the legendary John Buchanan who rejoined Northampton after scoring an impressive sixty-one goals in 266 games from the heart of the midfield.

The brothers Bennett donning the blue jersey at the same time coincided with the start of the Bluebird's first decent run of a miserable season, when they defeated Wrexham 3-2 at Ninian Park on 4 November. A narrow win over Norwich provided another welcome lift, but more turmoil followed when Morgan was relieved of his duties and moved into an 'administrative' role to allow former Wales defender Graham Williams to take over as 'coach' – though he was, in effect, the new manager. His first game in charge was a goalless draw at Watford, but he only had to wait a week for his first win, which came at the expense of Leicester. However, that result may have had more to do with luck than managerial ability because his team then proceeded to lose eleven of the next thirteen League matches. There were more shake-ups behind the scenes when Ron Jones wrote his name in the history books by becoming the first paid director of a football club, his job title changing from general manager to managing director.

On 2 January 1982, Cardiff were unceremoniously dumped out of the FA Cup in round three by Manchester

City, the only good things to come from the 3-1 defeat being Peter Maddy's goal and a share of the gate receipts from a 31,547 strong Maine Road crowd. Having already been knocked out of the League Cup by Exeter, Cardiff then went into free-fall; gates at Ninian Park had reached crisis point, and they badly needed a Cup run to restore some shattered faith (and some income) in the faltering club. As so often before, the Welsh Cup proved to be the answer and, even though they could no longer attest to being the best club in Wales, City powered through the early rounds with big wins over Bridgend Town, Newport and Billy Ronson's Wrexham. A semi-final meeting with Hereford proved slightly more problematic, but City eventually came through to reach their first final since 1977. It came as no surprise that their opponents were to be high-flying Swansea.

Though City performed near-heroics in reaching the Welsh Cup Final, by the beginning of March they were in deep relegation trouble. Desperate times called for desperate measures, and both Morgan and Williams were promptly dismissed. The City Board then turned to Len Ashurst, who had recently left Newport having accumulated vast managerial experience with Hartlepool, Gillingham and Sheffield Wednesday, and he readily agreed to become City's sixth manager in just nine years. The Cardiff public were less than impressed with all the off-field shenanigans, and the lowest League audience since World War II, just 3,249, showed up at Ninian Park to see Ashurst's first game against Cambridge. As fate would have it, it turned out to be an amazing match which City eventually won 5-4 with a Stevens hat-trick and a brace from Kitchen. A narrow defeat at Norwich was followed by a sequence of three straight home wins against Grimsby, Watford and Orient, and a draw at Charlton, as City climbed out of the drop zone.

Sadly however, they couldn't maintain momentum, and defeats by Leicester and QPR sent them reeling.

Hoping to benefit from the wildly-fluctuating transfer market, Ashurst responded with a rash of new signings, including Jimmy Mullen from Rotherham United and Mick Henderson from Watford. An unlikely 1-0 win at Grimsby in the penultimate match opened up a chink of light at the end of the tunnel, and once again City were left having to win their last game of the season to stay up. Fresh from a home draw against Swansea in the first leg of the Welsh Cup final, Cardiff entertained runaway League champions Luton, but were easily swept aside as the Hatters roared to an unassailable 3-0 lead. Though the Bluebirds gave the 10,227 crowd some hope with late goals from Kitchen and Micallef, to win was a huge ask, and City tumbled into Division Three. The only consolation was that they were joined there by Wrexham, who had suffered an even more miserable season than Cardiff. Therefore, it was a deflated Cardiff team that took to the Vetch Field for the decisive leg of the Welsh Cup final on 19 May, their last game of a traumatic season. Victory would at least give them some silverware, a morale-boosting (and fan-appeasing) win over their great rivals, plus European passage, but after a great start in which they took the lead through Gary Bennett, they were eventually overcome by ten-man Swansea. The Bluebirds' misery was complete.

Though Ashurst showed signs of promise, his appointment simply came too late to save City. In truth they had struggled ever since being promoted back to Division Two in 1976, and were lucky to have survived for so long. A general sense of anxiety around football grounds in the wake of the rise of football hooliganism had already led to a drastic drop in attendance figures all over the country. But a key reason for Cardiff's failure to consolidate was the untimely formation of the Rugby League club, which attracted crowds of just a few hundred and was a constant drain on resources. Combined with a hopelessly inflated transfer market, a constantly fluctuating playing staff, a few unwise investments, player unrest, injuries, and a distinct lack of managerial stability, it all meant that the writing had been on the wall for some time.

9

Kicking Up A Storm
(1982–90)

During the 1982 closed season, Len Ashurst appointed Jimmy Goodfellow, his former assistant at Newport County, as trainer/coach at Cardiff City and together they set about whipping the bedraggled Bluebirds into shape. To make way for new faces, Steve Grapes was released after making over 160 first team appearances; Peter Kitchen joined aptly-named Hong Kong outfit Happy Valley; Wayne Hughes went to Bath City, and Gary Stevens was sold to Shrewsbury Town. Club legend Phil Dwyer stayed only on a month-to-month contract, and many others were retained on reduced terms as a cost-cutting measure. Not surprisingly, there were limited funds available, so Ashurst was forced to raid the free transfer market, landing forward Jeff Hemmerman, midfielder David Tong, and defenders Roger Gibbins and Paul Bodin. That summer also saw previous management team Richie Morgan and Graham Williams paid substantial sums of compensation as a result of their dismissals, which didn't exactly help City's financial crisis.

1982–83 season
After losing at home to Wrexham in the opening game, a new-look City team travelled to Millwall on 28 August 1982 with a point to prove, and made it in no uncertain manner, winning 4-0 with goals from John Lewis, Dave Bennett (2) and Gibbins. However, the tables were soon reversed and they were humbled 4-0 at Leyton Orient in their next

outing, before embarking on a mini-run of four wins and a draw to stride into the promotion places. Luton-born Godfrey Ingram, who had reportedly cost a new record £200,000 from San Jose Earthquakes, scored the winner against Gillingham at Ninian Park on 16 October, and three days later Gary Bennett fired them to the top of the League with the only goal of the game against Bradford City. Early the next month, Hemmerman, Dave Bennett and Ingram all scored in a 3-1 home win over Preston North End, but within days Ingram was on his way back to San Jose just nine weeks after arriving in south Wales in one of the most bizarre transfer deals in history. Cynics have since suggested that the £200,000 transfer fee City reportedly paid for him was a false figure deliberately leaked to the media to appease anxious fans. In December, Ashurst acquired the services of veteran striker Bob Hatton on a free transfer from Sheffield United, and the new arrival marked his home debut with the equalizer against Chesterfield as City entered the crucial Christmas period in a good League position.

Unfortunately, City could not transfer their impressive League form to any of that season's Cup competitions. In the League Cup, which that year became the Milk Cup, City managed to put out Hereford United 4-2 on aggregate before being well beaten by Arsenal. In the FA Cup they needed a replay to beat Wokingham Town and progress to round two where they slumped to an embarrassing 3-2 home defeat by non-League Weymouth, despite leading 2-0 at half time. Newport contributed by dumping them out of the Welsh Cup at the first time of asking, to ensure that by the turn of the year Cardiff could concentrate solely on winning promotion.

On New Year's Day 1983, City entertained Bristol Rovers, won 3-1, and went on to notch up equally impressive wins against Brentford, Walsall, Exeter City and

Millwall, before the run came to an abrupt end at Sheffield United. Shortly afterwards, goalkeeper Andy Dibble was injured, and Ashurst was forced into using a succession of stoppers in a frantic search for a capable replacement. In the short term the search proved fruitless, and with an identifiable weakness for their opponents to exploit, City's confidence began to wane. On 4 April they made the short journey to Newport, and lost to a controversial John Aldridge goal. The result dropped Cardiff to fourth, and saw their Gwent rivals move up to first place. However, the loss seemed to have a positive effect on the team as their run-in amounted to little more than a stroll in the park. City won five and drew two of the last seven to claim runner-up spot behind Portsmouth, and automatic promotion back to Division Two at the first attempt. Ironically, Newport finished fourth. The success was especially sweet for newly-installed club captain Jimmy Mullen, as it was the third time he had captained a side to promotion.

Sadly, the Welsh public did not respond to the improved League form as it was hoped, and despite the club losing just one League game at home all season (the first) the average attendance hovered at a vastly disappointing 7,600. The parasitic Cardiff City Blue Dragons Rugby League side, then two seasons old, was also performing badly and a constant drain on resources, meaning that despite winning promotion there was still no money available for Ashurst to spend. His squad was further depleted during the summer months when Dave Bennett was sold to Coventry City for £120,000, Hatton retired, and top scorer Hemmerman sustained a serious injury in a collision with future City goalkeeper Phil Kite in the last game of the season. Though Hemmerman made a brief comeback, the injury effectively ended his professional career and he pursued an alternative path as a physiotherapist. The only arrivals of note were winger Gordon Owen and goalkeeper Gary Plumley, who were both landed on free transfers. Upstairs, illness called for Chairman Bob Grogan, to be replaced. He had been associated with the club since 1975 and been instrumental in ensuring their continued existence via links with his company Kenton Utilities. He died a few months later.

For the start of the imminent 1983–84 season, the Football League unveiled what, at the time, was the biggest sponsorship deal in British sporting history, a three-year, £3 million arrangement with Japanese-owned camera manufacturers Canon UK. However, the opportunity to bring live televised football to the masses was lost when advanced negotiations with BBC and ITV broke down, leading to a lengthy and costly stand-off. The ruling body also angered smaller clubs by introducing a second substitute (as was already the practice in international and European matches). Those clubs felt they couldn't justify paying a 'thirteenth man' a salary.

1983–84 season
Cardiff's new season began on 27 August with a 2-0 defeat at Charlton Athletic, but impressive home wins over Manchester City and Grimsby Town settled any early-season jitters. However, after losing Hemmerman and Hatton the team predictably struggled for goals and they failed to net in eight matches out of the next ten. Amazingly, they managed to win the only two games in which they did score (at home to Carlisle United and away at Fulham). These were worrying times for the City faithful, but in the midst of it all Ashurst and Newport manager Colin Addison negotiated a transfer 'swap' deal involving an unprecedented five players. Arriving at Ninian Park were mid-fielder Nigel Vaughan and utility man Karl Elsey, while Linden Jones, John Lewis and Tarki Micallef all moved in

the opposite direction. Additionally, Ashurst signed ex-Nottingham Forest defender Colin Smith, who had been plying his trade in Hong Kong.

The tide began to turn with a shock 5-0 home win over Cambridge on 12 November. City won their next home game 3-1 against Huddersfield Town, but then slumped to three consecutive defeats. Boxing Day brought a visit from John Toshack's Swansea City, who had just been relegated from the First Division, for a titanic and potentially volatile showdown. Player/manager Toshack scored for the Swans on his return to the Welsh capital, but the Bluebirds won the match 3-2 with Trevor Lee, a shrewd new signing from Bournemouth, becoming an instant hero by scoring the winner on his debut.

Cup-wise it was another bad year for Cardiff. After seeing off Exeter 5-3 on aggregate in the Milk Cup, they were beaten 3-0 over two legs by Norwich City, while their fellow East-Anglians Ipswich Town knocked City out of the FA Cup in the third round. Meanwhile in the Welsh Cup, City enjoyed one-sided home wins over Welsh League outfits Taff's Well and Maesteg Park Athletic (who were managed by ex-Bluebird Brian Clarke) before losing to 3-1 at home to Fourth Division Hereford in the quarter-final on 7 February 1984.

Despite some good League results, the long-awaited return of striker Hemmerman, and the arrival of left-back David Grant from Oxford United, City had already been sucked into a relegation scrap. Ashurst found the financial situation at the club intolerable and on 4 March he resigned to take over at Sunderland, where he had spent fourteen years as a player. The Cardiff Board handed temporary control of team affairs to Jimmy Goodfellow and Jimmy Mullen, and together the duo steered the club to important wins against Cambridge and Shrewsbury in their first two games in charge and managed to steer the Bluebirds away from the drop zone. After Swansea came back from two down to win 3-2 at the Vetch, City finally achieved safety with a 1-0 home win over Division Three-bound Derby County on Easter Monday, when Gordon Owen scored the all-important goal. Sheffield Wednesday were the visitors to Ninian Park in the final game of the season on 12 May shortly after Goodfellow had been installed as full-time manager, and won 2-0. The result meant that Wednesday left Wales with the Division Two title while Cardiff were condemned to fifteenth place and Swansea were relegated with Cambridge and Derby.

An modest increase in attendances combined with stringent cost-cutting measures ensured that for the first time in years City were able to announce a 'working profit' of £250,000. Unfortunately, the club still owed over four times that amount, meaning that yet again there was no money available to strengthen the team. In fact, the opposite applied. Because of the massive debt, City were again forced into selling their most prized assets. First to go was inspirational goalkeeper Andy Dibble, who joined First Division Luton Town for a new record 'received' fee of £125,000. Independent tribunals then set fees of £75,000 each for Gary Bennett, who joined Len Ashurst at Sunderland, and top-scorer Gordon Owen who went to Barnsley. Goodfellow then began the search for bargains and free transfers, eventually settling on Vaughan Jones from Newport, goalkeeper Lee Smelt from Halifax Town, and forwards Kevin Summerfield from Walsall and John Seasman from Rotherham United. There was much relief around Ninian Park that summer when the much-maligned Cardiff City Blue Dragons rugby League club left the city to set up home, albeit briefly, in Bridgend.

But the big talk in football was the demise of the British

International Championship, which had been contested ever since the 1883–84 season, after England and Scotland withdrew claiming that the competition had grown predictable and outlived its usefulness. The withdrawals were taken badly by Wales and Northern Ireland, who depended on the annual competition to generate income, but they had the last laugh, finishing the last-ever tournament in second and first place respectively, putting the 'mighty' England third and Scotland last!

1984-85 season

All four new Cardiff recruits played in the opening match of the season at home to Charlton on 25 August 1984, which City lost 3-0 before a crowd of just 5,000. They had to wait for the visit of table-topping Leeds United on 12 September for their first League win, when Paul Bodin and Phil Dwyer, who had just set a new record number of appearances for the club, scored the goals in a stunning 2-1 victory. Ex-England captain Gerry Francis also played in the match, which proved to be the only win in the seven matches he played for the Bluebirds as a free agent. After the Leeds game City lost their next five, a run that equalled their worst-ever start to a season (1921–22), and saw the departure of a beleaguered Goodfellow, who was formally dismissed on 27 September. According to managing director Ron Jones, Goodfellow's inexperience counted against him and within hours Port Talbot-born ex-Welsh international Alan Durban, who had begun his playing career with City, took over the reins while Jimmy Mullen continued as player/coach. It was hoped that Durban, who had won promotion with both Shrewsbury and Stoke City before a spell in Division One with Sunderland, would have a dynamic effect on the team. However, his first game in charge was a sobering 3-2 loss at Middlesbrough, and was quickly followed by a home defeat by Portsmouth as the awful run continued uninterrupted. City eventually ground out a win at Notts County on 14 October, but the result proved to be another false dawn as City lurched from one mini-crisis to another. It was another month before they won again, and after that they didn't win until February of the following year! Despite the acquisition of Coventry striker Graham Withey, by the mid-way point relegation was a near certainty.

The Cup competitions offered no respite whatsoever. For the third time in four seasons, City met Exeter in the first round of the League (Milk) Cup, this time running out 2-1 aggregate winners. In the next round they met First Division Watford, and lost 3-1 to a John Barnes hat-trick at Vicarage Road. Despite winning the second leg 1-0, the gulf in class proved too much. The third round of the FA Cup saw them travel to Division Three leaders Gillingham on 21 January 1985, where a Withey strike was not enough to save them from yet another embarrassing defeat. More was to come in the Welsh Cup where City powered past Merthyr Tydfil to set up a grudge meeting with Hereford at Ninian Park. There, the underdogs eclipsed their performance of the previous campaign to beat City 4-0 and equal their worst-ever result in the competition they had once dominated. The humiliation was complete.

On 2 February 1985, Cardiff's horrific run came to an end with a 2-1 home win over Middlesbrough, a match that was watched by only 2,564, their lowest post-war League audience. A narrow win at Oldham Athletic later in the month was followed by a home draw with Wolverhampton Wanderers and a 6-3 hammering at Grimsby, before City clocked up an unlikely 4-1 win at Charlton where Dwyer was amongst the scorers. The goal was his last in his beloved Cardiff colours, for as the season drew to a close he was released along with Smelt, David Grant and Vaughan Jones.

In the current era of footballing mercenaries it seems unlikely that Dwyer's phenomenal record of 573 competitive appearances for Cardiff spread over thirteen years, during which he scored fifty-four goals and represented Wales ten times, will ever be bettered. After his release, Dwyer saw out the season in Division Four with Rochdale, before enlisting in the South Wales Constabulary, where he eventually served with the CID.

With City entrenched firmly at the foot of the table, a run of three straight wins in April temporarily lifted the gloom, but a defeat at Birmingham City sealed their fate. After only two seasons back in Division Two, City were doomed to relegation along with Wolves and Notts County.

While City were becoming resigned to relegation, forces were at work elsewhere to ensure that the last days of the season would have tragic and widespread repercussions. During a match at Bradford City's Valley Parade, a stand caught fire killing more than fifty spectators, and 125 Leeds fans were arrested after rioting in Birmingham. During the chaos a wall collapsed killing a teenager.

Just weeks later at the season's finale, the European Cup final, thirty-nine people died and over 350 were injured at Heysel Stadium, Brussels, the neutral venue staging the game between Liverpool and Italian side Juventus. The disaster was believed to have been caused by Liverpool fans charging at the Italian contingent, causing a wall to collapse, and so they bore the brunt of the blame in the eyes of the media. As punishment, all English clubs (but not the Welsh, Scottish and Irish clubs) were banned from participating in European club competitions for five years, with Liverpool serving longer – even after it was revealed that Heysel Stadium had not been subjected to a full safety check since 1930. The disaster was considered a major international incident, prompting the intervention of the then-Prime

Minister Margaret Thatcher. But the Iron Lady was left seething when the Football League asked the government to foot the bill for extra policing despite, in her opinion, obviously being in strong financial positions after commanding astronomical transfer fees for players.

This chain of tragedies came only months after high-profile skirmishes between Celtic and Rapid Vienna supporters in the Cup Winners' Cup, and Millwall and Luton supporters in the FA Cup. The latter incident was described by FA Chairman Bert Millichip as, 'Probably the worst in the long catalogue that has blighted our game over the last twenty years'. The alarming upsurge of football-related violence prompted the government to spend millions on undercover operations, surveillance and information-gathering in a sustained effort to stamp out the terrace terrors.

Come the end of the season, money (or the lack of it) was of greater concern to City than ever before. By then, the average League attendance at Ninian Park had plummeted to 4,395 and the overall quality of the team was extremely poor, meaning that there were not even any assets to sell to balance the books. Goalkeeper Gary Plumley was released along with Karl Elsey and Paul Bodin who, frustratingly, would later emerge as an international-standard fullback. Another future Welsh international, striker Dean Saunders, had already been allowed to slip through the net after being sent back to Swansea after an unsuccessful loan spell in the Welsh capital at the end of the previous season. Predictably, Durban was forced into the free transfer market where he snapped up forwards Mark Farrington and Robbie Turner. Behind the scenes, club directors worked tirelessly to attract new investors but many potential backers shied away from the 'problem clubs' in British football, of which Cardiff was definitely one. In the words of Ron Jones, 'Who wants to invest in a club where you've got nutters smashing the place up every two minutes? I still don't understand why we had the football violence problem but it obviously discouraged people, especially families, from coming to our matches'.

1985–86 season

Such was the negative impact hooliganism was having at Ninian Park that the club was forced to kick off the new season away at Notts County on 17 August without any shirt sponsorship, having failed to attract any companies who wished to be associated with them. Supporters and pundits alike feared the worst. But not for the first time, City surprised everyone by playing out of their skins and winning 4-1 with goals from McLoughlin, Farrington, Vaughan and a Mullen penalty, to record their best opening-day win since their very first Football League game way back in 1920. After a home defeat to Chesterfield in the next match City registered another impressive away win, this time at Newport. The signs were encouraging, but the early season optimism was squeezed out of them during an excruciating 17-match run during which they won just once, at home to Wigan Athletic. At one stage, City failed to score a single goal in over 500 minutes of football, and attendances dropped even further to around the 2,500 mark. The team seemed to lack conviction, and players came and went with alarming frequency as Durban tried desperately to stem the tide. Ex-Bluebird David Giles rejoined the club from Newport, youngsters Jason Gummer, Paul Wheeler and Wayne Curtis were blooded, and Roger Gibbins was exchanged for Swansea's Welsh international midfielder Chris Marustik. Also on their way were David Tong who left for Cambridge, Graham Withey who joined Bath, and Brian Flynn, another Welsh star who had been a huge disappointment since signing from Burnley, who was offloaded to Doncaster Rovers.

On 10 September, in the midst of this shameful run, the Scottish national team visited Ninian Park to play Wales in a World Cup qualifier. Scotland won a late penalty to tie the match 1-1 and prevent the Welsh travelling to Mexico the following summer, but the night was memorable for a different reason. The Scotland manager, ex Celtic legend Jock Stein, sixty-two, collapsed and died of a heart attack on the Ninian Park touchline, minutes after seeing his side draw level.

As if their League form wasn't enough cause for concern, City suffered more indignation in the Cups. Bitter rivals Swansea knocked them out of the League (Milk) Cup 4-3 on aggregate in the opening round, and relegation meant that they entered the FA Cup at the first round stage, where they lost 2-1 at Fourth Division Exeter. A debut in a competition called the Associate Members' Cup (Freight Rover Trophy), created exclusively for Third and Fourth Division clubs, was an absolute disaster as they lost to both Newport and Swansea in the group stages. They fared marginally better in the Welsh Cup, beating Caerleon and Mold Alexandra on their way to a two-legged quarter-final with Welsh League champions Barry Town, which they won 2-0. A semi-final with Wrexham was the prize, but here the dream ended as City were humiliated 6-2 on aggregate.

Just before Christmas, City turned the form book on its head once again with a 4-0 victory at Lincoln City which they followed with a 4-3 win at Chesterfield to set up another titanic clash with Swansea on Boxing Day. The Swans were also struggling near the bottom of the League, and had just escaped being wound up by the High Court, but the Bluebirds were in an unsympathetic mood and a solitary Vaughan strike two minutes from time was enough to settle the tie before a baying crowd of almost 10,000, four times the Cardiff average. They carried their form into 1986 with an amazing 4-4 draw at Plymouth Argyle, a subsequent home win over Brentford, and a well-earned draw at Reading.

For a while it looked as if City might play themselves out of trouble, but it wasn't to be. After failing to permanently land Swansea's Welsh international defender Nigel Stevenson (he had played against the Swans in the Boxing Day showdown on loan) Durban opted for Bournemouth centre-half Phil Brignall instead, eventually paying £9,000 for him. The fee was allegedly partly funded by supporters and Durban himself. When Stevenson returned to the Vetch, City returned to their previous dire form and managed just two wins from the next fifteen. As they ran out of matches it became glaringly obvious that City were on their way to Division Four and tensions ran high. Only 1,893 turned out at Ninian Park to watch them draw with Walsall on 5 April (during which Chris Sander became the first Cardiff goalkeeper to save two penalties in the same match) and large sections of the crowd turned on Durban. There were persistent rumours of a takeover, and following an angry confrontation with a group of supporters, Farrington had his contract terminated. Durban introduced another succession of second-rate loan players, yet remarkably City recovered some form to win three of their last four. But by then it was far too late, and Cardiff were faced with the prospect of two relegations in two seasons. On 1 May, two days before the last game at home to Lincoln, Durban was unceremoniously sacked. He later claimed that his eighteen months at Cardiff had been 'disastrous', and, 'after ten very good years as a manager, I lost all credibility'.

Ron Jones retorted: 'If Durban thought he was going to come and spend a million quid which nobody had, then he was naïve in the extreme.' Three weeks after Durban's departure, chairman Tony Clemo approached Sunderland to assess the availability of their coach Frank Burrows, who readily agreed to become the next Cardiff manager.

Most of the headlines concerning the 1986 World Cup in Mexico centred around Argentina's Diego Maradona's infamous 'Hand of God' goal against England, even after his country went on to win the tournament. The debate about hooliganism raged on, with UEFA president Jacques George publicly saying that the behaviour of English fans had, if anything, 'worsened' since the Heysel disaster. As if to illustrate his point, Manchester United and West Ham supporters clashed on board a ferry bound for the continent where their clubs were playing pre-season friendlies, resulting in four people being stabbed and fourteen arrests. However, despite the exclusion of English clubs, the coming season's European competitions proved to be some of the bloodiest ever with followers of (mainly) Dutch and German clubs vying for the title of 'most unwelcome supporters' vacated by the British.

Back in the UK, the much-lauded Cardiff takeover eventually occurred in June when Kenton Utilities handed over control of Cardiff to Clemo, who had been a director since 1975. Ex-Newport manager Bobby Smith was employed as youth/reserve coach and Jimmy Mullen left to take up a player/manager post at the Gwent outfit after making over 150 appearances for the Bluebirds, many as captain. Meanwhile, Burrows busied himself scouring the country for new players to boost a thoroughly demoralised squad, and used his considerable influence to land Welsh international Alan Curtis from Southampton, winger Alan Rogers from Stockport County, and goalkeeper Graham Moseley from Brighton & Hove Albion, all on free transfers. But the real coup was the acquisition of another Welsh international, Terry Boyle, who was purchased from

Newport for a tribunal-set fee of just £22,000. Burrows also brought in Andy Kerr from Shrewsbury and Paul Wimbleton from Portsmouth, initially on loan, though both impressed enough to secure permanent deals. Finally, former manager Jimmy Goodfellow returned as physiotherapist and assistant manager.

1986-87 season

Cardiff's first-ever match in Division Four, the 'basement' of the Football League', was at Hartlepool United on 23 August. A Rob Turner goal earned a draw, but the result was overshadowed by fierce crowd trouble and all but forgotten in the media furore that followed these violent clashes. In the next eight games, City lost only once, but half of those games were drawn, meaning that the club seldom rose above mid-table. By that time Birmingham triallist Nicky Platnauer had begun to force his way into the team and young Mel Rees was pushing hard for the goalkeeper's jersey. But what the team needed most was a proven goalscorer. Burrows eventually managed to sign Kevin Bartlett, who he knew from his time at Portsmouth from non-League Fareham Town, and the live-wire striker made an immediate impact by scoring twice on his League debut for Cardiff in a 3-0 home win over Cambridge. To further beef-up his attack, Burrows borrowed Chris Pike from Fulham, but couldn't find the money to make the deal permanent and the Cardiff-born striker reluctantly returned to London. Meanwhile, young Turner found himself surplus to requirements and moved to Bristol Rovers.

Despite their indifferent League form, for once City enjoyed a good run in the League Cup, which had then been re-labelled the Littlewoods Challenge Cup. They met Second Division Plymouth in the first round and won an amazing game 5-4 at Ninian Park after trailing 4-1, before winning the away leg to complete an unlikely 6-4 aggregate victory. If the Plymouth result caused minor waves in the football world, what happened next must have given rise to a tsunami. City were drawn against Luton, who had banned all away support for League games at Kenilworth Road following persistent crowd trouble. The ban did not apply to Cup games, but due to the growing reputation of some Cardiff supporters, Luton refused to issue Cardiff's rightful ticket allocation. Cardiff complained, and the League Management Committee took the unprecedented step of kicking Luton out of the competition, handing City a bye to the next round where they met First Division giants Chelsea at Ninian Park. At a time when hooliganism was rife the tie brought together two of the most notorious sets of fans in the country, Cardiff's Soul Crew and Chelsea's Head-hunters. A massive police operation was staged but was barely called upon as City again came from behind to win with a Platnauer double. Three weeks later the dream ended when City lost 1-0 at relative minnows Shrewsbury.

City also performed well in that year's FA Cup, and made history when they travelled to the Rhondda Valleys to face Welsh League club Ton Pentre who had qualified for the competition against all the odds. Always the favourites, City won 4-1 and went on to knock out Brentford to set up a third round clash with Millwall. The tie needed two replays to find a winner, and was eventually settled in City's favour after loan star Pike scored on 26 January 1987 to grant City passage to round four and a showdown at First Division Stoke. There, City took the lead but Stoke recovered to win 2-1 and send the plucky Welshmen out. Sadly, there were no heroics in the Associate Members' Cup (Freight Rover Trophy) as City lost to both Wolves and Bournemouth in the group stages and limped out of the competition without so much as scoring for the second successive season. The

Welsh Cup was also a disaster. A third round tie with Taff's Well at Ninian Park drew a crowd of only 581, the lowest-ever recorded attendance for a first team game at Ninian Park in any competition. As expected, Cardiff comfortably beat the Welsh League side to progress to round four, where they tumbled out at the gleeful hands of Wrexham.

Back to League matters, and though their away form had improved with wins over Preston, Burnley, Lincoln, Hereford, Scunthorpe United and Crewe Alexandra, at home City were nothing short of atrocious. They confounded their shrinking blue army of supporters by going over four months without a single win in the Welsh capital, eventually breaking their duck on 18 April when ex-Newport forward Steve Mardenborough, Alan Curtis and Paul Wheeler all scored in a 3-1 win over Torquay United. It was Mardenborough's only goal in thirty-five appearances. Then, City's form guide was suddenly reversed and they lost at Swansea, Torquay and Cambridge while winning at home against Burnley and holding champions-elect Northampton Town. Tellingly, only 1,510 turned up to see the last home game on 7 May, a 4-0 hammering of Hartlepool United. A mediocre finish of thirteenth in their first-ever season in Division Four, one place below Swansea and four below Wrexham, was largely forgiven in light of their remarkable achievements in the Littlewood's and FA Cups, but even the staunchest Bluebird now had to admit that the club had plumbed new depths. Average home attendances dipped below 3,000 for the first time in half a century, compounding the ongoing financial crisis, and crowd violence erupted across the country on a semi-regular basis, most notably at Hartlepool and Exeter early in the season.

The club's hierarchy was quick to realize that another season in the Basement could finish them, so promotion quickly became imperative. To make way for new faces there was a player exodus in the summer of 1987; Andy Kerr joined Telford United, Chris Marustik went to Barry Town, Phil Brignull was signed by Newport, and teenage goalkeeper Mel Rees was snapped up by First Division Watford in a deal that eventually topped £100,000. To replace them, Burrows brought in Oxford winger Brian McDermott, Shrewsbury midfielder Mark Kelly, and Cardiff-born Brentford defender Phil Bater, all on frees. In addition, he finally landed long-term target Nigel Stevenson from Swansea and paid a bargain £17,000 for precocious striker Jimmy Gilligan after Lincoln City became the first club to suffer automatic relegation out of the Football League.

1987–88 season
New star Gilligan endeared himself to the Cardiff faithful by heading the equalizer on his debut in a 1-1 home draw with Orient on 15 August. After a narrow defeat at Bolton Wanderers, he was on target again to notch the only goal of the game against Swansea at Ninian Park. The result was marred by the shameful behaviour of one of the Swansea players who was dismissed for violent conduct, sparking a free-for-all on the Popular (Bob) Bank terrace. The scenes made the national news, and eventually led to a strict membership scheme being implemented at Ninian Park similar to that already in place at Luton as the club declared war on its hooligan element.

After a bitter contract wrangle, Nigel Vaughan was sold to Wolves for a knock-down price of £12,000, just in time to make his debut for the Midlanders at Ninian Park in early September. To rub salt into the wounds, Vaughan got on the scoresheet, but still finished on the losing side as City ran out 3-2 winners. Only 2,258 saw the game, largely because of a ban imposed on troublesome travelling Wolves supporters, who had seen their club relegated three times in as many years. After the Wolves win City were sent crashing back to earth with a 3-0 defeat at Wrexham (where Phil Bater became the first Cardiff player to be sent off on his debut) but recovered to win four and draw one of the next five to climb into second place. Jimmy Gilligan was proving a big hit with the fans, and cemented his growing reputation by scoring winning goals against Rochdale and Exeter. Wimbleton and Platnauer stole his thunder as City left Newport with all three points on 21 November, but he was back on form the following month with double salvo's that secured maximum points against Burnley and Tranmere Rovers.

As the Christmas benchmark approached, City found themselves in a useful fourth spot in the League. But then tragedy struck, as a car accident robbed them of the services of goalkeeper Graham Mosely, who was forced to retire through injuries received. Burrows moved to sign ex-Scotland international George Wood from Crystal Palace as a temporary replacement, and City's ranks were further boosted by the arrival of ex-Welsh international forward Ian Walsh from Grimsby. Wood made his League debut for Cardiff in a storming 4-0 home win over Cambridge on 30 January 1988, and after a goalless draw at Darlington, City thrashed League leaders Wolves 4-1 at Molineux to consolidate second place.

Cardiff put the previous season's exploits into context by bowing out of the League (Littlewoods) Cup in the first round 4-3 on aggregate to Newport. Shortly afterwards, they travelled to Peterborough United for a first round FA Cup tie which they lost 2-1, and then made their customary early exit from a restructured Sherpa Van Trophy (formerly the Freight Rover Trophy). They did, however, make some progress by qualifying from the preliminary stage for the first time by beating Wrexham and losing to Walsall, before going down 2-0 at Notts County in the first round proper. This left only the Welsh Cup and here, for once, Cardiff excelled, playing with the passion and confidence that only a sustained promotion bid can generate. They faced Ebbw Vale in the third round and edged out the reigning Welsh League champions before seeing off the challenge of fellow Welsh League outfit Port Talbot Athletic. They then beat Cup holders Merthyr in round five to progress to a two-leg semi-final meeting with Caernarfon Town, which they won 3-1. In the final (played in Swansea) Cardiff met Wrexham, and goals by Curtis and Gilligan ensured that Cardiff lifted the Welsh Cup for the first time since 1976.

Shortly after a heavy defeat at Orient, Bartlett stole the headlines with the winning goal at Halifax on St David's Day. He also scored the winner in the next away game at Hereford after Gilligan scored the first in a 2-1 victory. For a time City were in pole position to capitalize on any mistakes by League-leaders Wolves, but two draws and a home defeat by Scunthorpe put the skids under their title aspirations. However, City finished the season in fine style with five straight wins to claim runner-up spot behind Wolves. It was this run that led to Burrows deservedly being crowned Division Four Manager of the Month for April (the month in which a 17-year old called Alan Shearer became the youngest player ever to score a First Division hat-trick by netting three times for Southampton against Arsenal).

With promotion back to Division Three assured, an imminent return to Europe after a decade-long hiatus (the existing ban applied only to English clubs) and a lucrative new sponsorship deal in the pipeline, financial stability appeared to have been achieved at long last. The team had improved dramatically and attendances were up (almost 10,000 had watched the last home game of the season), mainly due to the tireless efforts of the shrewd and industrious Burrows. The new manager had worked wonders with a small pool of home-grown talent, a succession of journeymen, and a non-existent budget. Swansea also won promotion back to Division Three from sixth place in the League via the newly-introduced and highly controversial play-off system.

At the end of the season, Oxford bid £150,000 for Mike Ford, who had made almost 200 appearances for City, and although initially unwilling to break up his promotion and Welsh Cup-winning squad, the money was simply too good to refuse. Burrows reluctantly accepted the offer. His biggest buy that summer was Hereford's defensive midfielder Ian Rodgerson, who arrived for £35,000, but Burrows also picked up forward Steve Lynex on a free transfer from West Bromwich Albion and brokered a deal to keep the impressive George Wood at Ninian Park. Through the 'out' door went Steve Mardenborough, who joined Hereford on a free transfer having failed to hold down a regular place in the side. The only other major departure was that of high-earning managing director/secretary Ron Jones, who left to take up an executive position at Portsmouth to be replaced in the boardroom by Eddie Harrison, an ex-FAW administrator.

1988–89 season

Contrary to most people's expectations, City's return to the Third Division was not a happy one. Walsh's first Cardiff goal, in the opening match at home to Fulham, was cancelled out then bettered as City crashed 2-1, and worse was to come when they lost 4-0 at Bolton a week later. A first win of the season came at the expense of Huddersfield at Ninian Park, where a Walsh double and a rare strike from Nigel Stevenson led them to a 3-0 whitewash. However, those who thought City had acclimatized to the higher level were sorely disappointed, as that proved to be their only League win in the opening ten matches. On that form they looked early-season relegation candidates, but took full advantage of successive home games against Bury, Gillingham, Northampton and Brentford to take maximum points, all with shut-outs. The points haul dragged City clear of the drop zone, and with the partnership of Gilligan and Bartlett firing on all cylinders again, a new wave of optimism swept the club. Optimism that again turned sour as City failed to win another League match that year, though their blushes were saved somewhat when a Gilligan brace salvaged a home draw to Swansea on Boxing Day before 10,675 fans, easily Ninian Park's biggest crowd of the season.

For the first time ever, that season Cardiff were required to participate in no fewer than five separate Cup competitions. The most high-profile competition was the European Cup Winners' Cup, not least because as all English clubs were still banned, the watchful eyes of the world's media were fixed firmly on the Scottish, Welsh and Irish representatives. As fate would have it, City were drawn against Derry City, a tie problematic in itself because of the political unrest in Northern Ireland. Cardiff's first European game in eleven years against the Irish Cup winners was a frenetic goalless draw in Derry/Londonderry on 7 September. The return game was a more one-sided affair, with Brian McDermott heading the Bluebirds in front before Gilligan claimed a hat-trick (only the second Cardiff player ever to do so in Europe) to complete a 4-0 thrashing. The second round paired City with Danish club AGF (Aarhus), who played some devastating football over the two legs, winning 6-1 overall.

Cardiff were drawn against Swansea in the first round of

the League (Littlewoods) Cup and eventually scraped through 2-1 on aggregate, only to lose heavily to Queen's Park Rangers. City also pulled Swansea in a three-club preliminary group in the Sherpa Van Trophy, beating them 2-0 at Ninian Park. Even though City lost their other group game at Torquay they still progressed to the first round proper, where they lost at Bristol Rovers. Gilligan, who was attracting attention from a number of clubs, made an impression in the FA Cup by scoring in all three rounds as City breezed past Hereford and non-League Enfield before going down 2-1 at home to Hull City. In defending the Welsh Cup, City managed to beat Bath and Worcester before disappointingly going out to Kidderminster Harriers. Remarkably, City didn't play a single Welsh team.

A much-needed League win (and first away League victory of the season) came on 2 January 1989 at Aldershot, where Curtis scored the only goal. After a defeat at Wolves, City then recorded three wins out of four, including a storming 3-0 home success over Port Vale in which Bartlett scored a stunning goal to add to another Gilligan double. Transfer speculation involving the prolific strike pairing was rife, but a few eyebrows were raised when Bartlett became the first to leave in February, City having accepted a massive £125,000 bid from West Brom. Supporters were outraged, and the club was again accused of lacking ambition. One can only imagine their dismay when just days after the sale of Bartlett, controversial chairman Tony Clemo suddenly announced that he was putting the entire club up for sale!

Former directors Gerald McCarthy and Craig Burgin emerged in the local press as favourites to take over Clemo's controlling shares, while Burrows, mindful of a backlash, fought tooth and nail to keep Jimmy Gilligan on the books, despite bids reportedly reaching £330,000. He succeeded, for the time being, and even managed to draft in ex-Bluebird

Roger Gibbins as coach and steadying influence. City lost 1-0 at Bury on 15 April, but that result, along with every other that day, was overshadowed by the tragedy that unfolded that day at Hillsborough stadium, Sheffield, during the Liverpool v Nottingham Forest FA Cup semi-final. Ninety-five supporters were crushed to death and 150 seriously injured after a senior police officer allegedly ordered a gate to be opened, allowing fans to surge through unattended. It was Europe's worst-ever football-related disaster.

After the horrors of Hillsborough, the remainder of the season was played out in a very subdued manner, with a 2-0 home win over Chester on 9 May securing Cardiff's Third Division status for another year. They finished the season in sixteenth place. Scoring goals, especially on their travels, was proving a problem, despite the continued presence of Gilligan, who was proving to be one of the best strikers outside the First Division. City played a mammoth total of sixty-three League and Cup matches that season, their highest to date.

The uncertainty that was beginning to engulf the club at boardroom level certainly hadn't help matters, with the club at one stage claiming to be losing £2,000 per week. To help balance the books, Burrows was forced into selling skipper Terry Boyle to Swansea, while Nick Platanauer couldn't wait for a move to Notts County. Also, Paul Wimbleton was sold to Bristol City, Nigel Stevenson to Merthyr, and Phil Bater to Gloucester. As if this rash of departures wasn't enough, Ian Walsh fulfilled his ambition to retire at the end of the season to leave City's squad in utter disarray. To plug the yawning gaps Burrows finally landed ex-loan star Chris Pike from Fulham, and paid £40,000 for Hull City left-back Ray Daniel. The squad was still wafer-thin, but there was simply no more money to spend, and to make matters even worse both Burrows and star player Gilligan were refusing to sign new contracts, in protest. As the new season approached, a sense of impending doom descended on Ninian Park. The pessimism intensified when, after City lost their opening two games, Burrows decided that he had seen enough and left to take the role of assistant manager to John Gregory at Portsmouth. Almost immediately, Tony Clemo (still in place) offered the vacant post to Len Ashurst, who accepted the challenge for a second time.

One of Burrows' first acts at Portsmouth was to rip the heart out of his old club by instigating a £210,000 raid for the unsettled Gilligan. The popular striker, who never missed a single game in his two years at Cardiff and boasted an impressive forty-six goals from 121 League and Cup appearances, played his last game for Cardiff against Northampton on 26 September, a 3-2 defeat. After his year at Pompey brought just a handful of goals, he finished his career back in Wales at Swansea.

1989–90 season
Out of the proceeds of the Gilligan sale, Ashurst immediately paid Kettering £60,000 for striker Cohen Griffith and Swindon £25,000 for mid-fielder Leigh Barnard, while ageing crowd favourite Alan Curtis packed his bags and travelled down the road to Swansea. A haul of just two points from the first eight matches made it officially Cardiff's worst-ever start to a season, and they had to wait until the October before registering their first victory, 3-2 success at Huddersfield, where Griffith scored on his League debut. Ashurst was enjoying the temporary luxury bestowed upon him and, to the delight of the fans, carried on spending, bringing in Birmingham goalkeeper Roger Hansbury and Bolton winger Jeff Chandler.

However, despite the new arrivals and some solid performances, City remained rooted to the bottom of the table until reeling off wins against Bury, Fulham and Preston. The Fulham win was City's best away League win since 1968 which by coincidence, had also come at Craven Cottage. After a slight wobble, City recovered their poise to record successive away victories at Swansea and Walsall and a home draw against promotion-chasing Tranmere, before succumbing to another dire run that virtually undid all their good work.

The first competition Cardiff exited proper that season was the League (Littlewoods) Cup, in which they lost 3-2 on aggregate to Plymouth. In the AM (Leyland) Cup. City didn't even escape the confines of the preliminary group, losing heavily to both Walsall and Shrewsbury. In the FA Cup they managed to beat non-League Halesowen Town and Gloucester after a replay (which was marred by more crowd violence) only to bow out to First Division QPR. In the Welsh Cup they beat Newport AFC, Port Talbot, and Aberystwyth Town on their way to a two-leg semi-final with Hereford. After the first game at Ninian Park City found themselves 3-0 down, and though they won the second leg 3-1 the score proved a bridge too far and they made another graceful exit.

City's first League win of the 1990's came on 21 February at Brentford, where a goal from young defender Gareth Abraham secured the points. But then it was business as usual as they picked up just one more win (a 2-0 home defeat of Rotherham) from the next eight. By Easter, the situation was critical, and a 2-0 home defeat by Swansea on 16 April followed by another defeat at Notts County all but sealed their fate. As the season trundled on to its horribly inevitable conclusion, Cardiff found their hopes resting on a sequence of three home games inside a week against fellow strugglers Walsall and Fulham, and mid-table Reading. They managed to record two wins and a draw, scoring nine goals in the process and giving themselves a slim mathematical lifeline. Unfortunately however, the draw (a thrilling 3-3) came against their closest rivals Fulham, and meant that the Londoners left Wales in a superior League position and significantly better spirits than their hosts. The lifeline was severed once and for all at Bury, who beat the Bluebirds 2-0 in the final game of the season to condemn them to a swift return to the Fourth Division. City ended the season in twenty-first position, a single point behind Fulham and the safety zone.

The season had been nothing short of an unmitigated disaster, and chaos had reigned at all levels. The club was still technically 'up for sale,' though Clemo, who was taking a serious barracking from sections of the supporters over his treatment of the club, insisted that he had yet to receive any 'realistic' offers. The situation changed several times over the summer months with different parties showing an interest, but for one reason or another the envisaged takeover never happened. The cloak of uncertainty drew criticism from the local media, which acted as a forum for scores of disillusioned fans to lambaste the quality of the Cardiff team, the running of the club, and the dubious motives of Clemo.

The Lord Justice Taylor Report, published in January 1990 in the wake of the Hillsborough disaster, famously stated that crowd behaviour could be linked to the squalid state of some of Britain's football grounds. The 104-page report called for every League club to replace terracing with seats, and made a host of recommendations for other safety-oriented alterations. The government stressed that the football industry was responsible for cleaning up its own disgraceful image, and so the clubs would be expected to meet much of the cost, despite warnings that many smaller outfits could be bankrupt as up to 75 per cent of them were already making a loss. This was particularly bad news for Cardiff, who had a shockingly run-down ground in Ninian Park, no saleable assets, a dwindling fan-base, and were now faced with the very real possibility of an extended stay in the dreaded Basement.

10

Highs and Lows
(1990–2000)

1990–91 season

Whilst the cream of international football contested Italia 90, Len Ashurst was amongst the throng of panic-stricken lower-division managers scrambling for signatures. He eventually persuaded ex-Aston Villa and Newcastle United star Pat Head to sign for Cardiff City, along with Swindon Town midfielder Mark Jones and Blackpool utility man Neil Mathews. After kicking off their season with a goalless draw at Scarborough on 25 August, City remained unbeaten for the first seven matches (admittedly, five were drawn) before tasting defeat courtesy of unfancied Rochdale. Three days later, however, a Chris Pike goal handed City a vital win over Wrexham and on their next away trip, to York City, a Cardiff-born YTS player called Nathan Blake scored his first senior goals to gift the Bluebirds another win. By then, Ashurst had recruited Eddie May as his assistant, but this had little effect on the team as they went on to record just one win (at home to Chesterfield) from the next nine.

This terrible run encapsulated what has become known in some circles as Black November, though the rot had set in well before the eleventh month. In the League (now the Rumbelows) Cup, City managed to triumph over Mansfield Town 4-1, but then lost 4-2 on aggregate to Frank Burrows' Portsmouth. In the FA Cup, City were sent out at the first time of asking by non-League Hayes after a replay, and they again failed to progress in the AM (Leyland) Cup after losing to Exeter City and only drawing at Hereford United in the group stages. However, the worst embarrassment came in the Welsh Cup where, on 6 November, they were crushed 4-1 by Merthyr Tydfil at Ninian Park. Meanwhile, the heavily criticized Ray Daniel followed Burrows and Jimmy Gilligan to Fratton Park, and Ian Rodgerson joined Birmingham City, as Ashurst blooded a succession of youngsters including Damon Searle and Lee Baddeley. It was just as well that Cardiff had a capable group of teen prodigies to call upon, as the Football League had placed a temporary embargo on any other transfer deals involving the club until its financial crisis had been rectified.

The Bluebirds' form finally recovered on Boxing Day, when they secured a 3-1 home victory over Carlisle United. They went on to beat Halifax Town three days later before going down to successive home defeats by Lincoln City and Aldershot. On the day of the Aldershot game, Cardiff hit a new low when they were sued by the local council for unpaid interest bills on a loan and a winding-up order meant an imminent visit to the High Court. The players themselves were in for a nasty shock after the game when they discovered that all their payment cheques had bounced! Out on the pitch, however, City managed to put their problems aside and concentrated on playing some solid, uncompromising football (there's no place for silky skills in Division Four), embarking on an impressive nine-match unbeaten run culminating in home wins over Scunthorpe United and York. But just as they were beginning to threaten the play-off positions, away defeats at rock-bottom Wrexham and Carlisle pegged them back. In the Wrexham game, Cameron Toshack, son of the legendary John, made his full debut following several substitute appearances having arrived from Bristol City. Unfortunately, Tosh the Younger failed to live up to his father's considerable reputation and was soon off to non-League Weymouth.

Around this time Rick Wright, millionaire owner of the Majestic Holiday Camp, emerged as a financial benefactor and potential saviour of the club, having publicly vowed to wipe out their debts and make additional money available for new players. Although opinion was, and still is, divided on Wright's association with Cardiff, the club was in such dire financial straits when he first arrived that it is fair to assume that without his input, the club would almost certainly have folded. On taking the role of 'financial controller' in March, he went public and boldly announced a triple goal: to get the club back into Europe, to improve the ground, and to win promotion. Shortly after Wright assumed his rather ambiguous position, Cardiff were given a cash injection of £500,000 by the Football Trust for ground improvements in light of the Taylor Report.

1991–92 season
Initially, the team responded positively to the changes at the club by beating Northampton and Halifax to re-ignite hopes of a play-off spot. But then they lost momentum, failing to win any of their last eight to finish in thirteenth position, while little Darlington won the title. Although they had struggled for much of the season, there was a real belief that in young guns Nathan Blake, Damon Searle, Jason Perry and Gavin Ward, City had the nucleus of a talented team. With financial stability now apparently achieved via Wright's bulging wallet, it looked for all the world that the club was ready to go from strength to strength. However, at Cardiff, the next drama is never far away, and no sooner had the season ended, Ashurst decided to walk out having lost the backing of many supporters. His assistant Eddie May, a jolly Londoner who had appeared for both Swansea and Wrexham during his playing career, was installed as 'coach' to handle team affairs.

For the first time in quite a while there was money to spend and, after a disappointing opening day home defeat by Lincoln on 17 August 1991, May used the cash to bring in Paul Millar from Port Vale and Carl Dale from Chester City. Diminutive striker Dale initially arrived on loan, but was signed permanently for £95,000 after just one competitive game. The team was crying out for a midfield general, and May pulled off a major coup by securing the services of tenacious 14-cap Northern Ireland international Paul Ramsey from Leicester City for £100,000. May knew 28-year old Ramsey, who had played over 300 games for the Foxes in the top two divisions and gone to the 1986 World Cup Finals in Mexico with his country, from when he held a coaching position at Filbert Street under then-manager Jock Wallace. As an ingenious ploy to boost flagging attendances, the club then implemented a revolutionary 'pay as we win' admission scheme on a sliding scale, meaning that the higher the club were in the League, the more the supporters had to pay to watch them. As an incentive for the players, Wright also dangled the carrot of a £1million bonus should they win the League, probably knowing full well that they didn't have a chance!

Millar, Dale and Ramsey, all made their debuts in City's first away game of the season at Crewe Alexandra, where Dale scored in a 1-1 draw. A penalty from Mark Jones was enough to give City a first home win of the season over Carlisle, but then a run of one win in six left them floundering in mid-table. The turning point came when old sparring partners Wrexham visited Ninian Park in October and were ruthlessly put to the sword in a 5-0 defeat, Pike leading the way with a well-taken hat-trick. A temporary setback resulted in a 3-0 reverse at Mansfield, but that proved to be City's last League defeat of the year as they racked up an impressive sequence of four wins and four draws, the highlight being a home win over title contenders Rotherham United. Again, the all-important goal was scored by Dale, who was already proving a huge hit in a team that had lacked a reliable goalscorer since Jimmy Gilligan left.

Cardiff was seemingly doomed to mid-table obscurity, and the various Cup competitions offered the team no respite. In the first competition to start, the Football League (Rumbelows) Cup, City managed a 3-2 first leg win over Bournemouth only to lose the return match 4-1. The biggest disappointment, however, was saved for the FA Cup. They were paired with Swansea in the first round, and disappointingly lost 2-1 at the Vetch on 16 November, but the result told only half the story. Around 3000 Cardiff supporters travelled there, a large percentage of whom ran amok in the city centre and fought running battles with police and rival supporters. By the end of the day thirty-nine people had been arrested. Remarkably, just three days later the two sides met again at the same venue in a restructured AM Cup (Autoglass Trophy) where the teams laboured to a dour goalless draw. This time there was no trouble, and with many fans horrified and outraged by the previous weekend's events, the match only attracted a modest crowd of 2,955, less than a third of the number that had attended the FA Cup debacle. In the other preliminary tie, Cardiff drew with Bournemouth, who had just knocked them out of the Rumbelow's Cup, before going on to lose 3-0 at Stoke City in the first round proper.

At the height of their impressive mid-winter League run, City came up against no-hopers Macclesfield Town, who shocked everybody by winning 5-0 at Ninian Park on New Year's Day 1992. The next home game against Hereford offered the chance to make amends and Dale duly obliged, while the visit of Chesterfield shortly afterwards brought a glut of goals as the English side crashed 4-0. The result kick-started City's season, and they went on to win four of the next five before eventually succumbing to defeat before 16,030 supporters (the biggest gate at Ninian Park for over a decade) to table-topping Burnley. Instrumental in this run, during which the Bluebirds scored sixteen goals in just five games, was Chelsea winger Eddie Newton who had arrived on loan and made a startling impression with some powerful, direct displays.

After the Burnley defeat, City regrouped and managed a narrow win over Walsall, but then, with hopes of a high League position fading badly, so did the team, and they didn't win again until Halifax visited Ninian Park on 11 April. In a classic example of 'too little, too late,' they then remained undefeated until the end of the season, a run that included an avenging 3-1 win at Burnley and culminated in a satisfying 3-0 humbling of Wrexham. Going into the final League game of the season against Crewe at Ninian Park, City still had a good chance of making the play-offs, as long as they won and other results went their way. Blake scored to point them in the right direction, but the visitors grabbed a late equalizer to cruelly dash the Bluebird's hopes and force them down to ninth position.

But the season wasn't quite over. There remained the small matter of the Welsh Cup Final that could secure Cardiff a place in Europe after a four-year absence. Having dispatched Newport and Stourbridge Athletic in the early rounds, a Pike goal saw City through to the semi-finals at the expense of Swansea. There they easily beat Maesteg Park Athletic to guarantee a historic first appearance at the National Stadium (also known as Cardiff Arms Park) on 17 May. Hednesford Town were Cardiff's opponents, and put up a spirited performance, a Dale goal, his twenty-fifth of a remarkable debut season, being the only difference between the two sides. The win meant that City qualified for the

European Cup Winners' Cup for the thirteenth time, then a record for a British club. As a further indication of the progress being made, at the start of the season there were 291 Junior Bluebird members (a club set up for young supporters) but by the end that number had swelled to over 4000.

Qualifying for Europe helped soften the blow of finishing so low in the League, and the general feeling was that Eddie May had moulded a decent, solid team. Unfortunately, they were unable to hold on to talented Chelsea mid-fielder Eddie Newton, who returned to Stamford Bridge with a new-found confidence that landed him a place in their first team and England U21 honours. Also on the move were Gareth Abraham, who went to Hereford after making 109 appearances for City, and goalkeeper Roger Hansbury, who retired after playing 113 matches in all competitions in just three seasons. Unwilling to rest on their laurels, the club continued rebuilding throughout the summer, recruiting Irish 'B' international defensive starlet Derek Brazil from Manchester United for £85,000 and midfielder Nick Richardson from Third Division rivals Halifax. Experienced goalkeeper Mark Grew also joined, as did ex-Wales international Robbie James who, after being rejected by then-Cardiff manager Jimmy Scoular when a schoolboy, went on to have successful spells at Swansea and Leicester before joining Bradford City, where he won Player of the Year twice. As the clubs could not agree on a price, it was decided that a tribunal should set a fee for the 35-year old, who had amassed a total of forty-seven Welsh caps. Because of the player's advanced age, City were eventually ordered to pay just £17,500. These acquisitions ensured that City were installed as 9-1 joint favourites with Lincoln City to win the League. On the commercial side, Cardiff signed a lucrative shirt sponsorship deal with the South Wales Echo newspaper, and implemented some much-needed ground improvements.

At the latest European Championships in Sweden, Denmark beat a reunited Germany in the final to win their first major honour. The Danes only qualified for the tournament by default after UEFA decreed that war-torn Yugoslavia, who had finished above Denmark in their qualifying group, could not take part. Back home, there were wholesale changes in store for every club in England as the FA announced plans to introduce a streamlined breakaway 'Premier Division' in place of the old First Division, signalling the break-up of the 104-year old Football League. The move meant that every club outside the top tier moved up a League in status, ensuring that Cardiff kicked off the next season in Division Three after all. To spice things up further, the FA also revised the controversial 'back pass' law, forbidding goalkeepers to pick up a ball that had been intentionally passed to them by one of their own players. Players adjusted, but the new ruling played havoc with defences up and down the country.

1992–93 season

Expectations boosted by the clutch of close-season signings, a healthy (by Third Division standards) crowd of 8,399 turned out for City's first match of the new season on 15 August, which turned out to be a dour draw with Darlington. But then May's recruits began to gel, and a 3-2 win at Walsall was quickly followed by home wins over Halifax and Northampton. Paradoxically, City then suffered their worst run of form of the season, as over the next seven games they won only once, against Gillingham when Blake was among the scorers. Blake had also made the headlines after the previous match against Hereford at Edgar Street where, after scoring a late equalizer, he received a police warning in the changing rooms for 'over exuberant celebration'. Hereford supporters claimed that the winger had made obscene gestures, while Blake rather feebly maintained that he was merely making a 'V for victory' gesture. The tide turned when Scunthorpe were put through the horrors on Halloween Night as the Bluebirds ran out 3-0 winners, and both Colchester and Bury were dispatched in similar fashion. But while City thrived in front of their own supporters (a 2-1 defeat by Wrexham was their only home League defeat of the season) they often struggled on their travels, a rare victory at Doncaster Rovers on 11 December standing out as their only away success before Christmas. The Doncaster game was notable for another reason, as it was where soon-to-be-legendary Phil Stant made his Cardiff debut in place of long-term injury victim Carl Dale. Stant, a rampaging tattooed striker, was signed for £100,000 from Mansfield where he had scored thirty goals in a recent promotion campaign. His first club Hereford reputedly had to buy him out of the army, but persistent rumours that he was once a member of the fabled SAS remain unconfirmed.

By the time Stant signed for City, they were already out of three Cup competitions. Though Dale gave City a narrow first round, first leg win over Bristol City in the Football League (Coca Cola) Cup, they lost the return game 5-1. Their latest foray into Europe ended prematurely with a 3-1 aggregate defeat to Austria's Admira Wacker, and there was even worse to come in the FA Cup where they were humbled by non-League Bath, who won at Ninian Park in November. They fared slightly better in the A. M. Cup (Autoglass Trophy) where they beat Shrewsbury Town and Hereford, only to be undone by old rivals Swansea (naturally) after extra time. The match was a typically bad-tempered affair that ignited the Ninian Park crowd on a cold, windswept evening. There were seventy-six arrests as rival fans clashed in front of the Sky Sports cameras, despite the presence of 180 police officers with a full complement of mounted officers and police dogs. The trouble probably came in retaliation for the previous season's disturbances in Swansea.

As the New Year approached, City briefly threatened the promotion places, but a consistent run of positive results was crucial if the team was to improve on recent mediocrity. When Hereford visited Ninian Park on 2 January 1993, it was new hero Stant who stepped in with a crucial goal, a tally doubled by Nick Richardson's first for his new club. Three days later Cardiff secured a major coup when ex-Wales and Everton skipper Kevin Ratcliffe joined in a unique 'pay as you play' deal. The 32-year-old defender had been languishing in the Toffees' reserves after winning two championships, an FA Cup and a Cup Winners' Cup with them, but after an unsettled spell he was granted a free transfer. He made his Bluebirds debut at Carlisle on 9 January, where he headed the winning goal prompting May to label him, 'the eighth wonder of the world'. Previously, Ratcliffe had scored only twice before in over 350 League games. After the drama of Carlisle, City were faced with more difficult away ties at Gillingham and Halifax, but silenced their critics by winning both. Another away win at Darlington was sandwiched between home bankers against Walsall and Torquay United and a 2-1 win at Northampton, where Stant and Pike were the scorers. These made it eight League wins on the trot. In the process, City climbed to second in the table, meaning that for the first time, supporters were required to pay 'category A' admission prices under the club's revolutionary 'pay as we win' scheme, which were only applied if City graced the promotion places.

Before the home match against Crewe which, if City won, would see them equal the record of nine straight League wins set way back in 1946–47, several members of that historic Division Three (south) championship-winning side, including Arthur 'Buller' Lever, Fred Stansfield and Ken Hollyman, were introduced to an appreciative and vociferous crowd. Unfortunately, Cardiff City circa 1993–94 were stopped just short of the record and held to a draw, but were soon back on track and roared to the top of the League with wins over Scarborough, Colchester United and Chesterfield. There was a mini-outcry after the Colchester game when the Newport-based *South Wales Argus* rather cheekily printed a picture of Damon Searle in action, having removed the motif of rival newspaper and City sponsor the *South Wales Echo* emblazoned across the front of his shirt!

The likeable May deservedly picked up the Manager of the Month award for January after steering Cardiff to five victories to kick off 1993, and the local media crowed over the team he had assembled. With the added class of the talismanic Ratcliffe, who became the first Bluebird to represent Wales since Alan Curtis in 1987, and the hard-running enthusiasm of Stant, the team was scoring goals for fun. The highly-rated Brazil brought some skill and poise to the defensive unit and complimented aggressive partner Jason 'Psycho' Perry perfectly. Ramsey was the inspirational midfield catalyst, and Griffith and Blake, the penetrating wingers supplying the ammunition for deadly duo Dale and Pike. As the season intensified, Rick Wright continued to court the press with cryptic statements about the future of the club. He made no secret of the fact that his main motivation was money, and even hinted that the club could cease to exist if additional backing could not be found. There was a suggestion that the club could turn its back on the Football League and join the newly formed Konica League of Wales. His argument was that even though such a radical move would alienate much of Cardiff's loyal fan base, it would cut costs drastically and virtually guarantee domestic success leading to a complete monopolization of Welsh football.

City's thirteen-match unbeaten League run finally came to an end at unfancied Bury in late March. The team then got a slight case of the jitters, and won only once in the next four before recovering to beat Lincoln 3-1 at Ninian Park. Cardiff's form had catapulted them into the automatic promotion places, and a late slump by Barnet gifted them the opportunity for glory. They travelled to high-flying Wrexham on 17 April for the most important Welsh derby in living memory, and won with goals from Griffith and Perry. 17,253, City's biggest gate of the season, turned out for the penultimate League fixture against Shrewsbury at Ninian Park which resulted in a convincing 3-1 victory, and an estimated 3,000 travelled to Scunthorpe a week later to see the 3-0 win that made City champions of the (new) Third Division.

In winning their first League championship for forty-six years, the team had achieved a club record-equalling twelve away League wins, and the average attendance at Ninian Park rose sharply to 8,560. Stoke City won the Division Two title, Newcastle Division One, and Manchester United the inaugural Premiership. As in the previous season, after the scheduled League fixtures had been played out only the Welsh Cup Final remained, again to be contested at the National Stadium on 16 May. City had cruised through the earlier rounds against Ton Pentre, Caeru and Maesteg Park Athletic, before edging out Wrexham 2-1 in a two-legged semi-final. Their final opponents were Rhyl, and the weak seasiders were obliterated with a hat-trick from Stant and a brace from Griffith in a handsome 5-0 win as City retained their grip on the trophy with the minimum of effort.

The end of the season saw the departures of three of City's most influential players; Gavin Ward left for Leicester in a deal totalling £250,000, Paul Ramsey joined Scottish Premier Division side St Johnstone (where ex-Bluebird John McClelland was in charge) and goal poacher Chris Pike stayed in the Third Division with Hereford, while Roger Gibbins moved onto the Cardiff coaching staff. To replace them, May brought in goalkeeper David Williams, winger Wayne Fereday, and pint-sized striker Darren Adams. In an admirable gesture, on 2 July 1993, Rick Wright signed over his 86 per cent majority shareholding to the Junior Bluebirds and, for a short time at least, Cardiff were the only football club in the world owned by its own young supporters. But the squad looked weak, and cash rows with Rick Wright had seemingly eroded team spirit. Crowd idol Phil Stant started the new season's campaign on loan at Mansfield following a bitter dispute over bonus payments in the wake of the Welsh Cup Final triumph, and Ratcliffe left for similar reasons, though he soon returned.

1993–94 season

Before the new season kicked off, May strengthened his side by drafting in 34-year old veteran Welsh international defender Mark Aizlewood from Bristol City on a month-to-month contract. The arrival of the cultured ex Luton Town and Leeds United man provided a much-needed lift for the supporters, as did the acquisition of experienced striker Garry Thompson from Queens Park Rangers and goalkeeper Phil Kite from Sheffield United. The team got off to a bright start in Division Two of the Barclays League, with goals from Blake and Griffith giving them an opening day victory over Leyton Orient at Ninian Park on 14 August.

The following week they triumphed 3-1 at Fulham, where Thompson's first goal for his new club supplemented a brace from in-form Blake. The Fulham game also brought the first crowd trouble that season, as twelve Cardiff supporters were arrested in London. There were some reservations about the behaviour of some of the City faithful as they prepared for Division Two, but Fulham, along with every other club in the division, turned down an offer to supply extra stewards for certain matches to save on costs. When the dust of south London had settled, Cardiff reeled off three consecutive 2-2 draws, indicating that they at least had the ability to hold their own against their new peers. Their first League defeat of the season came at the hands of Hull City, who won 4-3 at Ninian Park on 11 September. From there, with a threadbare squad of just seventeen professionals, City embarked on a truly awful run and collected only three points from the next twenty-four available.

In the midst of this dire sequence, one of the most amazing transfer sagas in the club's history began to unfold when Paul Ramsey let it be known that he had failed to settle in Scotland and hinted at a move. Cardiff quickly stepped in with the required transfer fee of £75,000 (the amount St Johnstone had paid for him just months earlier) and Ramsey signed terms with his former club. It was a done deal, and he even played for the Bluebirds in an early Welsh Cup tie, but the move was blocked. It was adjudged that Cardiff had broken Rule 53, which stated that no player could return to his former club within twelve months of a transfer unless the League is informed prior to the event. The net result was a decent player in limbo and a club fined for breaching regulations.

Wright was planning a tactical withdrawal from ownership, stripping club assets and limiting investment.

He was already tightening his purse strings by placing many players on weekly contracts. One of these was Robbie James, who found the situation intolerable and joined Merthyr in the Vauxhall Conference as player/manager. Eventually Wright bowed to pressure and, after a 'strong recommendation' from May, reinstated Stant from his exile at Mansfield. It was clear that Wright wanted out, and for the best part of the next year the press was full of takeover talk. Around this time City also lost Ratcliffe for good. Having lost the impetus of the previous season and with his age catching up with him, he left to become player/assistant manager at Chester.

In spite of his patchy form, Stant was awarded one of only three 'foreigner' (non-Welsh) places in City's European squad, the others being Richardson and Kite. Unfortunately, the foreigner rule also applied to English, Scottish and Irish players – a fact that severely depleted the Cardiff team. Their latest European adventure kicked off with a Cup Winners' Cup first round, first leg tie in Belgium against Standard Liege. Teenage striker Tony Bird scored two magnificent goals as City took a half time lead in front of a partisan 25,000 crowd, but the Belgian giants proved too strong and ran out comfortable 5-2 winners. The real drama came when Cardiff fans clashed with police and Liege's notorious 'Hell Siders' despite a huge operation launched with the help of the National Crime Intelligence Service, the principal weapon in the war against hooliganism. Up to 200 of the 1000 travelling supporters were thought to have been involved, leading to seventy-seven arrests. Most, however, were released without charge and dispatched back to Wales en masse via specially chartered trains. There were no repeats of the violence in the return fixture two weeks later, but there were no heroics either as City went down 3-1. They suffered a similar fate in the Football League (Coca Cola) Cup where they went out 4-2 on aggregate to Bournemouth. And in the restructured (and needlessly complicated) AM Cup (Autoglass Trophy) where they beat Torquay but lost out to Bristol Rovers and Wycombe Wanderers.

All the hype, however, was saved for the FA Cup, where City for once turned giant-killers, despite needing a replay to ease past non-League Enfield in the opening round. Subsequently, Brentford were knocked out with the minimum of fuss and First Division Middlesbrough were sent packing after a replay. The first game of the New Year, a draw at Ninian Park on 8 January 1994, was another that erupted into violence with Middlesbrough, becoming another one of only a handful of clubs to visit Ninian Park intent on causing trouble, and leaving with their faculties largely intact. In the replay at Ayresome Park, Stant scored, despite being injured, but it was Blake who stole the thunder, tapping in the winner in the final moments of extra time. The unlikely victory put Cardiff into the fourth round, where they were paired with big-hitters Manchester City who sat atop the Premiership at the time. In a carnival atmosphere at Ninian Park before a capacity crowd of 20,486, Blake again grabbed the headlines, scoring a wonderful individual goal to bring down the house and book a place in the fifth round for the first time since 1971–72. Unfortunately, all the heroics counted for nothing and, despite being drawn at home, City went down 2-1 to Luton. Even worse, largely because of his FA Cup exploits, future Welsh international Blake was now a target for several larger clubs. The vultures were circling.

Meanwhile in the League, a Blake hat-trick settled a home tie with Stockport County and draws with Cambridge United and Bradford followed before Blake was again City's saviour, landing them three crucial points with a vital winner against Fulham. A satisfying home win over Swansea was followed by a 3-0 win over champions-elect Reading, but their nine-match unbeaten run came to an end two days later with a 5-2 defeat at Rotherham. They claimed a League double over Wrexham with an emphatic 5-1 drubbing at Ninian Park on 5 February but, typical of City's form, their only other League match that month was a defeat at Burnley. The Burnley game proved to be the last League outing for Blake in Cardiff's colours, as he was soon on his way to Sheffield United. The winger-turned bustling target-man had scored forty goals in 164 appearances for his hometown club, and his transfer sparked fury among the City faithful who yet again questioned the club's ambition. The mooted price was £500,000 (to be paid in instalments and add-ons), but in what proved to be a costly error, City lost out on almost half that amount when the Blades became one of the first clubs relegated from the Premiership, as the balance was only payable on the condition that they stayed up.

After Blake's controversial departure, a deflated City had to battle for every point. Wins over Plymouth Argyle, Burnley and Rotherham were the high-points of an emotional March which saw City's play-off hopes all-but evaporate. April saw them play an incredible ten League matches, starting with a disappointing defeat at Swansea which deepened the gloom threatening to engulf Ninian Park. Two draws followed, before City crushed Brighton & Hove Albion 5-3 on their own ground to lighten the mood, Millar leading the way with a hat trick from midfield. City managed to edge out Exeter in their next home game, but they crumbled shockingly when mid-table Cambridge visited, losing 7-2 to suffer their worst defeat in years. Just for good measure they also lost their last two fixtures of the season to settle into lowly nineteenth position, narrowly escaping the drop.

1994–95 season

There was precious little transfer activity at Ninian Park in the summer of 1994, the exception being the signing of Anthony 'Charlie' Oatway, a talented midfielder from non-League club Yeading. So it was virtually the same team that kicked off the new season with a 4-1 defeat at Stockport and a 3-1 home drubbing at the hands of Oxford United, before picking up their first point at York. City's dire form continued, with them collecting maximum points just once in the first twelve games, a 2-0 win at Chester where Stant and Aizlewood were the scorers. Stant banged in a hat trick against Cambridge at Ninian Park on 22 October in a 3-1 victory, and was on target again in the next match, along with Millar, as they won a 3-2 thriller at Bradford. But the wins were few and far between, and a 3-0 over Brighton was their only other League victory that side of Christmas.

City suffered the humiliation of being knocked out of the FA Cup in the very first round by non-League Enfield, and went out at the same stage of the League (Coca Cola) Cup to lower League opposition in the shape of Torquay. Somewhat surprisingly given their form, they managed to beat Plymouth in the AM Cup (Autoglass Windscreens Shield) but went out at Exeter, and were barred from entering the Welsh Cup. The row over City's non-involvement in the Konica League of Wales resulted in them, and the other Welsh clubs playing in the Barclays League, being excluded. Cynics complained that it wasn't fair that they represented their country in Europe, but didn't participate in their national League, overlooking the fact that Barclays League clubs were far better equipped than those playing in the comparatively inferior Konica League.

It all proved too much, and Eddie May was ousted to be replaced with 'general manager' Terry Yorath, the man who had won the hearts of a nation during his ill-fated stint as

Wales boss. As a player he had been a model professional, collecting fifty-nine Welsh caps during a glittering career with Leeds, Coventry City and Tottenham Hotspur. He was to form a managerial partnership with Mark Aizlewood, who would also continue playing. Soon, it emerged that Yorath was also a member of a consortium bidding to buy the club, and the speculation surrounding that issue was a constant distraction. Football-wise the team lurched from catastrophe to catastrophe. The experimental Yorath-Aizlewood partnership wasn't delivering, and City remained in the relegation places. Conflicting interests and the breakdown of takeover talks prompted Yorath to resign from his post, and a hurtful 4-1 drubbing by Swansea at the Vetch on 7 March 1995 epitomized the sorry state of affairs at Ninian Park.

Eddie May, always the fans' choice, was tempted back as temporary boss, but was faced with a virtually impossible task in keeping the Bluebirds up. May's return, however, undoubtedly had a positive effect as the team embarked on their best run of the season, losing just one in seven to give themselves a slim chance of avoiding the drop. But then defeats by Birmingham and Shrewsbury sealed their fate and a difficult season ultimately saw them relegated with Plymouth, Chester and Leyton Orient.

City's future hung in the balance, and the speculation intensified until, on 7 July, Samesh Kumar officially bought the club, took over as chairman, and recruited Bill Coldwell as director of football and Kenny Hibbitt as head coach. Kumar had enjoyed a successful stint as Birmingham chairman before losing most of his assets with the collapse of the BCCI bank. His first priority was to financially stabilize the club and get a commercial department in place, before turning his attention to the playing staff. The first acquisitions under the new regime were tenacious midfielder Paul Harding, who signed on a two-year contract from Birmingham, and Ian Rodgerson, who was a free transfer from Sunderland. Out went Paul Millar, who returned to Ireland with Linfield, Nick Richardson, who went to Bury, and ex-player/assistant manager Mark Aizlewood, who joined Merthyr. As the decks were cleared for the new arrivals Cohen Griffith, Wayne Fereday and Charlie Oatway were also released.

1995–96 season
Bird was on target twice, along with Dale, in an opening day 3-3 draw at Rochdale on 12 August, but City were edged out by Northampton in their next outing and had to wait to claim their first victory until a Dale penalty was enough to beat Darlington on 2 September to claim their first victory. In the early stages of the season their form was erratic, they would go from beating Mansfield 3-0 one week to losing 4-2 at Cambridge the next, as the new management team struggled to establish themselves. In November Eddie May was edged out of the equation and soon found himself in alternative employment at Konica League side Barry Town, and then on 8 December, director of football Bill Coldwell died suddenly from a brain haemorrhage following routine hip surgery. The very next day Dale fired off a double tribute as he scored the goals to beat Hartlepool at Ninian Park, but they were the only bright sparks in a very a grim period.

The gloom was temporarily lifted by a useful run in the League (Coca Cola) Cup, where City overcame Portsmouth before going out to Pompey's south-coast rivals Southampton 5-1 over two legs, largely due to the efforts of Matt Le Tissier at his sublime best. City progressed to round two of the FA Cup at the expense of non-League Rushden & Diamonds, but there they crashed out to Swindon. In another nondescript AM Cup (Auto Windscreens shield) they drew with Hereford and beat Gillingham in the group stages before losing to Northampton.

In the transfer window, Cardiff bought mid-fielder Steve Flack from non-League Cambridge City and 30-year-old striker Tony Philliskirk from Burnley, who immediately lapsed into a lengthy goal drought. In an attempt to create more goals, Crystal Palace winger Tony Scully was drafted in on loan, but his arrival did little to appease disgruntled fans who were growing increasingly impatient with affairs at Ninian Park. Hibbitt in particular came under criticism, and as his team continued to flounder in mid-table the need for a new manager became increasingly apparent. However, when Hibbitt was officially moved sideways to take the role of director of football early in 1996, it came as a huge surprise in the footballing world as his replacement was one of England's most decorated players. Phil Neal had won almost every major honour in the game with Liverpool, amassed 50 England caps (coincidentally, the first during a 2-1 win over Wales in March 1976), had once been the England assistant-manager, and had steered Coventry to twelfth place in the premiership. Neal arrived with pedigree, vast experience, a huge reputation, and with the club in a reasonable League position. But sadly, it wasn't the fairytale appointment many had anticipated. His first game in charge was a 3-2 win over Doncaster courtesy of a Dale hat-trick, but that was a rare highlight as they succumbed to three consecutive defeats. It wasn't until April that Cardiff's secured their status with a draw at Scunthorpe, by which time ex-England centre-back and Bristol City manager Russell Osman had been drafted in on a monthly contract from Brighton and defensive teenage prodigy Lee Jarman had emerged through the youth set-up.

It had been another tough season at Ninian Park, a fact attributed mainly to continuing problems in midfield.

Skipper Paul Harding, the man charged with the task of filling the void left by the departure of Paul Ramsey, had started the season an inspiration, but his form tailed off dramatically and he ended the season available on a free transfer. His remarkable decline was a mystery, and the only explanation the player himself could offer was that he 'wasn't happy.' Also released were goalkeeper David Roberts, forward Darren Adams, and defensive stalwarts Derek Brazil and Damon Searle, who had played over 400 games between them.

As per usual, there was a distinct lack of money that summer. In fact, Kumar claimed that the club was in such a perilous position that it was losing around £3,500 a week. Local businesses were slow to intervene to help City, which was now essentially a small club in a poor League with a very big ground in a state of severe disrepair. Despite the lack of funds, another attempt was made to plug the midfield hole by signing highly rated QPR youngster John Cross. Unfortunately, injury prevented him from ever making a first team appearance. The other big news was the arrival of a 37-year-old journeyman striker from Hereford. In all fairness Steve White, who had finished the 1995–96 season as Division Three's top scorer, proved to be one of Neal's better signings. White's former club mate, left-back Kevin Lloyd, also made the short trip to Ninian Park, and the new order was completed by defender Jeff Eckhardt who arrived from Stockport, Carlisle goalkeeper Tony Elliot, and Bristol City mid-fielder Jason Fowler. Another unpleasant surprise was in store for Bluebirds fans when the bookies announced the odds for the forthcoming season and made City rank outsiders while Swansea, managed by ex-Liverpool and Denmark mid-fielder Jan Molby, were installed as clear favourites to win the division.

1996–97 season

Injuries and a shortage of players meant that for the big kick-off, the misfiring Philliskirk was moved into midfield to accommodate the new strike pairing of White and Dale. City's opening game was against Scarborough, where ex-Bluebird Gary Bennett was player/coach, and the new-look team acquitted themselves well enough to return with a point. A debut goal from Eckhardt was enough to beat Brighton at Ninian Park in the next outing, before Wigan Athletic inflicted Cardiff's first defeat. Three wins from the next four catapulted them into the upper echelons and things were going well but on 7 October, Phil Neal abruptly packed his bags and left to take the role of assistant manager to Steve Coppell at Manchester City. His undignified departure prompted an investigation by the FA and a lengthy legal dispute as City sought compensation from the Division One giants. While another extended bout of media speculation and supporter unrest set in, Kumar began the search for a worthy successor with Kenny Hibbitt taking temporary charge. A High Court battle was avoided when the clubs settled out of court, but even that wasn't the end of the saga. Barely a month after Neal's appointment at Manchester City, Coppell resigned leaving Neal holding the reigns at the troubled club. He too resigned shortly afterwards.

Meanwhile at Cardiff, under the guidance of Hibbitt, the team boasted an impressive League record of four wins and two draws from eight games. But he was soon ousted in favour of Russell Osman, a rookie manager who had played fifteen games for the Bluebirds the previous season as his playing career ground to a halt. His first match in charge was a home first round FA Cup tie against Hendon which City won 2-0, but they disappointingly went out to Gillingham at the next stage. Their participation in the other Cup competitions was equally short-lived. Northampton accounted for them in the first round of the League (Coca Cola) Cup and, though they progressed to the second round of a re-structured AM Cup (Auto Windscreens Shield) at the expense of Gillingham (the match coming just three days after their FA Cup meeting), they went out to Exeter.

The unstable situation at Ninian Park reached almost farcical proportions on Christmas Eve when after only forty-three days at the helm, Osman was demoted to assistant manager with Hibbitt temporarily taking over his duties. Though given precious little time, the ex-England star had failed to win over the fans who were growing increasingly frustrated at the club's lack of progress and perceived reluctance to spend money. In response, Kumar blamed the 'worst injury crisis we have had', and took up many columns of newsprint bemoaning the financial plight of the club.

Shortly after Osman's departure, Cardiff acquired the services of Portsmouth's Deon Burton, possibly the brightest of all their loan-signings to date, just as a local prospect called Simon Haworth, started breaking into the team. The big forward, christened 'Bambi' by the fans because of his gangly runs, scored his first senior goal for City in a 2-0 win against Hull. On 11 January 1997, crowd favourite Phil Stant returned to Ninian Park with Lincoln and scored in a 3-1 win for the visitors. Hibbitt was so irate, he placed every member of his squad on the transfer list, a shock tactic clearly designed to shake up his beleaguered troops. However, the rest of the Football League were reluctant to splash out on City's players and to add insult to injury, Deon Burton, who was often the shining star in a poor team, opted to return to Portsmouth and play in their reserves rather than fight it out in City's first XI. A big-money move to the Premiership with Derby County followed.

The situation looked bleak, but Cardiff fans received a timely boost with news of a link-up with the people behind the Cardiff Devils ice hockey team. Celtic Leisure, fronted by local businessmen David Temme, Paul Guy and Bob Phillips, had made the Devils the most successful club in British ice hockey and planned to, in the words of chief executive Joan Hill, 'improve the financial structure of the club [Cardiff City] immediately.' Sure enough, soon there were changes afoot at all levels; Ceri Whitehead replaced ex-World Cup referee Jim Finney as club secretary, and Hereford mid-fielder Gareth Stoker arrived for an undisclosed fee. The battling 23-year old had a long list of disciplinary problems, and immediately made an impact against his former club first by scoring against them, then being sent off in a 1-1 draw. Three successive wins followed with the blossoming Haworth scoring in each as City began to threaten the play-off positions, and as the season drew to an exciting climax they notched a 2-0 win over already-promoted Carlisle to leave themselves needing a single point from their last match at Darlington to sneak in. As fate would have it they lost 2-1, but limped into the play-offs for the first time in their history thanks to other results going their way. Their opponents were Northampton, the only top six side City hadn't beaten that term, and sure enough the Cobblers proved too strong for the Bluebirds and won a fiery tie 4-2 on aggregate. The only consolation was the fact that Northampton beat Swansea in the final.

Apart from that disappointing finale, it had been a reasonable season for a young City team, the average age of which was just twenty-three. The form of Wales U21 captain Lee Jarman and emerging striker Haworth proved the catalysts for a late surge that was a vast improvement on previous seasons, but the promising squad could not be kept together and before the season ended City accepted a hefty

£500,000 bid for Haworth from Premiership strugglers Coventry City. Other notable departures included the long-serving skipper Jason Perry, who moved to Bristol Rovers, and Jimmy Gardner, who went to Exeter.

Despite the windfall from Haworth's sale, Hibbitt was given precious little to strengthen the team, his biggest purchases being Bristol City duo Kevin Nugent and Scott Partridge for a combined £115,000. The current vogue sweeping British football was the 'wing-back' formation that utilized a pair of deep-lying wide men who attacked or defended as the situation required. Consequently, converted wing-backs Chris Beech and Anthony Carss arrived on free transfers, as did defender Mark Harris, midfielder David Penney and experienced goalkeeper John Hallworth, who joined from First Division Oldham Athletic. The clutch of new signings, many of whom had experience of playing in higher divisions, prompted the bookmakers to make City 8-1 joint favourites with Swansea and Peterborough to win the newly-franchised Nationwide League Division Three.

1997–98 season
The bookies' estimation appeared to be justified when City won the opening game 1-0 with a Dale goal at Orient on 9 August, and stayed unbeaten for the first six games until Chester left Ninian Park with all three points. They then conspired to draw eight of the next ten, and long-term injuries to Dale and Nugent prompted the Board to part with the £75,000 necessary for Hibbitt to land Swindon's Irish U21 midfielder Wayne O'Sullivan. It was the highest fee paid by City since Phil Stant signed for them five years earlier, and there was soon another new arrival as journeyman striker Andy Saville signed for his ninth professional club.

Predictably, Cardiff exited in the first rounds of both the Football League (Coca Cola) Cup and the AM Cup (Autoglass Windscreens Shield), losing to Southend and Millwall respectively. The writing was probably on the wall when Jimmy Rollo, a bit-part import from Bath, knocked himself out cold in the act of scoring against Southend. There was more drama in the FA Cup, where City breezed past Slough Town before beating Hendon for the second year running. In the subsequent round, an impressive win against higher-division opposition Oldham set up an epic fourth round battle with First Division Reading. After the first match ended in a 1-1 draw on 24 January 1998, City reported their opponents to the Football League after learning that a feature had appeared in an earlier Reading FC programme branding Ninian Park 'unsafe,' and urging visiting supporters to be careful as 'violent incidents' often occurred there. The bad feeling between the clubs erupted at the replay and trouble flared, leading to thirty arrests (fifteen from each side) for a range of offences. The Royals eventually won the tie on penalties. That season also saw the introduction of a controversial new tournament. After expelling them from the Welsh Cup, the FAW were eager to capitalize on the comparatively large crowds the exiled Welsh clubs attracted, and devised the FAW Invitation Cup, with a modest amount of prize money up for grabs instead of European qualification. City progressed unbeaten from a group that included Wrexham, Merthyr and Newtown, and defeated Conwy United and Merthyr (again) on their way to a final showdown with Wrexham which they lost 2-1. Though unveiled in a blaze of publicity and championed by BBC Wales TV, the new tournament failed to capture the public's imagination and the average gate for City's group games hovered around the 1,000 mark. The much-hyped final drew only 3,700.

Shortly after the Reading FA Cup drama, newly-installed assistant manager Russell Osman was relieved of his duties and Hibbitt took full temporary control as Kumar searched for yet another new manager. The job was advertised, and around 50 applications were received, 'half from serious contenders, and half from fans and other people with little chance of landing the job'. On 16 February, Joan Hill announced that previous manager Frank Burrows would be leaving a coaching post at West Ham to take the Cardiff job for the second time. Billy Ayre, who had been Jan Molby's number two at Swansea until they were both dismissed in October 1997, was employed as his assistant.

Around this time, home-grown talent such as defender Lee Phillips and striker Christian Roberts were beginning to break into the team, and were given every chance by Burrows. After three draws and a defeat from his first four games, Burrows orchestrated a 7-1 demolition job of relegation favourites Doncaster at Ninian Park on 14 March, where Saville netted twice to complement goals by O'Sullivan, Beech, Penney, Roberts and Scott Young. Roberts also scored the winner at Hull the following week, but sadly that was the Bluebirds' last League win of the season. The final game was a 0-0 draw at Darlington, City's twenty-third of the season, a new League record. Their finish of twenty-first place was bitterly disappointing after the previous season's exploits. The chief reason for this low ranking was probably the constant managerial shake-ups. However, the introduction of the FAW Invitation Cup, meaning that City had to fulfil no fewer than sixty-five first-team fixtures, certainly didn't help.

At the end of the season, Burrows wielded the axe in no uncertain manner, releasing Tony Elliot, Anthony Carss, Chris Beech, Tony Philliskirk, Jimmy Rollo, Steve White, Mark Harriss and Carl Dale. Philliskirk had turned into the forgotten man at Ninian Park, but White had performed reasonably well, with only his advanced age counting against him. The greatest loss, however, was that of goal poacher Dale, who scored ninety-four goals in 253 appearances before his career was ravaged by injury.

To fill the gaps, Burrows exploited the new Bosman ruling, which meant that any player over the age of twenty-three was free to leave his club when his contract expired, with no transfer fee or compensation payable. In this manner he signed goalkeeper Seamus Kelly, defender Mike Ford, centre-back Graham Mitchell, midfielder Mark Bonner, and experienced striker John Williams, once famously dubbed the fastest player in British football. Another new arrival was right-back Mark Delaney from League of Wales (formerly the Konica League) side Carmarthen. At the time, Burrows was criticized for taking a gamble on Delaney, an untested player with no League experience, but the resilient Scot stood by his decision. The only player Burrows actually bought in that period was midfielder Richard Carpenter, who cost a conservative £35,000 from Fulham.

1998–99 season

As fate would have it, on the opening day of the new season at Hartlepool, all the new imports were upstaged by another of Burrows' young guns, 17-year-old striker Robert Earnshaw, who scored his first League goal with a spectacular overhead kick to salvage a point. A week later they lost their first home game 3-1 to Peterborough, and as it became apparent that more quality was needed, Burrows drafted in Caerphilly-born Watford striker Dai Thomas, who scored on his début as the Bluebirds registered their first win of the new campaign at Shrewsbury. After losing to Rotherham and Darlington, the team gradually began to gel, and lost only once in the next twelve games, but a bad-tempered 2-1 defeat at Swansea ended the run. City responded well to the Vetch setback to reel off victories against Southend, Carlisle, Scunthorpe, Mansfield and Shrewsbury, the Mansfield game seeing the debut of Welsh international midfielder Andy Legg, who had been added to the squad after finding himself frozen out at Reading. The versatile 32-year old was a long throw expert, and his drive and enthusiasm galvanized an already-strong midfield. As the New Year approached, City were top of the League and at the centre of a surge of interest that saw their average home attendance treble, while behind the scenes, officials frantically searched for ways to safely increase Ninian Park's capacity.

City made little impact in either the League (Coca Cola) Cup or the AM (Windscreens Shield) Cup where they lost out to Fulham and Millwall respectively. However, their good League form translated to the FA Cup where they demolished Chester and non-League Hednesford on their way to a third round showdown with another non-League side, Yeovil Town. The plucky underdogs forced a replay, which Nugent won in extra time to secure a trip to First Division Sheffield United where the Bluebirds lost heavily. In the FAW Invitation Cup (now dubbed the FAW Premier Cup), City were grouped with Bangor, Merthyr and Rhyl. In the very first game Bangor provided a shock by winning 1-0 at Ninian Park, but City claimed revenge by winning the return 4-1 and marching on to a quarter-final with old enemy Swansea. In this latest instalment of the saga, which attracted more than double the average gate of the competition, City won a thrilling match 3-2, but lost a subsequent two-legged semi with Wrexham 4-3.

On 9 January 1999, City thrashed Hartlepool, featuring ex-England legend Peter Beardsley, 4-1 to remain top of the League and later that month, City signed another Welsh international from Reading, right-sided mid-fielder Jason Bowen, on a two-and-a-half year contract. 26-year-old Bowen, born in Merthyr Tydfil, had previously played for Swansea, Birmingham and gained Premiership experience at Southampton. However, in March, City accepted a £500,000 bid from Villa for right-back Mark Delaney. Some fans disputed the move, and once again questioned the club's ambition, but no one can deny that it was a smart piece of business for a player who had cost nothing. A transfer to the Premiership capped a meteoric rise for the young player who was on the verge of a Welsh call-up after just nine months of League football.

After defeat at Rotherham, a Nugent double at Exeter kicked off a sequence of results that included wins over Carlisle, Southend and Scarborough and reaffirmed City's promotion hopes. In the penultimate game, City finally achieved promotion with a goalless home draw against Scunthorpe. Burrows declared this, his fourth promotion as a manager, as 'the best of the lot.' In just fourteen months he had transformed an ailing club from basement strugglers into championship contenders, but again controversy was just around the corner. No sooner had the season finished than Samesh Kumar announced his decision to step down as chairman and managing director. Kumar, who had bought the club for £800,000 in 1995, admitted to being disappointed at the way his reign ended, though he insisted he would temporarily retain his 37 per cent shareholding. Chief executive Joan Hill also left that summer to be replaced by general manager Ceri Whitehead, while Steve Borley took over as chairman.

Amid the chaos, Burrows quietly set about his task of fine-tuning his team in readiness for a difficult season in Division Two and released several players, most notably Wayne O'Sullivan. He also demonstrated his business skills by selling Graham Mitchell to Halifax and John Williams to York, both at 100 per cent profit as players who had cost nothing. His first purchase was the £20,000 acquisition of Wales U18 striker Jamie Hughes from League of Wales outfit Connah's Quay. The 22-year-old ex-postal worker once scored 164 goals in a single season in the amateur Leagues. Burrows also forked out £100,000 to prise Matt Brazier away from Fulham after he had impressed during a loan spell the previous season, and snapped up 23-year-old Republic of Ireland mid-fielder Willie Boland from Premiership Coventry, who, despite arriving on a free, was City's most expensive signing at the time because of expenses, add-ons and wage demands. Also arriving at Ninian Park were centre-back Russell Perrett from Portsmouth, right-back Winston Faerber from Dutch club Den Haag, and ex-Welsh international midfielder John Cornforth, who joined on a monthly contract from Wycombe. Just before the new season kicked off the club held a centenary dinner at the plush Marriott Hotel, which was attended by a host of celebrities including Cardiff players past and present. During an awards ceremony John Toshack was named as the club's 'greatest player' and Brian Clark scorer of the 'greatest goal' for his 1971 winner against Real Madrid, which won the 'most exciting match' award.

1999–2000 season
After a startling, goal-laden pre-season, Boland opened his account for his new employers with a penalty in his first competitive game, a 1-1 draw with Millwall. The result was unremarkable in itself, but the match made headlines for other reasons as violence swept the city of Cardiff. Web sites and internet chat rooms, the new-favoured medium for hooligans, carried running commentary on what was described on one (Millwall) site as 'the tear up of the year.'

Burrows still favoured the 5-3-2 wing-back system but unfortunately, the pool of players at his disposal didn't suit his ideology and he was often forced into playing midfielder Jason Fowler in the heart of the defence. Tellingly, in the first two games of the season Fowler was sent off, conceded a penalty, and scored an own goal. However, the team still held the imagination of the public as a 1-1 home draw with Wrexham on Friday 20 August attracted the highest crowd of the entire lower two divisions (11,164). Later that month, Kenny Hibbitt left the club after a four-year association. The 48-year-old Yorkshireman had filled a number of positions including manager. When he left he was Director of Youth Development. Shortly afterwards, Burrows borrowed £1.35 million-rated Manchester City defender Tony Vaughan, and the 23-year-old made such an impression that Burrows spent the rest of the season trying to sign him permanently. Sadly, it was to no avail. City looked solid in defence, but scoring goals was a problem. To try and remedy this Burrows signed Wales U21 winger Josh Low from Orient in the hope of turning him into a striker, while the search for a hit-man continued. Meanwhile, Cornforth and Jarman, who was then still only twenty-one, were allowed to leave.

On 12 November, City beat Chesterfield 2-1 at Ninian Park with a Bowen double to claim their first win in ten outings. Things were looking up, especially when Sheffield Wednesday agreed to loan out former England U21 Richie Humphreys. The forward, who had made over sixty Premiership appearances, scored twice on his debut in a 3-0 win at Colchester. City then spent £110,000 on 6' 5' German mid-fielder Jorn Schwinkendorf from Mannheim. The transfer raised many eyebrows as the club already had a wealth of midfield talent, but Burrows probably had aspirations to turn the bustling German into a centre-back. In fact, he was played in defence several times but looked so uncomfortable there that Burrows was forced to restore him to midfield.

City's last match of 1999 and the second millennium was a 0-0 draw with Cambridge at Abbey Stadium. Despite ending goalless, the match was full of incident as controversial referee David Elleray sent off all three of City's central defenders and awarded Cambridge a penalty, which was then saved by Hallworth. And as if that wasn't enough, Fowler was rushed to hospital at half-time suffering from concussion. The resulting suspensions left City woefully short of players in a squad that had already been reduced by injuries and ravaged by a flu bug. It therefore came as no surprise when they lost their first match of the new millennium 4-0 at home to high-flying Preston on 3 January 2000. The poor run continued, and a 2-1 defeat at Wrexham three weeks later erupted in violence as the fans grew ever more impatient with the team. There were seven arrests, but more worryingly, police were alerted to fans' plans to engage in combat with like-minded individuals at other games before the end of the season, in particular at Stoke.

More strange managerial decisions occurred in the New Year, when Burrows sent all of his young strikers out on loan: Earnshaw went to Greenock Morton in the Scottish First Division, Hughes to League of Wales club Cwmbran Town, and Roberts to League of Ireland side Drogheda, which was managed by ex-Cardiff boss Eddie May. In addition, Middleton was sent to Plymouth while the fading Dai Thomas had already been farmed out to the Spanish Second Division. The latter soon returned, only to be sent to Ireland to link up with Roberts and May. This string of managerial clangers probably ultimately cost Burrows his job, because shortly after a meeting with Steve Borley, it was announced that Burrows and the club were parting company. The tough-talking Scot paid the penalty for not living up to the club's high expectations and doggedly sticking to the same systems (like the controversial wing-back formation), refusing to change even if the team struggled. Apparently, he also lost his famed motivational powers, as out of the last forty-six League games with him in charge, his team won just nine times. Burrows was replaced by Billy Ayres.

They also tumbled out of the large Cup competitions, falling at the first hurdle of the AM Cup (Auto Windscreens Shield) to Northampton, and going out of the League (Worthington) Cup to Wimbledon after seeing off the challenge of QPR. A mini-charge in the FA Cup that disposed of Orient and Bury was halted in the third round by Bolton Wanderers, leaving only the FAW Premier Cup to spare their blushes. There, they didn't disappoint. They progressed from a group featuring Newtown, Merthyr, and Barry Town, and beating Aberystwyth Town and Caernarfon Town on their way to a final rematch with Wrexham.

By this time, a proposed £2.5 million takeover investment by a consortium was the talk of the town, and Billy Ayre's first task as caretaker-manager was to assess the squad on their behalf. Despite his attacking philosophy (Ayre immediately changed to a 4-3-3 formation) his first match in charge was a goalless draw at Scunthorpe that left the Welsh club sixth from bottom. Then, largely due to the disruptive boardroom influence of ex-chairman Kumar, who apparently thought the club was being sold on the cheap, the proposed takeover collapsed. Outraged supporters formed the Bluebirds 2000 club, with the primary aim of raising the £300,000 needed to buy enough shares to force Kumar's shareholding below 25 per cent, ensuring that he would be unable to block any future investments.

On the pitch, the team didn't notch their first League win

of the new millennium until 17 March when they beat Colchester 3-2 with goals by Bowen (2) and Nugent. Days later Wales B and former U21 international striker Kurt Nogan was signed from Division Two rivals Preston for £100,000, the move partly funded by the Bluebirds 2000 group and the official supporters club. The inflated transfer market meant that most quality players were simply out of City's price range, and they tried to address their goal-scoring problems by getting pint-sized ex-Newcastle striker Paul Brayson on loan from Reading. Nogan made his debut at Reading's Madejski Stadium on 25 March, where Bowen scored a memorable goal against one of his old clubs to hoist them out of danger.

Just when a reprieve was looking likely, the footballing Gods once again pulled the rug out from under City's collective feet; Nogan scored on his home debut but his new club still lost to Burnley, this was followed by a draw at leaders Preston and home defeats by Cambridge and Bury. As predicted, a 2-1 defeat at Stoke on 29 April provoked more crowd disturbances that had to be quashed by police with mounted officers and riot gear, and resulted in twenty-three arrests. The game had been earmarked as a potential powder keg even before the gravity of the situation had been established. A crushing 4-1 defeat on 2 May at promotion-chasing Gillingham, where City actually took a first minute lead through Bowen, finally condemned them to an eleventh relegation. With the pressure lifted, Cardiff managed to win their last League match of the season over Bristol Rovers to restore some pride and finish a solitary point behind Oxford and safety. Yet again the game was overshadowed by violence, as marauding Rovers supporters clashed with heartbroken City followers in the city centre. There were complaints, not for the first time, that the police had been unnecessarily heavy-handed with the distraught

City supporters. City ended the season with a whimper on 14 May as they lost the FAW Cup final 2-0 to old foes Wrexham, who won the trophy for a second time.

So, Cardiff's centenary year ended not with jubilation and celebration, but with more misery and despair. Despite improving the playing staff immeasurably in the past year, the club apparently suffered from the air of uncertainty surrounding it, a lack of cohesion on the field, questionable tactics, and several disastrous forays into the transfer market. To help balance the books, Middleton was sold to Halifax, teenage sensation Christian Roberts signed for Exeter, and skipper Mike Ford, Lee Phillips and Seamus Kelly were all handed free transfers. The disappointment was compounded when it was confirmed that they would be exchanging places in the Football League with Swansea, who had won the Third Division title.

11

Miracle Worker
(2000–2005)

This is not a football club – it is a Welsh institution (and) I burn with a passion to make it something for the whole of Wales to be proud of.

Sam Hammam

In the summer of 2000, 52-year old Lebanese businessman Sam Hammam emerged as a surprise contender in the take-over saga. The ex-Wimbledon supremo, who spectacularly guided the Dons from the old Fourth Division to the Premiership and an unforgettable FA Cup Final win over the mighty Liverpool, first became interested in Cardiff City after a chance meeting with former villain-of-the-piece Samesh Kumar at a Worthington (League) Cup Final. The vast majority of fans were behind Hammam from the outset, having long since grown tired of all the cloak-and-dagger boardroom shenanigans, but a minority voiced concerns over plans to change the club's name, crest, and playing colours. Hammam was insisting on an obvious Celtic/Welsh theme to stir up interest in the club, but opinion polls showed that most fans were against any radical changes. These concerns were mirrored by the directors who, though keen to secure the club's future, were equally keen to protect its identity. As a safeguard, 'heritage clauses,' agreed upon by all concerned parties, were written into all binding legal documents, delaying the £3.1 million bid and temporarily enraging the would-be benefactor. Even with these safeguards in place, the club crest was later quietly changed to a new design incorporating a single Bluebird and a St David's cross. At last, on 21 July, a deal was verbally agreed between ex-chairman Tony Clemo, who was acting as Hammam's representative, and the 'take-over committee' consisting of chairman Steve Borley, vice-chairman Michael Isaac and director Paul Guy. Happily, the deal coincided with the club being handed a £1 million grant for ground improvements from the Football Foundation, enabling Ninian Park's capacity to be raised to15, 500.

As the kick-off to the new season approached, Hammam spent considerable time courting the local media, to which he gave passionate and often rousing interviews. He also met with sections of the hardcore fan-base, a fan-base having been the only thing missing from his time at Wimbledon. To the derision of the press, he even made a concerted attempt to win the respect of the troublesome hooligan element, called the Soul Crew, by meeting with representatives. In monetary terms, Hammam's cash injection cleared £1.5 million of various accumulated debts, secured all losses for the foreseeable future, and left around £600,000 for team building, which was a lot of money for a basement club. Consequently, they were quickly installed as clear favourites to win Division Three, even before the high-profile appointment of ex-Wales boss Bobby Gould as Director of Football. However, before a ball had even been kicked in anger, hooligans made a mockery of the term 'pre-season friendly' when Cardiff and Newport County supporters clashed after a Bluebirds win at their Gwent neighbours. Luckily, only small numbers were involved and the flare-up led to just seven arrests, but the unfortunate incident happened just weeks after striker David 'Dai' Thomas, a lifelong Cardiff fan, was caught on TV footage rioting alongside known English and Welsh hooligans at the

Euro 2000 finals in Brussels, Belgium. Consequently it was the beginning of the end for him as he was first suspended then packed off to non-League Merthyr Tydfil in disgrace, eventually agreeing to a permanent transfer there.

The re-building continued with the signing of full-back Andy Thompson from Tranmere Rovers and rookie Wales U21 right-back Danny Gabbidon from West Bromwich Albion for a fee that would eventually total around £800,000. Shortly after, fellow defender David Greene joined from Colchester United, Wales U21 midfielder Kevin Evans was recruited from Leeds United, Welsh goalkeeper Mark Walton signed from Brighton & Hove Albion, and left-back Scott McCulloch arrived from Dundee United. The dramatic events unfolding at Ninian Park certainly stirred up public interest and the media were quick to capitalise, revelling in Hammam's rebel-rousing antics. It soon became apparent that for all his front and showmanship, this multi-millionaire with an interest in British football was absolutely serious about propelling City into the upper echelons of the Football League. Many before him had tried and failed, but not many shared his passion, determination and insight. It's fair to say that when he first breezed into Ninian Park that summer on a tide of hope and optimism, most people just couldn't help but be swept away on it.

2000–2001 season

Hammam predicted an average gate approaching 7,000 would turn up to watch the 'new' Cardiff play their home games, and pledged that every penny raised by additional attendances would go towards team building. The managerial structure took on a more fluid approach, with Gould and Billy Ayre jointly picking the team. The first match under the new regime on 12 August 2000, saw City face three former players at Exeter City's St James' Park – John Cornforth, Steve Flack and Christian Roberts – while Cardiff gave full debuts to Walton, Greene and Thompson. Goals from Paul Brayson and Josh Low settled the match and ensured a winning start. A week later a Kevin Nugent strike salvaged a point from City's first home game which, incidentally, was watched by 11,019, proving Hammam's estimated attendance figure of 7,000 to be somewhat conservative!

A sequence of four more draws followed, as people worked tirelessly behind the scenes to smooth over Hammam's arrival and finalise the biggest development in the club's recent history, while the management team identified a list of priority transfer targets. For his part, Hammam travelled the length and breadth of Wales speaking to various groups of supporters about his hopes and plans for the future, even extending the hand of friendship in Swansea, where he outlined his vision of a 'United Wales', maintaining that there were 'Eighty-nine other (non-Welsh) clubs to hate.' He then reiterated his new-found passion for Cardiff by smashing their existing transfer record to bankroll a £300,000 deal to land powerful striker Leo Fortune-West from League rivals Rotherham United. Even though he had paid only £35,000 for the player just eighteen months earlier, Rotherham's manager, ex-Bluebird Ronnie Moore, was 'fuming' at Fortune-West's decision to sign for his old club. The fact that the Welsh club offered Fortune-West the highest wage in their entire history probably helped persuade him. Meanwhile, City's previous highest-earner, the German, Schwinkendorf, was released from his contract to return to his home country where he linked up with VFL Osnabrück after making only five underwhelming appearances in a Cardiff shirt.

On 12 September, City registered their first home win of

the season with a resounding 4-2 victory over Halifax Town, the goals coming from Scott Young, Jason Bowen, Rob Earnshaw and Fortune-West on his debut. Three days later, the takeover deal was made official and Steve Borley stood down to allow Hammam, who had quickly become the people's choice, to take the chair. On his first full day in office his new charges won 2-0 at Scunthorpe United to climb to third in the League. Tellingly, it was only their third League win at Ninian Park since the sale of Mark Delaney in March 1999. The team had lacked confidence and impetus for far too long, but it seemed that now even they could not help but be swept away on a patriotic blue tide of euphoria. The encouraging start to the season came to an abrupt end in a nightmare match against at Hull City where City lost to a brace of own goals, one coming from Greene, who was later sent off in what proved to be his last League appearance for the club. Though City had made a solid enough start to Hammam's reign, they were already falling into the old trap of drawing too many games. Soon after the Hull game, Ayre, who had just been demoted from assistant manager to head coach, was unceremoniously sacked altogether. His replacement as Gould's sidekick was Alan Cork, Wimbledon's all-time record goalscorer, and one of only a handful of players to have played in every division of the Football League. Though unproven in management circles, Cork's arrival further strengthened the Wimbledon 'Crazy Gang' link, as did the appointment of physiotherapist Clive Goodyear who was hired to work alongside existing physiotherapist Jimmy Goodfellow.

As part of his overall vision, Hammam was keen to acquire the best Welsh, Scottish and Irish youngsters available, which he dubbed his 'Celtic Kids'. It was this strategy that lured Andy Jordan (son of the Scotland legend Joe) to the club from Bristol City, and 20-year-old Welsh international defender Rhys Weston from Arsenal. Weston made his Cardiff debut against old-boy Phil Stant's crisis club Lincoln City on 22 November, with City on an unbeaten run of five, and fresh from a 4-0 drubbing of York City. An injury-time own goal added to strikes from Earnshaw and Brayson to see the Bluebirds win 3-2 against the man who once said that Cardiff supporters were 'The most fanatical I've ever played in front of.' The win saw City climb to fifth in the League with a team containing no fewer than eight Welshmen, the average age being just twenty-three. Three days after the Lincoln game the young guns beat Hartlepool United 3-2 at Ninan Park, again with an injury-time winner. The good results continued with Earnshaw scoring his first League hat-trick at Torquay United in a 4-1 demolition, and Cheltenham Town and Macclesfield Town both capitulating at Ninian Park.

By mid-season, City had assembled one of the largest and best squads in the lower divisions, and competition for a starting place was intense. However, there were small but worrying signs of unrest. In the press, the new regime continually bemoaned a perceived lack of public support (the Hartlepool match drew only 6,251) and in December Ian Butterworth, who had made 293 appearances as a player with Norwich City, was brought into the increasingly abstract management structure. Loosely defined, his role was assistant to Cork who was the team manager, while Gould was the club manager. And still Hammam wasn't finished rebuilding. Where possible, he preferred to have prospective new signings on loan to have a better look at them before pledging any money, otherwise he would try to soften the financial blow by negotiating staggered deals based on performances or appearance-related add-ons. The latest player to arrive at the club in this kind of structured deal was young striker Gavin Gordon, who was signed from

Lincoln for an initial £275,000 (rising to a possible £550,000). Gordon, who had scored twice at Ninian Park already that season for his former club, made his debut in a 2-0 home win over Macclesfield. Christmas saw the Bluebirds sitting pretty in third place in the League after an amazing run of twelve consecutive home wins in all competition. However, the unbeaten run came to an end at Plymouth Argyle on Boxing Day with a 2-1 defeat, a game which proved the last hoorah for Jeff Eckhardt who moved on after making a total of 164 appearances for the Bluebirds.

Under Hammam, the first competition City were eliminated from was the Football League (Worthington) Cup, where Crystal Palace put them out in the first round. They also kept up their tradition of barely contesting the AM Cup (now the LDV Vans trophy) by losing in the first round at Brighton. They fared slightly better in the FA Cup, where they thumped Bristol Rovers 5-1 in the first round thanks to Earnshaw's first competitive hat-trick (pre-dating his treble at Torquay by two weeks). The young striker, whose mother was a prolific goalscorer for a team in Zambia and a professional boxer, scored twice more in the next round in a 3-1 win over Cheltenham that set up a clash with First Division Crewe Alexandra. Young's goal at Ninian Park took the tie to a replay where yet another Earnshaw strike was not enough to prevent his side slipping to a 2-1 defeat. This left only the FAW Premier Cup, where Cardiff had been expected to cement their reputation as the biggest club in Wales but sadly, perennially underachieved. This time, although they progressed with a 100 per cent record from a group including Cwmbran Town, Merthyr Tydfil and Llanelli, they met the Martyrs again in the quarter-finals and promptly lost 1-0. All their previous good work came undone and embarrassingly, their last and most realistic chance of silverware disappeared.

City got back to winning ways in style with a 6-1 home demolition of Exeter on New Year's Day 2001. Since Cork had taken charge the team had collected twenty-nine from the thirty-six points available and the average home attendance had risen by almost 30 per cent. Hammam repeatedly stressed the need for a new 30,000 all-seated stadium, which he claimed would enable Cardiff to compete against the elite on a European stage, and was also keen to secure the futures of some of the nation's hottest emerging talent, announcing ambitious plans to build the 'finest youth development structure in the UK,' and tying starlets like Earnshaw and Weston to lucrative long-term contracts. But it wasn't all plain sailing, as a knee injury forced highly-rated keeper John Hallworth into premature retirement, and misfit defender David Greene was shipped out to Cambridge United. Hammam then attracted yet more controversy when he offered cut-price City shirts and Welsh flags to anyone handing in rival English club shirts at the club shop, and incurred the combined wrath of police and racism campaigners when he jokingly suggested burning the surplus shirts on a makeshift bonfire. Around this time the club was threatened with legal action by local journalist Grahame Lloyd, who reported the club for common assault after being doused with water by some over-zealous youth team players. Evidently Lloyd, who had just written the club's centenary book, was new to the 'Crazy Gang' culture; who knows what damage the incident may have done to already fraught relations between the club and the media.

City claimed revenge on Plymouth for the Boxing Day defeat by winning the return match 4-1 at Ninian Park on 20 January with goals from Earnshaw (2) Fortune-West and McCulloch (his first and only for the club), and followed it a week later with a 5-2 success at Macclesfield. Though they remained in the top four, February brought the season's first dry spell as City failed to score in the three games leading up to a 3-0 home win over Scunthorpe. Gabbidon scored his first goals for the club, Brazier grabbed the third, and City's latest recruit, 23-year old Wales B defender David Hughes, a £450,000 acquisition from Shrewsbury Town, made his home debut. Three days later a Brayson double guided Cardiff to victory at Halifax, before they celebrated their first-ever League game against Kidderminster Harriers with a 4-2 win at Aggborough. A 4-1 home win over Carlisle then left City in second place with games in hand on leaders Chesterfield, who were then a mammoth sixteen points clear.

City had claimed an impressive seventy-one points from thirty-seven matches and no side in the entire Nationwide League had bettered their haul of eighty goals. But then, inexplicably, the team began to stutter. An April Fool's day defeat at Cheltenham was followed by narrow home wins over Barnet and Torquay, and again City's away form became their undoing as they went down 2-0 at Darlington. That match saw Alan Cork begin a nine-game touchline ban for comments made to officials at Brighton the previous month and, to rub salt in the wounds, ex-Bluebird John Williams was among the scorers for the club then managed by another old boy, Gary Bennett.

Just when their promotion hopes were beginning to suffer, fate dealt Cardiff a welcome hand when Chesterfield were hit with a hefty nine-point deduction and a substantial fine after being found guilty of giving illegal payments. The points-deduction was especially damaging to the League-leaders as they prepared for a do-or-die encounter at Ninian Park. On that day City rode their luck, scoring a stoppage-time equaliser to draw 3-3 before a vociferous crowd of 13,602, and in their next outing a Fortune-West hat-trick salvaged a point at York to cement City's second promotion in three seasons. It was a timely retort by the player dubbed

'Costa Fortune' by fans who felt his transfer fee and inflated wages didn't reflect his ability. They were probably amongst the group that reportedly stayed in York celebrating for five days after the match!

With promotion a formality, City took their foot off the pedal and lost at both Mansfield, and then at Hartlepool in the last game. Sandwiched between these two defeats was their last home match, a 3-1 success over Kevin Ratcliffe's Shrewsbury, in which Young scored twice to take his tally for the season to twelve, the biggest haul ever by a Cardiff defender. That season the Pontypridd-born Wales B international also became the clubs longest-serving player. The other goal against the Shrews was scored by Earnshaw, his twenty-fifth League of a season in which he collected a clean sweep of 'Young Player of the Year' awards. City finished runners-up to Brighton, and were the only club in the entire Football League to end the season unbeaten at home. When the figures were added up, the haul amounted to ninety-four goals from forty-six games, more than any Cardiff outfit before them. Despite their off-field problems, Chesterfield finished third, two points behind Cardiff, and joined the promotion party. The general feeling was that City had assembled a squad better equipped for life in the Second Division than the rough and tumble of the Third, and their average gate was altogether more fitting for a higher-placed club. At the end of the season Jason Fowler was released having scored twenty goals in 169 appearances, and Danny Hill joined Oxford United. They were soon followed by Andy Jordan, Scott McCulloch, Andy Thompson and Russell Perrett, all of whom found themselves surplus to requirements.

During the summer of 2001, the club began the biggest marketing exercise in its history, contacting every person on its database to offer discounted deals on season tickets.

Work to upgrade the computerised ticketing system was also undertaken, as were steps to improve the drainage on the pitch and cover the Grange End of Ninian Park. Sections of previously disused terracing on the Popular (Bob) Bank was dusted off with the intention of increasing the ground capacity to 20,000 (including 2,000 away fans), and the club shop was extended and refurbished to cope with increased demand for merchandise. It all added up to a concerted effort by the club to raise its status, but of course all the frills would be meaningless without a decent team representing it on the pitch. To this end, midfield play-maker Graham Kavanagh became City's first £1 million man when he signed from Stoke City. The 27-year-old Republic of Ireland international was immediately installed as club captain and became symbolic of City's drive for success.

Another player with vital Premier League experience, centre-back Spencer Prior, arrived from Manchester City for £700,000, and was soon joined by a third, powerful mid-fielder Des Hamilton, who arrived from Newcastle United on a free. Other free transfers included Welsh wingers Leyton Maxwell and Leonne Jeanne, and Chesterfield left-back Mike Simpkins. It was a fresh start for the talented Llanrhymni-born Jeanne after a string of well-documented drug and alcohol problems had almost finished his career at Queen's Park Rangers before it had properly begun. With the profile of the club climbing rapidly it was proving easier to attract quality players, none better than goalkeeper Neil Alexander who turned down a host of clubs to move to south Wales from Livingstone, which had just won promotion to the Scottish Premier League. As the Scottish U21 international was under twenty-four, Cardiff were required to pay £135,000 compensation, a good price for a player of his calibre.

2000–2001 season

Alexander, Kavanagh, Simpkins and Hamilton all made their full Cardiff debuts in a 1-0 opening day home win over Wycombe Wanderers on 11 August, the goal scored by Gabbidon. The following day Cardiff's Millennium Stadium was the venue for the Charity Shield contest between Liverpool and Manchester United. The intense rivalry between the two English sides combined with Cardiff's bad reputation was expected to lead to violent three-way clashes, and the hooligan element didn't disappoint with a total of twenty-two arrests spread over the weekend. It later emerged that thirteen of the twenty-two were Welsh.

Kavanagh scored his first for Cardiff in a 1-1 draw at Peterborough United on 18 August, and Earnshaw and Fortune-West scored their first goals of the season in a 2-2 draw with Bournemouth at Ninian Park a week later. Their next League game brought their first away win, an impressive 2-1 success at promotion-favourites Reading, but City then slumped to their first League defeat of the season at Cambridge, four days after the atrocious terrorist attacks on America. Cambridge, rock bottom of the League, with a squad assembled at a cost of around £65,000, took great delight in beating the 'Big Time Charlies' from Ninian Park.

Making his Bluebirds debut at Cambridge was one of Kavanagh's old Stoke team-mates, Peter Thorne, a quality front-man who cost a staggering £1.77 million, at the time the biggest fee ever paid by a Second Division club for a striker. The 28-year-old's arrival took Hammam's spending to over £6 million in just twelve months, during which time he broke the club's transfer record no fewer than three times. And still he wasn't finished. Shortly afterwards he hired ex-Carlisle United manager Ian Atkins as head coach and joint assistant manager, and tried (unsuccessfully) to incorporate him into the existing set-up. After a win over Northampton Town, City's unbeaten home run, which stretched back to the penultimate home game of the 1999–2000 season, was finally ended by Huddersfield, despite Thorne scoring his first Cardiff goal. The run had lasted an astonishing twenty-seven games, but the reality of Second Division football was about to set in.

City didn't win another League match until a storming 3-0 at Swindon Town a month later in a televised match against the highly-fancied side that included former Liverpool legend Neil Ruddock. The victory was quickly followed by a win at Port Vale, their first there for fifty-five years. Tranmere held City to a draw at Ninian Park and then they were on the road again, this time only as far as Wrexham's Racecourse Ground where Kavanagh, Gordon and Fortune-West scored in a handsome 3-1 victory. The win against their historic rivals pushed City up to tenth in the standings, while forcing their struggling north Wales neighbours further down the table. However, Cardiff grew complacent and were well and truly humbled in their next game at struggling Bury. Consistency was proving a problem. The team was failing to live up to inflated expectations and languished in mid-table. There were also a multitude of other issues to contend with. By this time, the club had parted company with Ian Atkins, whose methods and work ethic conflicted with Cork's. Jeanne, the wide boy described by Hammam as 'my special signing,' catastrophically failed a random drug test leaving the chairman with a generous helping of egg on his face. The club vowed to stand by him, the youngster answered a misconduct charge at a FAW disciplinary hearing and was ordered to undergo treatment at the famous Priory clinic at the club's expense.

Elsewhere, Cork was beginning to feel the strain and withdrew his representative team from a fund-raising quiz after pleas were made by disgruntled supporters via the internet for crowd members to inundate him with questions regarding tactics and team selection. This was a sure sign that the club faced a fan revolt, a fact reiterated by a turn-out of only 8,013 (the lowest of the season for a home League game) for a 1-1 draw with Colchester. Remarkably, Cork was still keen to add to the bloated squad, and persuaded England B and U21 fullback Dean Gordon to sign a short-loan contract from Middlesbrough. After being told he had to sell before he could buy, Cork then responded by placing the bulk of his first team squad on the transfer list, echoing the actions of several Cardiff managers before him. Unfortunately however, other clubs weren't exactly queuing up to buy any of them. On the plus side, the goal against Colchester was scored by James 'Ginger Monster' Collins, a product of the youth structure who was making his first start for City in attack, though he would later make his mark as a sturdy central defender.

There was a revival of fortune on 1 December, when Oldham Athletic visited Ninian Park and were soundly beaten 3-1. Three days later, Brentford were the guests, and were despatched by the same scoreline. Loan star Dean Gordon then rescued points out of difficult trips to Blackpool and Stoke, and an Earnshaw double secured a share of the spoils when Reading visited south Wales on Boxing Day to propel City into a play-off place. The crowds returned to Ninian Park in force for the Reading game with 16,708 going through the turnstiles, and a similar number turned out for the Bristol City game four days later. They were to be disappointed however, as the Robins vanquished the Bluebirds 3-1 to remain unbeaten at Ninian Park for more than thirty years.

City's faltering League form was transmitted to the League (Worthington) Cup, where they went out to First

Division Millwall in the very first round. However, they made a blistering start to the AM Cup (LDV Vans Trophy) where they annihilated Third Division Rushden and Diamonds 7-1 with Gavin Gordon hitting five goals, the first Cardiff player to do so since Jim Henderson in 1933. This feat served as a timely reminder by the expensive striker, who was quickly becoming the forgotten man. City played virtually the same record-breaking team in round two against Peterborough United two weeks later. This time, however, there were no heroics and City exited 3-1. Again, most of the drama that season was reserved for the FA Cup, despite the campaign starting innocuously enough with a 3-1 win over non-League Tiverton Town, the first-ever meeting between the clubs. Round two saw Port Vale return to the Potteries on the back of a 3-0 hiding that put City into the third round for the fifth consecutive year. They were drawn to play Premiership leaders and champions-elect Leeds United at Ninian Park on 6 January 2002. Both clubs have a John Charles suite at their respective grounds in honour of the greatest footballer Wales ever produced, which was where the pre-match press conferences were held. That legend, who had recently been awarded an MBE, also had the honour of leading both teams out into the vociferous atmosphere created by the seething 22,009 capacity crowd.

Leeds, the Premiership aristocrats, fresh from a convincing 3-0 win over West Ham United, had spent lavishly and were at the height of their powers, fielding a team bristling with household names like Rio Ferdinand, Robbie Fowler, Alan Smith and Mark Viduka. The favourites started confidently and took an early lead, but then Smith was dismissed for violent conduct, Kavanagh equalised with a stunning free kick, and Young tucked in a dramatic winner moments from the end to give City arguably their best result since they had toppled the mighty Real Madrid in 1971. The defeat spelled the beginning of the end for the Yorkshire club, who were hit with financial problems and forced to sell off their stars, resulting in a catastrophic slide down the League and relegation.

If the game itself was laden with drama and incident, then events surrounding it were equally controversial. After his customary pre-match stroll around the pitch, Hammam stood accused of inciting the crowd, and the behaviour of a small minority, culminating in a good-natured mini pitch invasion, was blown out of all proportion by the national press. True, there were a few minor skirmishes leading to four arrests, but as the game was a Sky Sports show piece with a television audience of millions, steps had to be seen to have been taken. The next few weeks saw South Wales Police launch 'Operation Base,' and arrest a further ten suspects using CCTC footage, while the club itself was ordered to lower its capacity for future matches to 17,000, meaning a substantial loss in revenue. Hammam rightly felt harshly done by and said, 'In my twenty-five years in football I have never witnessed an orchestrated and vicious media campaign like the one Cardiff City is having to face.' There was yet another sub-plot to be uncovered when it was revealed that one of Hammam's minders, Neil MacNamara, was known to the National Crime Intelligence Service, the division set up by the government to combat football-related violence. He was unceremoniously sacked by the security firm he worked for, Unisec, even before it emerged that he had been responsible for letting off fire alarms and water sprinklers in the Leeds team's hotel as they prepared for the match.

For all their heroics, hopes of a third FA Cup final appearance (to be staged at Cardiff's new Millennium Stadium after the temporary abandonment of Wembley) were dashed by Tranmere in the next round.

The FAW Premier Cup was restructured that season to ease the burden on Wales' Football League clubs, and Cardiff were amongst those given a bye through the group stages. Therefore, their first match of the tournament was a quarter-final at Newtown, which they won 3-0 to set up a semi-final grudge match with competition kings Wrexham. City won a tight game on penalties to book a third appearance in the final, where a stunning Kavanagh freekick was enough to settle the latest derby encounter against Swansea and win City the trophy for the first time. However, the game was predictably marred first by the Swansea fans jeering a minute's silence for the recently departed Billy Ayre, followed by the Cardiff fans retaliating with extreme violence.

Almost unnoticed in the (largely) unwarranted media outcry after the Leeds game, Lennie Lawrence was appointed Director of Football, but to everyone's frustration the team's performances remained mixed. Morale-boosting home wins over Stoke and Swindon were preceded by a disappointing defeat to Peterborough and followed by grim away days at Brighton, Brentford and Wigan. Finally, the pressure told and Cork left the club to have his duties taken over by Lawrence. A new approach seemed to be all that was needed, as a penalty by dead-ball specialist Kavanagh was enough to beat Bury on 19 February and start another thrilling run. New loan signing Andy Campbell, a pacey striker from Middlesbrough, made a match-winning debut as a substitute at Northampton then blasted a hat-trick in the next away game at Oldham, which the Bluebirds won 7-1. Gabbidon, Young and Thorne pounced for the crucial goals against Wrexham on 22 March while Fortune-West and Campbell grabbed the headlines a week later at Chesterfield, where latest signing Gary Croft made his debut at left-back. The wins kept on coming, and Port Vale, Colchester, Notts County and Tranmere all fell by the wayside as City charged into the play-off semi-finals unbeaten in thirteen.

There, they were paired with the club lying immediately below them, Stoke, and won the away leg 2-1. With a goal advantage and the home game to come, a place in the Second Division play-off final looked a certainty. However, Stoke had other ideas and scored in injury time before a sell-out crowd of 19,376 to level the tie before going on to win it in extra-time to break City hearts. Post-match violence flared once more as police reportedly baton-charged around 600 'hostile' home fans on Sloper Road, despite the presence of women and a group of children amongst the fans. The complete absence of any Stoke supporters, who were still locked inside the ground at the time, lends weight to claims that the police again resorted to strong-arm tactics when there was little need.

At the end of the season, Earnshaw won his first full international call-up, and in true fairytale fashion scored the winner for Wales against Germany at the Millennium Stadium. The news wasn't as good for Leonne Jeanne who, after completing rehabilitation, refused to take another drug test and was bombed out of the club in disgrace with his career in ruins, while Josh Low, Brayson and Nogan all found themselves out of contract. Meanwhile, Campbell, who had made a spectacular start by scoring seven times in his first eight games, was signed on a permanent contract for £900,000, while the other big signings were ex-Bradford City holding midfielder Gareth Whalley and £600,000 full-back Chris Barker who, despite being only twenty-two, had made over 120 appearances for Barnsley in Division One. In addition, Croft's loan move was made permanent. On paper the new and improved squad was one of the strongest in the division, with Hammam having spent something in the region of £8 million during his short time at Cardiff. This made those players deeply unpopular with their less affluent peers. Hammam's endeavours certainly gripped the imagination of the Welsh public, with the average home attendance at Ninian Park climbing to 12,522. But there was concern over the violence that had disrupted so many fixtures, and club officials eventually declared a 'zero tolerance' policy on anti-social behaviour in and around Ninian Park, leading to a rash of banning orders. The sheer volume of orders issued against Cardiff supporters certainly didn't help the club's attendance figures.

2002–2003 season
The explosion of interest meant that almost half of the 8,033 crowd at Oldham on the opening day of the next season were travelling Cardiff supporters, and they were not disappointed as Campbell and Earnshaw struck to seal the points. However, a confident 3-1 win against Port Vale in their first home game on 13 August was quickly followed by their first defeat away at Northampton, and they didn't win another League match until Stockport County visited the Welsh capital a month later. Earnshaw, dubbed 'the True Prince of Wales,' was on target again in the next home game (a 2-0 win over Brentford), scored twice in the 2-2 draw at Plymouth Argyle that saw City climb to the top of Division Two for the first time in twenty years, then scored both goals in a 2-1 win over Crewe. With Earnie the potent weapon up front and the steadying influence of Kavanagh, they mixed it with the big boys admirably, but fell to a 3-2 defeat at Barnsley on 9 November, where Earnie scored both goals, before recovering to beat Chesterfield and QPR. The QPR game was a 4-0 route, Earnie again leading the way with a hat-trick in what would turn out a record-breaking season. As Christmas came and went, City found themselves firmly embedded in the play-off positions, and a

4-0 pasting of Huddersfield reinforced their deserved 'promotion challengers' tag.

Earnie was nothing short of a revelation that season, and had scored a hat-trick in just sixteen minutes of his first start, a 5-1 defeat of Boston United in the League (Worthington) Cup on 11 September. However, he was powerless to stop his side going out in the next round at Premiership Tottenham Hotspur. The LDV Trophy was equally unremarkable as City beat Exeter 3-0 only to bow out at Bournemouth. And it was a similar story in the FA Cup where City needed a replay to edge out Tranmere before going out to Coventry City. Cardiff then relinquished their grip on the FAW Cup they had won so controversially the year before by losing to Newport County on penalties in the semi-final after seeing off the challenge of Total Network Solutions.

On 4 February 2003, another Earnie goal at Northampton handed City an important victory, and the crowds flocked to Ninian Park for draws with Barnsley and Plymouth. Then came a sequence of three crunch away games at Port Vale, Stockport and Brentford, and City defied their critics to return with a haul of seven points, only to lose their way slightly before returning to winning ways with a 2-0 home defeat of Blackpool. They won three of the next four before slipping to consecutive defeats against Peterborough, Colchester and Bristol City, without scoring a single goal as their play-off ambitions came under threat. The drought continued into the next game against Wigan, but Earnie's thirty-fifth goal of a remarkable season not only smashed Hughie Ferguson's and Stan Richards' long-standing scoring records ('most goals' and 'most League goals' in a season respectively), but also salvaged the point they needed at Crewe to secure a play-off semi-final spot against bogey team Bristol City. The English side had notched up a League double over the Bluebirds, with Christian Roberts coming back to haunt his hometown club, but true to his blue roots, when he scored against them he never celebrated and looked, in all honesty, a little bit dejected. Thankfully, he never got a chance not to celebrate in the two-leg tie which was settled courtesy of a Thorne goal that set up a final meeting with QPR and a rare excursion to the Millennium stadium on 25 May, which was settled by an even rarer extra-time goal from the fading Campbell. The 66,096 supporters, easily the biggest crowd in living memory assembled to witness a Cardiff match, were ecstatic as the Bluebirds claimed a place in the second tier of the Football League for the first time since the 80s.

There was a mini-media frenzy in the wake of City's play-off success as their popularity reached an all-time high, reflected by another rise in their average home attendances resulting in their best total for twenty-six years. Also, website Cardiff City World was voted top out of seventy-five other websites in terms of, ahem, 'penetration against returning visitors'.

However, the step-up in class would require a complete overhaul of playing staff. Out-of-contract Mark Walton, Leo Fortune-West, Andy Legg and Andy Jordan all packed their bags to make way for new blood in the form of experienced Welsh international winger John Robinson who arrived on a free from Charlton, versatile Australian international defender Tony Vidmar, and Wales B 'keeper Martyn Margetson. However, the Bluebirds missed out on a host of other big-name targets who opted to join other clubs instead, suggesting that City weren't as attractive an option as they had once been, or that the financial incentives just weren't there any more. At the end of the summer, Cardiff City councillors met to discuss proposed plans to build a new stadium and gave their initial approval.

2003–2004 season

With Thorne spending a lot of time in the treatment room and Campbell continually misfiring, the signing of a proven striker to partner Earnie up front became paramount, especially when their first game in the Nationwide League Division One (and their first at this level for eighteen years) was a goalless draw at unfashionable Rotherham on 9 August. A week later a crowd of over 16,000 went home from Ninian Park disappointed as City slumped to a 2-0 defeat. Playing for Rotherham on the opening day was want-away hit-man Alan Lee, and within weeks he had signed for Cardiff in a deal that could potentially rise to £1.2 million. On the same day City announced another significant signing, the £400,000 capture of QPR Jamaican international midfielder Richard Langley. By the time the duo were unveiled, many pundits were predicting the worst for Cardiff, but the doubters were forced to reconsider when City returned from Nottingham Forest with all three points, then inflicted a damaging 4-1 on Derby County just forty-eight hours later with goals from Alan Lee (his first for the club), Kavanagh (a penalty), Earnie (of course) and James Collins. The two surprise wins steadied the ship and instilled some confidence as City followed a serviceable draw at Walsall with a crushing 5-0 home defeat of Gillingham, when Earnie continued to write his name all over the back pages with a four-goal salvo. The partnership the young Welsh international was forming with cult figure Peter Thorne was proving good enough to cause problems for the best teams in the division, but even so City went on to produce just one win from the next six. A 3-1 win at Coventry then heralded a much-improved run of form that encapsulated wins over Watford, Stoke (both home and away, where Thorne scored a hat-trick against his former club) and Wimbledon. But then in the run-up to Christmas,

City lost four on the spin to slide into eighth. Hammam was enraged and publicly accused his players of underachieving, going on to say that he was refusing to part with any more money and that the season had been 'wasted'. As it was barely halfway through, and all the top clubs were busy strengthening their teams further, these remarks were met with a mixture of confusion and derision by the fans. Hammam stood accused of lacking ambition, and for the first time his support in the Welsh capital began to waver. Even more worryingly, internet message boards began carrying speculative claims of impending financial meltdown.

City's promotion meant that they were now excluded from the LDV trophy (AM Cup), so that season's extra-curricular activities began with the Carling (League) Cup and a 4-1 home defeat of Orient, where Earnie celebrated his first game as captain with yet another hat-trick. However, West Ham proved just too strong in the next round, and Cardiff slumped to a 2-3 defeat despite two more goals from the little striker. The FA Cup campaign was equally forgettable, with City bypassing the early rounds only to lose their first game in the competition to Sheffield United. In a restructured FAW Premier Cup City progressed past Newport County but lost out to Wrexham in the subsequent round. Hammam did little to disguise his growing contempt for the competition where City often fielded a combination of first-teamers, youngsters and fringe players, which might go some way to explaining their constant failings.

The Bluebirds finally returned to winning ways in the League with a 3-2 home defeat of Rotherham on 10 January 2004, where Earnie was again amongst the scorers along with the usual suspects of Thorne and Kavanagh. A Langley goal was enough to beat Bradford a week later, but City had to wait over a month for another win, a 4-0 thrashing of highly-fancied Sunderland at Ninian Park on 21 February witnessed by a seasonal best crowd of 17,337.

The win came the day after the death of Gentle Giant John Charles MBE, who had been in a coma since collapsing in an Italian TV studio two weeks earlier. The fact that his minute's silence was disrupted by lowlife Sunderland supporters perhaps explains the ferocity with which City went about their task that day. By then, City had been awarded 'Academy' status, meaning that their reserve and youth players could now compete with the best in the country. This was hailed as a landmark event, and it certainly boded well for the future, but elsewhere there were signs that all was not well.

The latest additions to the first XI were York midfielder Lee Bullock, who initially signed on loan amid rumours that City couldn't afford his transfer fee, and left-winger Paul Parry who arrived from non-League Hereford United. The duo were acquired at a combined cost of less than £150,000, a far cry from the millions Hammam had previously been throwing around. Parry soon followed in Mark Delaney's footsteps by making his full Wales debut just seven weeks later. The international, a 4-0 friendly trouncing of Scotland, was also notable because Earnie scored his first international hat-trick. At his new club, Parry was a direct replacement for the departed Crystal Palace loan-signing Julian Gray, and was seen by some as a cheap alternative, but proved his critics wrong by scoring his first-ever League goal at League-leaders Norwich before setting up Earnie (naturally) for the winner. City then recorded wins over Crewe, Sheffield United and Gillingham, but with safety virtually assured and a place in the play-offs a distant dream, the League season petered out and City settled into thirteenth place.

The official line that summer was that no money would be made available for new players until the go-ahead was given for the new stadium at the Leckwith site. With hindsight, however, this, along with the cancellation of a pre-season tour to Scandinavia, the decision to put new replica shirts on sale three months early, and several senior players complaining of being denied bonus payments, indicated that there could be some truth in earlier rumours of impending financial difficulties. Influential midfielders Mark Bonner and Gareth Whalley both left the club under clouds, and it was implied that Gary Croft was being purposely left out of the team because he was due a large bonus if he played one more game, though Lawrence dug his heels in on that one and eventually handed him a new contract. It was also suggested that a fit-again Alan Lee was dropped for the last two games to avoid paying Rotherham an appearance bonus under the terms of his transfer.

2004–2005 season

Probably the best anyone could hope for in the way of new arrivals were a few high-profile free transfers, which duly came in the form of Welsh international centre-back Robert Page from Sheffield United and Millwall goalkeeper Tony Warner, who was generally considered one of the best outside the Premiership. With him between the sticks, however, the team endured a miserable pre-season, culminating in defeats by continental outfits Racing Santander and Lazio, which resulted in the new 'keeper, reputedly the new highest-earner at the club, being dropped in favour of Margetson for the opening-day 2-2 draw at Crewe. Three days later City notched their first win of the newly-sponsored Coca Cola Championship over Coventry at Ninian Park with goals by Earnie and Bullock. However, that proved to be the last League goal for 'the True Prince of Wales' in a Cardiff shirt, as he was soon on his way to Premiership strugglers West Brom in a £3 million-plus deal.

There was very little resentment over the transfer as most fans accepted that the livewire striker had simply outgrown his hometown club and needed a move to further his career, and there was a feeling that it might even be advantageous when Hammam promised that 'three or four' significant new signings would be joining new right-winger Joel 'Jobi' McAnuff at the club. The highly rated ex-Wimbledon and West Ham player was another of Hammam's 'special' signings, and went some way to filling the void left by the inspirational John Robinson, who had left for Gillingham.

The promised new additions to the squad never came. And with the focal point of their attack now gone, City set off on a nightmarish run that saw them pick up just one point from the next twenty-one as only winless Rotherham kept them off the foot of the table. Assistant manager Ian Butterworth and fitness coach Clive Goodyear were both dismissed, and Watford assistant Terry Burton (who had captained and scored for Arsenal in the team that beat Cardiff in the 1971 Youth Cup Final) was drafted in as Butterworth's replacement. The run didn't come to an end until a daunting visit to Molineaux, where form side Wolverhampton Wanderers were beaten 3-2 with goals from Parry, Thorne and Kavanagh. The squad that won at Molineaux also included new loan signings Darren Williams, whose move from Sunderland would eventually be made permanent, and England U21 captain Gary O'Neil, who was borrowed from Portsmouth. After a midweek slip-up at Burnley the Bluebirds put together a run of two wins and five draws, the highlight being a 4-1 thrashing of West Ham in Cardiff on 2 November. The West Ham win came just over a week after City were named by the Home Office as official leaders of the 'league of shame,' by picking up more arrests and banning orders than any other club in the League. Figures released to the press put their 2003–04 total at 160 banning orders and 107 arrests, compared to second-placed Stoke's showing of 126 and 28 respectively. This would appear to be a direct result of the club's clampdown on anti-social behaviour that evidently only served to reduce attendances and generate yet more bad publicity.

On the pitch, a team weakened by injuries and suspensions began to struggle and won only once in the next nine, a 3-1 home win over Gillingham. The win did little to lift their spirits however, and they lost their next two games. With the impressive O'Neil's loan from Portsmouth at an end, reinforcements were urgently required, and soon arrived in the most unexpected fashion. 25-year-old Japanese World Cup star Junichi Inamoto was recovering from injury in West Brom's reserves and a loan deal was secured via the Home Office, who processed his work permit application in world-record time to allow him to make his debut for the Bluebirds in a Boxing Day draw with Wolves. Not only was the ex-Fulham midfielder an experienced international with undisputed class, but the move was hailed as a marketing master-stroke, capitalising on Cardiff's sizeable Asian community and broadening interest in the club in the Far East.

For the record, Earnie's 107th and last goal for Cardiff came in a League (Carling) Cup tie at Kidderminster Harriers, which Cardiff went on to win on penalties. They progressed through the subsequent rounds at the expense of Milton Keynes Dons (formerly Wimbledon) and Bournemouth, only to crash out at Premiership outfit Portsmouth. The Bluebirds' FA Cup involvement didn't begin until round three, where they drew with another Premiership side Blackburn Rovers at Ninian Park, only to lose the replay 3-2. There was more disappointment in the much-derided FAW Premier Cup, when a young Bluebirds side travelled to Bangor City and lost 1-0.

City's next League win came on New Year's Day 2005 at Derby County, and was followed two days later by a thumping 3-0 home victory over relegation-haunted Forest courtesy of a Thorne brace and a Kavanagh strike. Burnley and Brighton also fell by the wayside at Ninian Park before Millwall returned to London with all three points on 22 February. The 1-0 defeat was shrouded in controversy because, just as all eyes were on the potentially explosive crowd, all hell broke loose on the pitch, with three players seeing red and the match officials running a gauntlet of hate as they tried to leave the ground after ending the game a full 90 seconds early, with City on the attack.

Just days after the Millwall game, and to the horror of the supporters, financial accounts were published detailing the period between May 2003 and May 2004, which revealed the true extent of Cardiff's much-rumoured financial difficulties. The figures showed that a £9.8 million annual wage bill was being offset against an annual turnover of £9.5 million, creating a rolling shortfall that constantly added to accumulated debts of £29.6 million. It left the club unable to pay employees' wages, and had financial experts and journalists predicting (not for the first time) that the club would struggle just to survive: a ten-point penalty deduction routinely incurred by going into administration would mean certain relegation. In reaction to events, director David Temme bizarrely issued a statement saying that, 'We can clarify that there is no problem'. Subsequent events showed this to be blatantly untrue, and whether he was misinformed or simply lying, the incident serves as a prime example of the sort of comments made by Cardiff representatives in recent times that caused a near-complete breakdown of trust between the club and its supporters with the media hovering somewhere in between.

With speculation rife, the only certainty was that City

would again be forced into selling their most valuable assets, and sure enough within days Robert Page was sold to Coventry, having just returned from captaining Wales to a 2-0 win over Hungary. At his regular press conference, Lawrence said that no more players would be leaving before the next match (an emotional 1-0 home victory over Sheffield United on 5 March) but even as he spoke a deal was being thrashed out to take club captain Graham Kavanagh to Premiership-bound Wigan for an initial £300,000. The Irish international had become symbolic of City's renaissance under Hammam, and made no secret of his unwillingness to leave the club for which he had made 165 appearances scoring thirty-one goals, mainly from free kicks and penalties. The remaining players and staff (those who kept their jobs) were instructed not to talk to the press about the crisis, but were reassured that the problems were not as bad as had been depicted. Even so, the vultures from rival clubs began circling Ninian Park in the hope of landing City stars 'on the cheap'. One unnamed City player told the Western Mail that he and his fellow-players knew no more about the matter than the public, and hinted that as a result many felt betrayed and let-down by the club. This couldn't have done much for team spirit.

In direct contradiction to what Temme had said at the beginning of the week, Hammam then went public to say, with no trace of irony, 'We have mismanaged on the financial side.' He was forced to borrow money from the PFA to pay outstanding wages, and brought in Peter Ridsdale (who had been the chairman at the centre of Leeds' near-death experience) in an effort to sort out the club's finances. This in itself drew criticism from some quarters, as people immediately asked how much money Ridsdale was being paid and whether it was justified when money was apparently such a concern. Hammam's reputation had already suffered irreparable damage and was hanging by a thread. His attempted media manipulation had backfired on him badly and he was now the target of supporter unrest, with some Internet message boards turning into virtual abuse forums. The tension was compounded when it was revealed that despite the club's predicament, he had paid his own company (Rudgwick) over £500,000 for supplying 'management services,' and provided loans to the club at 6 per cent above the base rate. Hence for the first time ever, anti-Hammam chants echoed around Ninian Park. With the club haemorrhaging money and a debt believed to be in the region of £30 million, plans for the proposed new stadium were halted as it became clear that Hammam couldn't fund the project.

Amid all the chaos and unrest, long-term target Neal Ardley was persuaded to sign from Watford (creating yet more uproar as City's relegation rivals rightly questioned how they were able to sign new players in the midst of the worst financial crisis in their history) and City introduced youngsters Cameron Jerome and Joe Ledley to the team. It was Ledley, Kavanagh's 17-year old replacement, who scored the vital goal against Sheffield United while Jerome made his name by scoring twice at Stoke a month later in a 3-1 win that eased any lingering relegation fears. An interest-free loan of £1 million from director Michael Isaac secured the club's short-term future, but a daunting visit from Kavanagh's Wigan ended in defeat, as did a trip to Preston. To their credit City regrouped and Ardley scored his first goal for the club to salvage a point at Leicester, before strikes from Thorne and Jerome were enough to beat Reading and lift City to seventeenth position with fifty points, traditionally the safety benchmark. Another draw at Gillingham in the penultimate game was followed by a 1-0 home win over QPR courtesy of McAnuff, who rather poignantly scored what would be his last goal for City against the club that poached him a few weeks later.

All things considered, Cardiff were lucky to claim sixteenth place. With the team performing so badly and so much negative publicity surrounding it, the average home gate fell to11,200, a slightly misleading figure in itself when you consider that 8,200 of these were season ticket holders who paid all their money up front at the start of the season, leaving only 3,000 fans paying on the day. This meant that from every match barely £50,000 was being created through new ticket sales, which wasn't even enough to cover the cost of stewards and policing. On a match day the club made additional money through merchandising and catering, and then there was sponsorship and TV revenue, but to all intents and purposes the club was operating at a loss and had been for some time. Eventually, the gap between income and expenditure had become a chasm. Football-wise, the single most devastating blow was the loss of the talismanic Earnie, his goals being the difference between a struggling team and one gunning for promotion.

With the season over, wholesale changes were required if Cardiff was to avoid following Swansea and Wrexham into administration. The first casualty was Lennie Lawrence himself, who was replaced with ex-Southampton and Wolves boss Dave Jones. The appointment raised a few eyebrows as most fully expected Lawrence to keep his position, but generally it was met with widespread approval. Most critics agreed that a change of direction was needed and Jones was a capable, proven manager. Hammam later defended his actions by saying that the team had to be disbanded because they had, 'underachieved on the football front every year since I came to the club five years ago.'

12

So Near, Yet So Far
(2005–2009)

As expected, a flood of players left Cardiff in the weeks following the conclusion of the 2004–05 season. Cult hero and record signing Peter Thorne was allowed to join League rivals Norwich for £200,000 (unbelievably, the fee payable only if the Canaries achieved promotion within the next two years). Talented Welsh international defensive pairing Danny Gabbidon and James Collins joined play-off winners West Ham for a combined £3.1 million, Jamaican international Richard Langley went back to his spiritual home of QPR, his international team mate Jobi McAnuff was sold to Crystal Palace for £600,000, Tony Vidmar was transferred to NAC Breda in Holland, and both Lee Bullock and Darren Williams went to Hartlepool.

Most of the money the club received in fees was used to pay off outstanding debts, but Jones was given a modest amount for some much-needed team strengthening. Even with quality players available on Bosman free transfers, the main worry was that with players demanding ever-increasing wages that the club couldn't afford, they might struggle to attract the required calibre. The other concern was that with the City management team reluctant to sign players too long before the new season started in order to save on the wage bill, they ran the constant risk of losing out on top targets. A lot of fears were allayed with the acquisitions of West Brom duo Darren Purse, who was bought for £700,000 and immediately installed as club captain, and Welsh international Jason Koumas, who arrived on a season's loan. Since making a big name for himself at Tranmere Rovers, the midfield maestro had found things tough in the top division. It was suggested that the double swoop was part of the deal that took Earnshaw to the Hawthornes, and included the possibility of future link-ups.

In addition to the WBA duo, as the summer went on, Dave Jones also signed centre back Glenn Loovens from Dutch side Feyenoord (initially on loan), battling midfielder Jeff Whitley on a free from Sunderland, his Northern Irish international team mate Phil Mulryne from Norwich, Kevin Cooper from Wolves, and Watford defenders Neil Cox and Jermaine Darlington. Also, Neal Ardley earned himself a two-year contract after putting in some impressive displays in the turbulent closing months of the previous season. A clutch of City's highest earners agreed to take substantial pay cuts to remain at the club, and Peter Ridsdale took the post of Chief Executive having performed his initial task of reducing the wage bill with aplomb. City ended a three-year association with sportswear giant Puma and instead changed to Spanish company Joma, while housing firm Redrow continued as main shirt sponsor. These were encouraging signs, and there was little doubt that Jones was stamping his authority all over the club.

2005–2006 season

If pre-season results were anything to go by, City, having completed an unbeaten friendly tour of Scotland, appeared to have stabilised. However, they lost their first competitive game under Jones at Ipswich on 6 August 2005. Three days later, they scraped a home win against Leeds United with goals from Purse and Koumas, but two losses and two draws followed, despite the blossoming forward Cameron Jerome scoring in each of the four games. To share striking duties, Michael Ricketts arrived on loan from the financially-stricken Elland Road club, and scored vital winning goals at Ninian Park against Leicester City and Crystal Palace. The ex-England international, whose career was beginning to nosedive, was to enjoy a good spell at City, and on 22 October he scored again, along with Jerome, Ledley, Cooper, Purse and Koumas, in the club's biggest win of the season, a 6-1 home demolition of Crewe,. Bizarrely, after the hatful of goals, City didn't score again for three games, finally rediscovering their scoring touch in a 3-1 win at Sheffield Wednesday. Results over the frenetic Christmas period typified City's form that season. Disappointing defeats to Plymouth and QPR were made more palatable by an impressive 2-1 home win over promotion favourites Southampton, when Ledley and Jerome were the scorers.

The League Cup followed a similar pattern, as City bombed out in the third round to Leicester after beating Colchester and Macclesfield. The FA Cup saw them narrowly beaten at the mighty Arsenal before a bumper crowd of 36,552 on 7 January 2006, where Jerome scored a consolation goal in a 2-1 reverse, but humiliation awaited in the FAW Premier Cup. Despite entering the competition at the quarter-final stage, a young City team was beaten 2-1 at Carmarthen Town before a crowd of fewer than 1,000.

When the mid-season transfer window opened, Scottish international striker Steven Thompson was signed from Glasgow Rangers for £250,000 to replace Michael Ricketts, who went back to Leeds at the end of his loan spell, and Ricardo Scimeca arrived from West Brom to bolster the midfield. After a stinging 1-5 drubbing at Reading, Thompson scored twice on his debut in a 3-0 route of Burnley as the Bluebirds settled into a decent run of form, losing just one from seven, and threatened to move up the table. Thompson was on target again in a 1-0 win at Plymouth on 18 March, but unfortunately that proved to be

City's last win of the season as they tumbled down the table and came to rest in twelfth place. The brightest point of the season was the scoring exploits of target man Cameron Jerome, who notched an impressive twenty goals from forty-seven games in all competition. The vultures were soon circling, and just weeks after the season came to a close he was sold to Birmingham for a club record £3 million. Also shown the door were Rhys Weston, Jermaine Darlington, Neil Ardley, Neil Cox, Willie Boland and Andy Campbell, who had struggled badly since his famous goal against QPR in the play-off final. He left the club and head to the Scottish Leagues with Dunfermline with a final record of twelve goals from seventy-three League games for the Bluebirds.

The marquee signing that summer was Michael Chopra, a lively forward who arrived from Newcastle for £500,000. Despite scoring the then-fastest Premier League goal of all time 15 seconds after coming on as a substitute against the Magpies' arch rivals Sunderland, he had struggled for first-team football in the north east. The goal against Sunderland was the only one he managed in 21 Premier League appearances, and he had spent the previous season on loan at Barnsley. The highly-rated wide-man Willo Flood also arrived from Manchester City for an undisclosed fee believed to be around £200,000, centre-back Roger Johnson was brought in from Wycombe Wanderers for £250,000, ex-Arsenal and Everton striker Kevin Campbell and Scottish international full-back Kevin McNaughton were signed on frees, and Jones struck a deal with Feyenoord to keep Glenn Loovens in the Welsh capital permanently. He would prove a key acquisition.

2006–2007 season
So it was a very changed team that took the field at Barnsley on 5 August. Jones was building a solid side, further

evidenced by a confident 2-1 win courtesy of goals from Ledley and Thompson. The team was playing fast, attacking football with a rigid 4-4-2 formation, and picked up some fantastic wins in the first half of the season. Leeds, Birmingham, Wolves, Crystal Palace and Southampton were all put to the sword as City roared to the top of the League. The run of form brought thirty-five points from fifteen games, culminating in a 2-1 defeat of Sunderland away at their Stadium of Light where Chopra returned to the north east to bag a brace as he was voted Championship player of the month for both September and October. However, immediately following this splendid run, for some reason City fell away badly, managing just one win from the next thirteen games as they slipped down the table into mediocrity. Just before Christmas, Sam Hammam, who was rapidly losing the support of the fans, sold the club to Peter Ridsdale for the sum of £27 million. Ridsdale then took over as chairman.

The Cups offered little respite, as the Bluebirds crashed out of the League Cup to League Two side Barnet and the FAW Premier Cup to The New Saints. They did manage, however, to go one better than the previous year by beating Carmarthen Town at the quarter-final stage. All the drama that season was reserved for the FA Cup, when City drew Premiership Tottenham Hotspur in the third round. A crowd of 20,376 turned up to witness a goalless draw at Ninian Park on 7 January 2007, where City had chances to win, but simply failed to put the ball in the net. For all their endeavour they were well beaten in the replay ten days later, where they went down 4-0. In February came the biggest news to concern the club for quite some time when it was announced that with planning permission received and finances in place, construction work could finally commence on the new 30,000-seater stadium in the

Leckwith area of the city. The lead developer was revealed to be Cardiff-based firm PMG developments, led by club director Paul Guy and ex-Wales Rugby Union captain Mike Hall.

City finally got back to winning ways in the League with an impressive victory at Wolves on 20 January, where Jason Byrne, a £75,000 buy from Shelbourne of the Irish League where he had scored an impressive eighty-three goals in 122 League games, scored the winner on his debut. A week later, Michael Chopra scored his first hat-trick for the club in a home win over Leicester, and was on target in the next game against Barnsley where Peter Whittingham, a new £350,000 signing from Aston Villa, opened the scoring with his first goal for the club. Whittingham, a 23-year old left-footed attacking midfielder, was held in high regard by many, but deemed surplus to requirements at Villa Park, despite making over half a century of appearances in the highest division, and had not been offered a new contract. His arrival coincided with another sudden upturn in fortunes, as in the wake of the Leicester match City won four and drew one from the next seven. However, a 1-0 home win over Norwich on 10 March, gifted to them by way of a Paul Parry goal, turned out to be their last win of the season as they drew two and lost seven of the last nine. Despite topping the table early on, City finished in disappointing thirteenth place.

Chopra was top scorer with twenty-two goals, a feat which saw him named in the Championship team of the year. At various points in the season, Dave Jones was forced to fill out a thin squad with players promoted from the flourishing youth system, giving local youngsters Chris Gunter, Joe Jacobson and Darcy Blake, game time alongside Joe Ledley, who had cemented his position in the centre of the park and made his Wales debut the previous season.

Wonder-kid Aaron Ramsey also made his debut in a City shirt, coming on for the last minute of the defeat at Hull City on 28 April 2007, the Caerphilly-born midfielder becoming the youngest City player ever at just sixteen years and 124 days, beating the previous record holder John Toshack. Just under a month later, Chris Gunter became the youngest Cardiff City player to ever play for Wales when he turned out in a friendly against New Zealand at Wrexham's Racecourse Ground.

In the closed season, the club parted company with a host of players. The most high-profile of them, Kevin Campbell and Welsh international goalkeeper Martyn Margetson, both retired. Chris Barker and Neil Alexander failed to agree new terms. Alexander would prove a particularly telling loss, the Scottish international goalkeeper moving to Ipswich after making more than 200 appearances for the Bluebirds in his five years at the club. Willo Flood was also farmed out on a season's loan to Dundee United, having failed to make an impression at City.

Season 2007–2008
Ross Turnbull was brought in on loan from Middlesbrough to take Alexander's place between the sticks, and Michael Oakes signed on a free from Dave Jones' old club Wolves to act as cover. Over the summer, various other additions were made to the squad, all on free transfers. Midfielders Trevor Sinclair and Gavin Rae arrived from Manchester City and Rangers respectively, along with defender Tony Capaldi from Plymouth and striker Steve MacLean from Sheffield Wednesday, as City played out an impressive pre-season programme that included five wins from six games. Michael Chopra continued his impressive scoring form by snatching both goals in a 2-0 win against Merthyr Tydfil, but

unfortunately that proved to be his last action in a City shirt as he was transferred shortly afterwards to Premier League Sunderland for £5 million. The deal caused anger amongst the Bluebirds' support, who once again accused the club of lacking ambition. However, nobody could deny that the deal was good business for a player who had cost just £500,000 a year earlier. It wasn't to be Chopra's last association with the club.

To plug the yawning gaps up front, Jones signed legendary Liverpool and ex-England international Robbie Fowler and ex-Holland international Jimmy Floyd Hasselbaink on free transfers. Despite undoubted pedigree, the ageing pair's best years were clearly far behind them, and concerns were immediately raised about the duo's fitness levels. In the case of Fowler, his commitment was also brought into question when he was pictured rather the worse for wear in a Cardiff pub before he had even played a game for his new club. Still, the general consensus was that their experience around the dressing room would be vital.

Steve MacLean was another striker with a good scoring record at his previous clubs, and was famous for never having missed a penalty. Therefore, it was almost written in the stars that he should miss a spot kick on his City debut against Stoke on 11 August in a game City ended up losing 0-1. It was the first time City had been given a home tie to kick off the season in eleven years. MacLean made amends for the gaff a week later when he scored his first goal for the club in a 2-0 win at QPR, with Parry also on target. A surprise home defeat to Coventry was followed by a win at Norwich, where Whittingham and Johnson notched their first goals of the season, but from that point on City's form spluttered and they registered just two more wins from the next fifteen, taking them into December. The goalkeeping duties continued to be a problem, with City certainly missing the consistency of Neil Alexander. Kasper Schmeichel, son of the Manchester United legend Peter, was drafted in on loan from Manchester City as a possible solution and performed well, though ultimately City failed to sign him permanently.

It is quite possible that a series of off-field problems contributed to City's abysmal form during this period, adding to the frustration and uncertainty surrounding the club. Back in August, financial backers Langston, under the chairmanship of Sam Hammam, initiated legal proceedings against Cardiff City over claims that the club had not repaid a £30 million loan, and Mike Hall resigned from the board over a possible conflict of interest between Langston and his own company, PMG Associates, who were involved in the construction of the new stadium. Peter Ridsdale reduced the monies owed to the creditors by £9 million by selling them the naming rights from the new stadium, and the Cardiff Blues Rugby Union club signed terms to become paying tenants, playing their home games there instead of at Cardiff Arms Park.

In November, a board meeting handed Dave Jones a vote of confidence, so often a kiss of death in managerial circles. The board promised Jones more time in the job as long as results improved. And they did, slowly. Parry scored the only goal of the game against Ipswich on 24 November to temporarily lift spirits, but draws against Leicester and Hull put the pressure right back on. The team's performance in a 0-2 home reverse to unfancied Charlton drew harsh criticism from the media and fans alike. With the Bluebirds languishing near the foot of the table, this was the lowest point in many a season, and some sections of the support began jeering the team when they took to the field and calling for Jones to be relieved of his duties. However, the club turned a corner with a thumping 4-1 home win over

Colchester and went on to win six of the next nine stretching into the new year to haul themselves into mid table, Dave Jones even winning the Manager of the Month award for January. Perhaps more deserved was Joe Ledley's award for Championship Player of the Month, following a series of spirited midfield displays.

In the transfer window, goalkeeper Peter Enckelmen was loaned in from Blackburn Rovers after Kasper Schmeichel went back to his parent club despite desperate attempts to keep him, and young Polish stopper Erwin Sak was signed from Sokol Pniewy on a free. Through the door went Jason Byrne and Kevin Cooper on free transfers, Steve MacLean, who was sold to Plymouth for £500,000 after a largely unproductive stint in south Wales, and highly-rated teenage right-back Chris Gunter, who went to Tottenham for £1.5 million after making thirty-three appearances in all competitions.

City put in some much improved displays in that season's League Cup, seeing off Brighton and Leyton Orient on the way to a thrilling third round tie at West Brom which City won 4-2 with goals from Hasselbaink, Sinclair and a brace from Fowler, as the old guard showed glimpses of the talent that once took them to the top of the footballing tree. The win set up a mouthwatering fourth round clash against Fowler's past employers Liverpool at Anfield where 41,780 saw them go down 2-1 despite a goal from captain Darren Purse. The FAW Cup was less spectacular, where a narrow win at Welshpool Town was followed by a home defeat on penalties to Newport County in the semi-final.

All the drama that year was saved for the FA Cup. The dream began on 5 January 2008 with a 3-1 win at Chasetown, the lowest-ranked club to ever reach the third round, where Ramsey scored his first senior Cardiff goal to add to strikes by Whittingham and Parry. Hereford were duly dispatched in the next round, before Wolves visited the Welsh capital in round five, only to be sent packing with goals from Whittingham and Hasselbaink. Wales was now firmly in the grip of FA Cup fever, and the fever only intensified when City marched into the semi-final of the oldest football competition in the world by winning 2-0 at Premier League outfit Middlesbrough. The semi-final drew City against Barnsley, the tie to be played at Wembley Stadium, where a crowd of 82,752 turned up to see the Bluebirds squeeze past their Championship rivals with a single goal by hometown hero Joe Ledley, on the way to their first FA Cup final since they won the competition way back in 1927. The final was played at Wembley on 17 May against Premier League strugglers Portsmouth. There, the Bluebirds' dream ended as Nwankwo Kanu scored the decisive goal on thirty-seven minutes in front of a crowd of 89,897 to hand the south coast club a narrow victory.

Paradoxically, after David Jones won Manager of the Month for January, the Bluebirds remained winless in the League until 12 March, when a solitary McPhail goal was enough to scrape a home win against Hull. This result heralded a much-improved run of form, during which City also notched wins against Bristol City, Southampton and Blackpool. They then lost two and drew one before winding up the season with a convincing 3-0 home win over Barnsley, when Parry, McNaughton and Ledley were the scorers. Despite all the big-name strikers at the club's disposal, Parry and Ledley finished the season as joint top-scorers with 11 each in all competitions as City settled into twelfth position, one place higher than the previous season. Player of the year was defender Roger Johnson.

It was universally agreed that the club were not progressing as it was hoped, so the summer saw another mass clear-out as many highly paid and under-performing stars were moved on. Trevor Sinclair, Michael Oakes and Jimmy Floyd Hasselbaink all retired, fading forward Robbie Fowler moved on a free transfer to Blackburn having made just thirteen League appearances, David Forde moved to Millwall where he was a big success, Glenn Loovens was sold to Celtic for £2.5 million after making a century of League appearances, and both Willo Flood and Warren Feeney were sent on loan to Dundee United. The biggest loss that summer was undoubtedly that of Aaron Ramsey who, after being courted by several Premier League giants, eventually signed for Arsenal in a deal worth £4.8 million. Although the club, and the supporters, would have preferred to keep the teen star, the sheer amount of money involved made it a difficult deal to turn down for a player who at that stage wasn't even a first team regular, especially when one considers the costs of the new stadium and other ongoing financial concerns. At the final reckoning, the prodigy had made just twenty-one total appearances for the Bluebirds, scoring two goals.

Clearly, there were now gaps to be filled within the squad. First priority was a goalkeeper, and to this end Enckelman was signed on a permanent deal from Blackburn while Tom Heaton was drafted in on loan from Manchester united to provide competition. Target man Jay Bothroyd arrived for £350,000 from Wolves, Hungarian international defender Gabor Gyepes was signed from Northampton Town for £200,000 where he had been recuperating after a career-threatening injury, 21-year-old forward Ross McCormack was signed from Motherwell for a bargain £120,000, Guadeloupe international Miguel Comminges arrived from Swindon Town, and left winger Mark Kennedy signed on a free. In addition, USA international striker Eddie Johnson was signed on a season's loan from Fulham, and handed the number nine shirt. The Cardiff fan-base were initially underwhelmed by the new signings, especially as the club had raked in almost £8 million in player sales that summer. But a solid pre-season during which City won the Algarve Cup in Portugal by defeating Scottish champions Celtic did a lot to allay any fears.

2008–2009 season

A crowd of 19,749 flocked to Ninian Park on 9 August to see the curtain-raiser against promotion contenders Southampton, and were treated to a rip-roaring spectacle that the Bluebirds won 2-1 thanks to Steven Thompson's last goal for the club before his move to Burnley, and an injury-time winner from Roger Johnson. McCormack scored his first goal in City colours to salvage a point at Doncaster three days later, then scored both goals in a 2-2 home draw with Norwich. The team was looking solid, losing just once in the opening fourteen League games with McCormack leading the club's scoring charts with eleven strikes, but then a mini-slump saw them suffer three defeats in four games. However, the Bluebirds remained firmly in the play-off zone. During the lean spell, crowd favourite Michael Chopra returned on loan just a year after moving to Sunderland when Bothroyd suffered an injury, and fired a penalty on his second debut during a valuable 2-1 home win over Crystal Palace on 15 November. England U-21 winger Wayne Routledge also arrived on short-term loan from Aston Villa to add some flair to a midfield temporarily reduced by injuries to key players Ledley and Whittingham. Routledge made an instant impact, setting up Chopra for a consolation goal at Plymouth then scoring the equalizer against Reading three days later at Ninian Park. The stage was then set for the first south Wales League derby in some time, as City travelled to Championship new boys Swansea on 30 November. The match was a stormy affair, and ended in a 2-2 draw with both sides reduced to ten men after referee Martin Atkinson sent off Stephen McPhail and Darren Pratley. A home win over Preston was followed by another 2-2 draw at Burnley, where City reject Steven Thompson scored the equaliser for his new club. As the winter weather set it, Cardiff won five of the next seven to move up into fourth place.

Cardiff City's League Cup campaign kicked off away at League Two side Bournemouth, where City won with a pair of goals from Paul Parry. After navigating past MK Dons in round two, they were handed a third round tie against Swansea at the Liberty Stadium on 23 September where they narrowly lost a heated affair to a deflected free kick. In the first south Wales derby in almost a decade, midfield general Stephen McPhail was sent off after receiving two yellow cards, only to be sent off again in the League match between the two clubs two months later. Predictably, trouble flared after the match when fans of both clubs clashed with police.

The discontinuation of the increasingly unpopular FAW Cup meant that the only other silverware City could challenge for was the FA Cup, where unfortunately there was to be no repeat of the previous seasons heroics. After knocking out Championship rivals Reading in the third round at Ninian Park on 3 January 2009 with goals from McCormack and Ledley, City were drawn against Premier League giants Arsenal. Though they scraped a goalless draw at Ninian Park, they were put to the sword at the Emirates where they lost 4-0.

In the January transfer window, midfield misfit Willo Flood signed a permanent deal with Celtic for an undisclosed fee and City made a much-publicized £3 million bid to sign Routledge permanently, who had impressed greatly during his loan spell. However, the terms were rejected by the player, who chose instead to sign for rival Championship club QPR and he left Ninian Park under a cloud. Having lost out on Routledge, the City hierarchy shifted their attention to other targets, eventually settling on 25-year-old Scotland international right-winger Chris Burke who signed from Rangers having made over 130 career appearances for the Glasgow giants. He was shortly to be joined by Greek international goalkeeper Dimitrios Konstantopoulos and Ghanaian international midfielder Quincy Owusu-Abeyie, who arrived on loan from Coventry and Spartak Moscow respectively. Despite arriving with big reputations, and presumably commanding big wages, they both made a limited impact at Ninian Park. Konstantopoulos in particular, brought in after injuries to both Enckelman and Heaton, was responsible for several high-profile clangers including scoring an own goal on his debut, prompting Jones to bring in Aston Villa's Stuart Taylor on yet another short-term loan deal before the end of the season. Michael Chopra's loan agreement was also extended, the deal being struck just fifty-five seconds before the mid-season transfer window slammed shut.

City's outstanding League form came to a shuddering halt at Southampton's St Mary's Stadium at the end of February where they went down to a David McGoldrick penalty, but they recovered well to reel off good home wins over Barnsley and Doncaster Rovers. The former match was notable because it was the first time all season City that had scored more than two goals in a match, and latter was notable because on-loan forward Eddie Johnson, who was becoming something of a terrace hero due to his high work rate and sheer determination, scored his very first goal in British football, to add to strikes by Bothroyd and Chopra in a handsome 3-0 victory. The Bluebirds' form remained erratic, as evidenced by a defeat at Norwich and a draw at Bristol City where McCormack scored a late goal to spare

City's blushes. The Scot was developing a useful habit of scoring vital late goals, none more so than the injury time penalty that salvaged a point against Swansea at Ninian Park on 5 April in the third south Wales derby of the season, and the last to be played at the 'Old Lady.' In the next home game three days later, City thrashed Derby 4-1, with Eddie Johnson suffering the ignominy of scoring at both ends. However, as City made a late charge to consolidate a play-off spot, their form remained unpredictable. A good 3-1 win over Burnley meant that City needed just two points from the remaining four games, but this was followed by their worst defeat of the season, a 6-0 mauling at the gleeful hands of Preston. As City spluttered over the finish line, with a 2-2 draw at Charlton giving them their only point from the last four matches, the Preston result would come back to haunt them in the final reckoning. The last game ever played at Ninian Park, where a capacity crowd of 19,129 turned out to say goodbye to the old ground, was a 0-3 reverse to Ipswich on 25 April 2009. Heartbreakingly, the Bluebirds finished the season in seventh position on seventy-four points, one place out of the play-off zone. They surrendered sixth spot to Preston, who scraped into the play-off's at City's expense by virtue of goals scored.

Despite the season ultimately ending in disappointment, it was Cardiff's highest League finish for thirty-eight years, and David Jones had built the nucleus of a strong team. The stand-out performer was Ross McCormack, who plundered twenty-three goals from forty-four games, while Roger Johnson, Kevin McNaughton, Gavin Rae, Peter Whittingham, Paul Parry, Joe Ledley and Jay Bothroyd also made huge contributions, missing just a handful of games between them. City used four different goalkeepers at various stages, the lack of cohesion in such a crucial area of the pitch proving costly on more than one occasion.

As the club readied itself for the big move to the new stadium, several notable playing personnel moved on. Paul Parry went to Preston in a £300,000 deal after six years at the club during which he scored twenty-seven goals in a total of 214 competitive appearances, Darren Purse moved on a free to Sheffield Wednesday, and in the deal of the summer, fellow central defender Roger Johnson was snapped up by Premiership Birmingham for a fee of £5 million after being named Cardiff's Player of the Year for the second time running. In addition, several players were sent out on loan, including local youngsters Darcy Blake and Adam Morris, who went to Plymouth and Newport County respectively to gain first-team experience, striker Warren Feeney, who went to Sheffield Wednesday in search of first-team football, and Tony Capaldi who went to Leeds after finding himself slipping down the pecking order at Ninian Park.

To take their places, in came highly-rated goalkeeper David Marshall from relegated Norwich, right-back Paul Quinn from Motherwell, central-defender Anthony Gerrard (cousin of Liverpool legend Steven) from Walsall, and young midfielder Soloman Taiwo from Dagenham & Redbridge. They were joined by 27-year-old central defender Mark Hudson, who joined for £1.1 million from Charlton and was soon installed as club captain, and strong midfielder Kelvin Etuhu who arrived on a season's loan from Manchester City. However, the marquee signing that summer was not a new signing at all, but the permanent return of Michael Chopra from Sunderland for £3 million, smashing the club's transfer record which had stood since the acquisition of Peter Thorne for £1.75 million back in 2001.

13

Red is the New Blue
(2009–2013)

2009–2010 season

During the summer, the club agreed a lucrative new five-year kit manufacturing deal with sportswear giant Puma, and signed a short-lived shirt sponsorship with 777.com. That season's home kit was the traditional blue shirt with white shorts and socks, while the away kit was yellow and blue, and a third kit was solid yellow. On 22 July, the new 27,000-capacity Cardiff City Stadium (CCS) was officially opened with a 0-0 friendly draw against Celtic, where many of the new signings were unveiled. The first competitive game at the stadium followed on 8 August, the Cardiff team taking the field on that historic day consisting of Marshall in goal, full-backs Quinn and Kennedy, centre-backs Hudson and Gerrard, a midfield of Whittingham, Ledley, McPhail and McCormack, and the strike pairing of Chopra and Bothroyd.

Cardiff's eighty-third consecutive year in the Football League got off to a splendid start as a brace from returning hero Michael Chopra and further goals from Bothroyd and Whittingham saw City run out convincing 4-0 winners over Scunthorpe before a crowd of 22,264. It was very much the perfect start in the Bluebirds' new home, and after a draw at Blackpool and a win at Plymouth they romped to a home 3-0 win over Bristol City before suffering their first defeat at the CCS to promotion favourites Newcastle by virtue of a solitary goal from Argentine international Fabricio Coloccini. Dave Jones said afterwards, 'We made a mistake in the first half that cost us. When you play top teams, that's what happens.'

There were also issues to be addressed off the pitch, as 777.com withdrew their sponsorship due to licensing problems, to be replaced by online bookmaker SBOBET. Even this development caused problems. Due to concerns raised by representatives of the Premier League, who were anxious about exposing youngsters to gambling, the SBOBET logo was soon removed from the shirts of the youth team academy players and replaced with that of the Tŷ Hafan children's hospice.

On the footballing front, City lost two of the next three to slip to ninth place in the League, before having the chance to make amends in a 6-1 mid-week rout of Derby at the CCS where Chopra bagged an incredible four goals. The good times didn't stop there. In the next game City hit four without reply at Watford, including a stunning 50-yard free kick from Welsh Under-21 right back Adam Mathews, who had recently broken into the side. It was his first-ever goal, and what a way to score it! The good form continued with a draw against Crystal Palace and a win over Coventry before an amazing game took place at Sheffield United's Bramall Lane on 24 October, where Whittingham scored a hat-trick from midfield in a 4-3 win as the Bluebirds roared up to second place behind Newcastle and Dave Jones won Manager of the Month for October. However, November passed without a single win, the low-point being a 3-2 defeat at Swansea's Liberty Stadium where Ross McCormack made his first start in three months. City got back to winning ways at the beginning of December when they reeled off three consecutive wins against Preston, West Brom and Middlesbrough without conceding a single goal, with Chris Burke scoring in each game. A home defeat to Plymouth followed, and then a sequence of three draws taking them into the new year.

The Football League Cup kicked off with a routine 3-1

win over Dagenham and Redbridge. Bristol Rovers, the smaller of the two Bristol clubs, were dispatched by the same scoreline in the second round with Whittingham scoring in both ties to keep up his impressive scoring record. However, City's participation in the competition came to an end with a 0-1 defeat at Aston Villa. In the FA Cup, City were drawn against Bristol City in the third round and needed a replay to overcome their Championship rivals, eventually going through by virtue of an own goal. In the next round City were paired with more Championship opposition in the form of Leicester, who they beat 4-2 at CCS on 23 January 2010. It took more than a little luck, with the decisive two goals coming from Burke and McCormack in injury time. Three weeks later they travelled to Stamford Bridge, where a strong Chelsea side dumped them out of the competition 4-1, with City's consolation goal coming from Chopra.

Back to League matters, and barely a week after knocking Bristol City out of the FA Cup City faced them in the League, and registered their biggest win of the season at Ashton Gate where McCormack and Chopra scored two each to add to a strike from Whittingham and an own goal in a storming 6-0 victory. City left it late in the next game where an injury-time winner from Bothroyd sealed a dramatic home win over Doncaster, before they travelled to table-topping Newcastle on 5 February. There, largely due to the efforts of Andy Carroll, they found themselves 3-0 down within 15 minutes. They could find no way back, and eventually went down 5-1, a late goal coming from youth player Aaron Wildig, which proved to be his one and only goal for the club. The Newcastle game was also notable because it marked the return to first team action of Steve McPhail after being diagnosed with stage one lymphoma, a rare form of cancer, three months previously. His return could not have been timed any better, as City had recently lost the services of Riccy Scimeca, who had been forced into retirement after making a total of eighty-two appearances for the club over an injury-ravaged five years.

City recovered well from the setback at St James' Park to beat rock-bottom Peterborough 2-0, but didn't win another game until March, when an early Bothroyd strike was enough to see off Middlesbrough. After away defeats at Ipswich and Leicester, City went on to stay undefeated for the next ten games. The highlight for many was a 2-1 revenge victory over Swansea at the CCS on 3 April, where the Bluebirds came from behind to beat their arch-rivals with a brace from Chopra, his first League goals in three months. It was Cardiff's first win over Swansea since 1997, which more importantly, gave them an eight-point cushion in the play-off zone. A last-day defeat at Derby's Pride Park on 2 May did little to spoil the party as City settled into fourth place in the League with an impressive total of seventy-six points from forty-six games, despite much of the season being played under threat of High Court winding-up orders.

And so, Cardiff City entered the play-offs for the first time since their promotion to the Championship, with a place in the Premier League at stake. They were drawn against Leicester in the semi-final, and won the away leg on 9 May with a stunning free kick from Championship top-scorer Whittingham, his twenty-fifth of the season. The home leg three days later finished 3-2 to the visiting team after extra time, but City went through to the final after a penalty shoot-out. The play-off final was to be played against Blackpool, winners of the other semi-final against Nottingham Forest, at Wembley Stadium on 22 May before a crowd numbering 82,244. City started the match as favourites, and took the lead twice, through Chopra and

Ledley, but eventually went down 3-2 to the battling Seasiders whose manager Ian Holloway was moved to comment, 'You can't write a script like that.' His team joined Newcastle, who won the division at a canter with 102 points, and West Brom, in the Premier League, while Sheffield Wednesday, Plymouth and Peterborough were relegated. The average attendance in City's first year at the CCS was 19,413, a figure which disappointed many. The plan and overall layout of the new stadium, which some said made it difficult for the fans to create much of an atmosphere, coupled with the upheaval of the move from Ninian Park and some poor results at vital times of the season, were possibly all contributing factors.

Just days after the play-off final disappointment, Malaysian businessman Dato Chan Tien Ghee (TG) took over as chairman, having been on the Board of Directors since the previous November. The affable Malaysian made initial contact with the club when his son, Nick Chan, was offered a trial. TG installed Gethin Jenkins from the Newport-Gwent dragons rugby club to act as Chief Executive. Non-executive directors Paul Guy, U-Jiun Tan and Michael Isaac joined Steve Borley and Alan Whiteley on the board as TG's consortium immediately took financial control of the club with a £6 million initial investment and more promised. Peter Ridsdale stepped down, along with former directors Alan Flitcroft and Keith Harris. During the summer, TG addressed the long-standing cash flow problems at the club, including paying a £1.9 million debt to HM Revenue & Customs which led to the winding-up petition being formally withdrawn. Further unpaid tax issues led to a transfer embargo being imposed on the club, but TG assured the fans that these were temporary hitches. The extent of the club's money troubles prior to TG's investment was made apparent by legal action taken against the club by Motherwell, when Cardiff failed to pay agreed instalments for the Paul Quinn transfer. The outstanding amount was finally paid, but relations between the two clubs were damaged and the Bluebird's reputation suffered as a result of that saga.

In the wake of the financial insecurity surrounding the club, no fewer than eleven players left that summer. Ross McCormack was sold to Leeds for £400,000 after finding his first-team opportunities limited by the form of Chopra and Bothroyd. McCormack had scored thirty goals in eighty-eight games. and fading left-midfielder Mark Kennedy joined Ipswich for £75,000. Tony Capaldi, Warren Feeney, Peter Enckelman, Aaron Morris and Darren Dennehy all came to the end of their contracts and were not offered new terms, while one player who was offered new terms but rejected them was local boy and midfield mainstay Joe Ledley, who left the club where he had played his entire career so far to sign for Scottish giants Celtic. At the age of just twenty-three, Ledley had made a total of 256 appearances, scoring thirty goals. The fact that he signed for a club outside the English League system meant that Cardiff did not receive the compensation fee they would have been entitled to otherwise, despite Ledley being in talks with a number of other clubs. In addition, Solomon Taiwo and Anthony Gerrard left the club on long-term loans.

The transfer embargo limited Cardiff's activity for most of the summer, the only permanent arrivals being Tom Heaton, who had impressed during his loan spell, and defenders Chris Riggott and Lee Naylor, who arrived on free transfers. With a weakened team, the club endured a miserable pre-season, winning just one game at Bath, and losing to Notts County and Spanish giants Deportivo in a glamour tie at the CCS.

By the time the embargo was lifted, most transfer targets

had been snapped up. Dave Jones was forced into the loan market, where he secured the services of legendary Welsh international duo Jason Koumas (for a second time) and Craig Bellamy for the season from Wigan and Manchester City respectively. The fans and media were especially excited by the arrival of 31-year old forward Bellamy, who was highly rated, if considered a little temperamental, and had played for some of the biggest clubs in the country. Manchester City manager Mark Hughes had paid a reported £14 million to secure his services from West Ham just eighteen months earlier. Having been raised in the Trowbridge area of Cardiff before leaving to launch his footballing career at Norwich, the move was billed as Bellamy's homecoming. Upon arrival he was immediately installed as 'team captain,' with Mark Hudson assuming the role of 'club captain.' Midfielder Seyi Olofinjana also arrived on loan from Hull City, and was immediately nicknamed 'the Wardrobe' due to his imposing physical presence. Also brought in on loan deals were midfielder Danny Drinkwater from Manchester United, and Republic of Ireland striker Andy Keogh from Wolves.

The new campaign was dubbed, 'I'll be there,' in honour of one of City's earliest terrace songs to celebrate 100 years under its current incarnation. As BAFTA award-winning actor and City fan Jonathan Owens explained in a promotional video celebrating City's famous 2008 FA Cup run:

> This song was first sung by Cardiff supporters on the terraces way back in 1926 at the time of the General Strike. It was a miners' song, and coal was the link between the valleys where it was dug out, and Cardiff docks where it was shipped. One of the verses tells of the coal coming from the Rhondda on the Taff Vale

railway line. It was therefore a song which linked people from the valleys and the city and it has stuck ever since. Now it really is one football song that is unique to Cardiff fans. We're the only fans who sing it and that's why it's so special.

Chief Executive Gethin Jenkins added:

One of our main objectives this season is to ensure that the club actively embraces the wider community through a number of methods. Cardiff City has a proud tradition, and the 'I'll Be There' campaign illustrates the close links between the city and surrounding areas. The lyrics emphasise the collaboration and hard work of the whole community in South Wales. Testament to this relationship is the fact that the song is still sung with pride by our supporters at venues across the country today.

2010–2011 season

The Centenary season kicked off with a draw against Sheffield United at the CCS on 8 August. City then made a mockery of their pre-season form by reeling off four wins in a row against Derby, Doncaster, Portsmouth and Hull City, as Dave Jones' new-look side began to gel. Local hero Bellamy made an instant impact when he scored from a curling 35-yard free kick against Doncaster in a 4-0 rout, to add to goals from Burke and two from Bothroyd. It was the third time Bellamy had scored on his debut for a club. Despite the early-season promise, they then slumped to defeat at Leicester and Ipswich, as the Tractor Boys sneaked above them into the second automatic promotion place. Six wins and a draw followed, as City roared to the top of the table with an impressive thirty-two points from fourteen games. On 16 October they came from 0-2 down at home to Bristol City to win 3-2, but the highlight of this run was probably an emphatic 4-0 victory over Leeds, their biggest ever win at Elland Road, where Bothroyd (2), Chopra and Naylor were the scorers. Dave Jones won another monthly award to add to his growing collection, and Jay Bothroyd's form was in such good vein that he not only won the Championship player of the Month award for November, but was called up by the England squad to play a friendly against France on 17 November, the first time a current Cardiff player had been selected to play for the England national side in the club's 111-year history.

However, a 3-1 home win against Norwich proved to be the last for a while. Swansea won the first Welsh derby at the CCS, which was followed shortly after by damaging defeats to Nottingham Forest, table-topping QPR, and Middlesbrough. A much-needed Boxing Day win, their first for over a decade, over Coventry, temporarily settled nerves before City capitulated once more, suffering heavy defeats against Watford and then Bristol City.

The Bluebirds fared little better in the Cup competitions. In the League Cup they needed extra time to overcome Burton Albion of League Two, where they were helped by Ross McCormack's last two goals for the club. City then went out in the second round at Peterborough. In the FA Cup City held Premier League Stoke to a draw at the Britannia Stadium on 8 January 2011 thanks to a Chopra goal, but lost the replay 0-2 at the CCS ten days later.

Manchester United recalled Drinkwater after he had made a total of twelve appearances, only to loan him out again to Watford days later. To replace him, Cardiff pulled off something of a coup by re-signing Aaron Ramsey on a month's loan from Arsenal, as he continued his rehabilitation from a badly broken leg. Young striker Jay

Emmanuel-Thomas, was also signed from the Gunners until the end of the season to bolster the front line. Before the transfer window closed, Israeli international defender Dekel Keinan arrived from Blackpool for £300,000, and 29-year-old target man John Parkin, nick-named 'The Beast,' was brought in from Preston for £100,000 to act as cover for Bothroyd. Miguel Comminges moved to Southend on a free after making thirty-five total appearances, and Chris Riggott had his contract terminated by mutual consent due to ongoing injury concerns after appearing just twice. He never played professional football again.

After the Bristol City defeat, City got back to winning ways in the League with a 2-1 home win over Leeds to lift them back into the automatic promotion places, a result which extended their unbeaten run over Leeds to twelve games stretching back to 1983. City then won three and lost three, the much-improved form relaxing the pressure on under-fire Dave Jones, who in recent months had divided fans and drawn criticism from some local media outlets. This would soon lead to a long-standing feud, with the manager often refusing to give interviews to certain newspapers or reporters in retaliation for negative comments they had made, a strategy that would prove counter-productive to say the least. Football clubs develop a symbiotic relationship with the local press, and when it becomes so fractured it is never a good state of affairs.

A draw at Norwich where Parkin scored on his debut was followed by an emphatic 4-2 revenge win against Watford and a home draw with Reading where Bothroyd's seventeenth goal of the season and a spectacular injury-time winner from Bellamy wasn't enough to prevent the Bluebirds dropping to fifth in the table as arch-rivals Swansea moved above them.

The stage was set for the most important south Wales

derby in living memory, as the Bluebirds, in fifth place, travelled to the Liberty stadium on 6 February to face Swansea in third. There, local hero Ramsey set up Bellamy for a late winner as Cardiff leapfrogged the Jacks into third. It was only the sixth goal the Swans' defence had conceded all season, and Cardiff's first win on the road since November. City then beat Scunthorpe and drew against Burnley in two vital home games before losing at Nottingham Forest in a mixed sequence that typified their form that season. Picking up maximum points against Leicester and Hull consolidated their play-off place, before they went the whole of March without registering another win. Suffering a goalkeeping crisis, City signed two back-up keepers on short-term loan deals in Stephen Bywater and Welsh international Jason Brown within days of each other, and defender Jlloyd-Samuel also arrived from Bolton before the end of the month.

In contrast to the woeful March, the Bluebirds picked up five wins and a draw in April, the highlights including a 3-1 win at Doncaster, where Jason Koumas wowed the fans with a late double, and a narrow victory at Preston where a Whittingham strike was enough to seal the points. They were brought back down to earth with a bump when Middlesbrough visited the Welsh capital at the beginning of May and left with all three points, a defeat that virtually ended their automatic promotion hopes. A draw at Burnley in the last League game saw them sink to fourth in the table with an 80-point haul, as Swansea's 4-0 win over relegated Sheffield United saw them move above the Bluebirds into third with the same points total but with a better goal difference. QPR and Norwich achieved automatic promotion, while both Welsh clubs faced the lottery of the play-offs. The average attendance at CCS swelled to 22,091, and the top goal-scorer was Jay Bothroyd, who finished the season with eighteen in the League and twenty overall. The Player of the Year award went to fans' favourite Kevin McNaughton.

In their second successive play-off appearance, City met Reading in the semi-final, the first leg being played at the Madejski stadium where, despite losing star man Craig Bellamy to a hamstring strain in the seventeenth minute, City held firm to hold the Royals to a goalless draw. The score was predictable enough, as both League meetings between the clubs that season had ended in draws. The result meant that something had to give in the second leg at the CCS, and 'give' it certainly did as Cardiff endured the heartache of a 0-3 defeat, despite having more on goal than their opponents. To add insult to injury, the demolition was rounded off by ex-City player Jobi McAnuff, who scored a marvellous individual goal. As fate would have it, Reading met Swansea in the final at Wembley, where the Welsh club won 4-2 to cap a meteoric rise into the Premier League.

The play-off disappointment proved the final straw for the club's Board, as on 30 May Dave Jones was fired following an end-of-season review. Shortly afterwards, his staff, including assistant manager Terry Burton, first team coach Paul Wilkinson, and fitness coach Alex Armstrong, were all placed on gardening leave until the end of their contracts. Jones had been in charge for six years, and overseen over 300 games with an overall win ratio of 41.90 per cent. Statistically, he was one of the most successful managers the club ever had, but he ultimately paid the price for his team under-performing at crucial times since the Malaysian takeover, despite being backed with sizeable transfer kitties and one of the largest wage budgets in the division.

In the wake of Jones' dismissal, it was widely reported that ex-England captain Alan Shearer was offered the manager's job at the CCS, a development that surprised many as although he was highly respected within the game, Shearer had very limited managerial experience and since his playing days ended had become better known as a TV pundit. As it happened, Shearer turned down the job, prompting the board to look to then-Watford manager Malky Mackay, who eventually signed terms on 17 June forcing City to pay his old club compensation. At just thirty-nine, the ex-Scottish international defender became one of the youngest managers in Cardiff City's history. By the end of the month a new cast of back-room staff had been appointed in the form of assistant manager David Kerslake, first-team coach Joe McBride, and head of performance Richard Collinge. They were soon joined by Iain Moody as head of recruitment.

To complement the new management regime, there was an overhaul of playing staff during the summer. The biggest sale was that of Michael Chopra, who had been plagued by various off-field problems, and was subsequently off-loaded to long-term admirers Ipswich for £1 million. During his second spell with the club he made 110 appearances in all competitions, scoring forty-one goals. Jay Bothroyd soon followed his strike partner out of the door. After refusing to sign a new contract, he signed for Premier League QPR after scoring forty-six goals in 136 games for the Bluebirds. In all honesty, the fans were not sorry to see the back of the duo, who had been making grumblings of discontent all season. A far bigger loss was that of 19-year-old right-back Adam Mathews, who despite being courted by several Premier League clubs, eventually followed Joe Ledley to Celtic on a free transfer, the deal having been struck as early as February. Ironically, he made his Wales debut against Scotland just prior to his switch. As with the Ledley deal, because the player moved to a club outside the Football League Cardiff were not entitled to any compensation, a fact that rankled with many supporters. Scottish international pair Gavin Rae and Chris Burke also left the club when their contracts ended, going to Dundee and Birmingham respectively. Burke, in particular, would be missed, Dave Jones once claiming that the right-winger was 'an integral part of what we do.'

To replace Burke, another Scottish international winger was recruited on a free, 26-year old Craig Conway from Dundee United. He had made over 160 appearances for the Scottish club, and on arrival at Cardiff was immediately handed Burke's number 11 shirt. He was joined by fellow Scottish international midfielder Don Cowie, who was drafted in from Watford after being convinced to sign by his ex-manager, and yet another Scot soon followed when Mackay spent £840,000 on Kenny Miller. The striker had endured an unhappy time at Bursaspor in Turkey after good spells at Rangers, Celtic, Wolves and Derby. He was expected to form a partnership with Wales legend Robert Earnshaw, who had re-signed for his boyhood club on a free from Nottingham Forest after failing to agree a new contract. Young strikers Joe Mason and Rudy Gestede were signed from Plymouth and French club FC Metz to provide competition for places. In addition, highly-rated Icelandic international Aaron Gunnarsson was brought in from Coventry after his contract talks there broke down. Despite being only twenty-two, the tenacious midfielder was already firmly established in the national side, but because of his age City were forced to pay £350,000 in compensation. Gunnarsson's former team-mate at Coventry, centre-back Ben Turner arrived at the CCS later that summer for a fee in the region of £750,000, to join a defence already boosted by the signing of England Under-21 international left-back Andrew Taylor, who was brought in on a free from Middlesbrough. To complete the new line-up, Slovakian

Under-21 midfielder Filip Kiss was brought in on a season's loan from Slovan Bratislava with a view to securing a permanent move.

2011–2012 season

With so many new signings at the club, plus the new management team experimenting with tactics, it was hardly surprising that the Bluebirds endured an indifferent pre-season, with a narrow win over Charlton and a goalless draw at the CCS in a glamour tie against Italian giants Parma being the only positives. However, City surprised everyone with a win at promotion favourites West Ham in the first competitive game of the season on 7 August where an injury-time goal from Miller made him an instant hero. Also making their debuts that day were Taylor, Cowie, Conway, Gunnarsson and Gestede from the bench. It was the first time City had won at Upton Park since 1950. They proved the win was no fluke a week later in their first home game of the season when they triumphed over Bristol City, finding themselves three goals to the good after just thirty-six minutes through Hudson, Conway and Earnshaw, to register two wins from the first two games of the season for the first time in nine years. However, a midweek game against unfancied Brighton handed City their first defeat, which was followed by draws at Burnley and Plymouth before City got back to winning ways against Doncaster. On 1 September, a club record ten international call-ups were made, including Rob Earnshaw and Darcy Blake, who were called up to Gary Speed's Welsh squad, and no fewer than five linking up with the Scotland squad.

Following the Doncaster win came two more draws, against Blackpool and Leicester, before a Miller brace settled a pivotal home match against table-topping Southampton on 28 September. However, City didn't win another League match until Barnsley visited the Welsh capital on 22 October, a shocking run that saw them plummet to twelfth in the table. The Barnsley match was one of the most thrilling the CCS had ever witnessed, the Bluebirds eventually running out 5-3 winners with goals from Gunnarsson (2), Miller, Mason and Cowie. Danny Drinkwater, who had been at loan at Cardiff the previous season, was among the scorers for Barnsley. The result proved to be a turning point, and City went on to lose only one from the next fifteen, registering home wins over Crystal Palace, Nottingham Forest, Birmingham, Reading and Portsmouth in the process as Mackay picked up the Championship manager of the Month award for November.

One of the main criticisms of Dave Jones had been his inherent unwillingness to experiment with tactics. Perhaps mindful of this, Mackay seemed keen to buck the trend by utilizing a diamond formation during the first half of the season, as opposed to Jones' orthodox 4-4-2, with a holding midfielder protecting the defensive unit and an attacker 'in the hole' behind the strikers flanked by two attacking wingers. As the season ground on, Mackay would increasingly fall back on a safer and more solid 4-5-1, with Kenny Miller often deployed as a lone striker. City lodged several unsuccessful bids for wide players during the transfer window, eventually taking advantage of the financial problems at Portsmouth to land Republic of Ireland international Liam Lawrence on loan. City were also keen to build for the future. Several players from the youth system were promoted to the first team squad, and youngsters Kadeem Harris and goalkeeper Elliot Ward arrived from Wycombe Wanderers and Aston Villa. Perhaps the most important signing, however, was that of Mackay himself, who signed a three-year contract extension to keep him at the club until 2016.

On 7 January 2012, City crashed out of the FA Cup at Premier League West Brom at the third round stage, and later that month terminated the contract of Gabor Gyepes after he fell out of favour with the new management regime, allowing the centre-back to pursue his career elsewhere. He eventually found himself with Vasas SC in Hungary. Most of City's success that season came via the League Cup. They dispatched Oxford and Huddersfield in the first two rounds to set up a titanic battle with Championship rivals Leicester at the CCS. Normal time ended 2-2, and after a goalless extra time the match went to penalties, which Cardiff won 7-6 to heap misery on their opponents, who they had beaten on penalties in the 2010 play-off semi-final. Next up were Burnley, who were beaten by a solitary Mason goal to set up a mouthwatering quarter-final clash with Premiership strugglers Blackburn in which City were drawn at home for the fourth consecutive round.

It was the first time City had reached the quarter-finals of the competition since 1965, and proved an emotional night in Cardiff, the game coming just days after the death of Wales legend Gary Speed. (Ironically, just seventeen days earlier the venue had played host to the last game the international team manager was involved in, a 4-1 friendly win over Norway.) On the night, City did not disappoint, as Miller and Gerrard scored the goals to put City through to a two-leg semi-final against Crystal Palace, who had eliminated the mighty Manchester United in the previous round.

The first leg was played at Selhurst Park on 10 January, where Cardiff lost 1-0 to an Anthony Gardner goal, despite having more possession, corners, and shots than their opponents. In the second leg two weeks later, Anthony Gardner, of all people, scored an own goal to level the tie, and City went on to win on penalties when extra time remained goalless. The hero of the day was Tom Heaton, who saved Palace's first two penalty attempts to seal Cardiff's fourth Wembley appearance in as many years and their first-ever League Cup final. In the process they became the first second-tier team to reach the League Cup Final since Birmingham in 2001, and ironically, they faced the same opponents, Liverpool.

The final was held on 26 February and despite being definite underdogs, the Bluebirds had the audacity to take the lead through a sublime Joe Mason strike to stir the Anfield outfit, now boasting Craig Bellamy within their ranks, into action. Kenny Dalglish's team equalized to take the game into extra time, then scored again to take the lead before Ben Turner bundled the ball over the line at the death to force another penalty shoot-out. And it was there, unfortunately, that Cardiff's luck ran out. Despite missing their first two penalties, Liverpool won the shoot-out 3-2 to win a record eighth League Cup. The decisive kick was missed by Anthony Gerrard, younger cousin of Liverpool's Steven, who also missed his attempt. After the game, Anthony Gerrard took to the social networking site Twitter to say, 'I can't close my eyes wid out (sic) seeing that penalty!! It's goin to haunt me for the rest of my days.'

Possibly because of the continuing distraction of the League Cup and the ultimate disappointment, Cardiff endured a miserable February in the League, during which they managed to win just one game, a 3-1 home win over Peterborough when Whittingham, Gestede and new short-term loan signing from Newcastle Haris Vuckic scored the goals. By the beginning of March the team's form had stabilised and a creditable draw at Brighton was followed by a crucial win at Bristol City where they were gifted two own goals to take the spoils. A damaging 0-3 defeat to Hull was followed by a sequence of four draws taking their tally to just two wins from fourteen as they dropped to eighth place, two points away from the play-off zone. Everyone connected with the club realized the need for solidarity, and support had remained strong despite the club's questionable League form. Another draw was in the offing when City travelled to Middlesbrough, who lay one place above them, on the 7 April, as the two clubs had drawn a total of thirty-one games that season. However, early goals from Turner and Mason settled the match as City moved tentatively back into the play-off places.

The result was put into perspective by the death of former manager Eddie May, who passed away a week later at the age of sixty-eight.

The games were coming thick and fast, and after being held to a draw by Watford, City reeled off wins against Barnsley and Derby but dropped points at home to Leeds in the penultimate game of the League programme. The final game was away at Crystal Palace, where they needed maximum points to guarantee a play-off place. The target looked in doubt when they fell behind to a Wilfried Zaha strike, but City rallied to take the spoils through goals from Whittingham and Mason to finish in sixth place with seventy-five points as Reading and Southampton took the automatic promotion places. Top scorer was Peter Whittingham, who had firmly established himself as the creative catalyst of the team and finished with thirteen goals, twelve of which came in the League. All-told, the Bluebirds had done extremely well and far exceeded expectations in what had been predicted to be a season of transition under the new management structure. Mackay, who had been through the play-off's as a player with West Ham, Norwich and Watford, told the press, 'We are ten games unbeaten going into the play-offs so there is real momentum. It's about staying calm and having a game plan.'

In their third consecutive play-off semi-final appearance, City were given a tall order when matched with third-placed West Ham, who had finished with eleven points more than City. The first leg was to be played at the CCS on 3 May where Welsh international midfielder Jack Collison scored twice to hand the Hammers control of the tie. Unfortunately, there was to be no epic comeback in the second leg, where the Bluebirds lost 3-0 to go out 5-0 on aggregate as West Ham avenged their opening day defeat and made an instant return to the Premier League.

Several notable players left the club that summer when their contracts came to an end and were not renewed, as Mackay attempted to impose his mark on the team. Among them were Lee Naylor, Tom Heaton, who moved to Bristol City in search of regular first-team football, Paul Quinn, who moved to Doncaster after making a total of fifty-seven appearances, Solomon Taiwo, who agreed terms with Mansfield, John Parkin, who went to Fleetwood Town after spending much of the season out on loan, and Dekel Keinan, who ended up at Maccabi Haifa, one of his former clubs. In addition, Kenny Miller, who hadn't hit the heights expected of him after his arrival, once going twenty-two matches without a goal, was sold to Vancouver Whitecaps for around £560,000. His final tally was eleven goals from fifty games. Cardiff also received fees for the sales of defenders Anthony Gerrard and Darcy Blake, who moved to Huddersfield and Crystal Palace respectively for a combined £700,000. Blake had made 118 appearances in seven years at the club, yet never managed a goal. He did, however, score for Wales in a friendly defeat to Australia in 2011. Fellow youth team products and fringe players Alex Evans, Aaron Wildig and Ibrahim Farah were also released after making twenty-three appearances between them. City turned down at least one substantial bid for Whittingham during the summer, who was seen as an integral part of the team.

The Malaysian owners backed Mackay to the hilt during the close-season, as he spent over £10 million on new players, an enormous sum for a second-tier team. The marquee signings included 25-year old striker Nicky Maynard from West Ham for a reported £2.75 million. Ironically, his last goal for the Hammers came against the Bluebirds at Upton Park in the 3-0 play-off defeat. Combative midfielder Jordan Mutch was signed from Birmingham for £2 million after impressing Mackay during a loan spell at Watford, and the manager beat off stiff competition from other clubs to land young South Korean sensation Kim Bo-Kyung from Cerezo Osaka for £2.5 million. The Bluebirds also finally landed long-term target Craig Noone from Brighton for £1 million, and yet another million-plus signing was Slovenian international striker Etien Velikonja from Maribor, where he had scored twenty-eight goals in sixty-four games. Mackay made a triple swoop on QPR as they prepared for life in the Premier League, taking experienced forwards Tommy Smith and Heider Helguson, as well as versatile defender Mathew Connolly to the CCS. Still, the rebuilding wasn't finished as Filip Kiss signed permanently, and goalkeeper Joe Lewis arrived from Peterborough. Ironically, his last game for Posh was the 3-1 defeat by Cardiff on 14 February. Perhaps the biggest signing of all was the return of hometown hero Craig Bellamy on a two-year contract. His manager at Liverpool, Brendan Rodgers, was quoted as saying, 'He is thirty-three and has travelled around the country all his life, so there are compassionate reasons.'

All the transfer talk that summer was eclipsed by a re-branding programme that involved changing the club's primary playing colour from blue to red, in order to make it more appealing to Asian audiences who view red as a 'lucky' and dynamic colour, while also having more of a national significance for Wales. It was the first major alteration since 1910, taken at the behest of principal backer Vincent Tan, who vowed a £100 million investment package. It was insinuated that should the re-brand not go ahead, the Malaysians could possibly withdraw their financial support, which would effectively send the club into administration as it was reportedly losing around £1 million a month and was no closer to paying off its huge debt. There was also now the added financial burden of a new stadium.

Eventually, no fewer than six new kits were unveiled before the start of the season: two versions each of the new red strip, the new blue away strip, and a third strip, which was primarily black. In rather a strange move, and obviously a further attempt to appeal to the potentially lucrative Asian market, there was no shirt sponsor as such. Instead, the word 'Malaysia' was emblazoned across the front of the shirts. The re-branding also included modifying the club badge to emphasise the dragon element at the cost of marginalizing the bluebird, until then a central component. Chief executive Alan Whiteley said at the time:

> The change of colour is a radical and some would say revolutionary move which will be met with unease and apprehension by a number of supporters, along with being seen as controversial by many. There is no getting away from the fact that history and tradition are the lifeblood of any club and as such should be jealously guarded and preserved. The changes to the home kit and badge introduced as a consequence of the investment package are designed to help the club to develop its brand and to allow it to expand its appeal to as wide an audience as possible, with a view

to delivering local success via an international and diverse market.'

Predictably, when the plans were first announced there was a mixed reaction, with many opposed to the changes. There were organized protests, and lively debate across all media platforms. The 1927 Club, formed in 1990 by Cardiff fans exiled in England and further afield, and so-called in honour of the club's FA Cup win, withdrew their support from the club and effectively disbanded in protest. Former player Jason Perry told BBC Wales that the club risked 'selling its soul.' In time, and when confronted with the options available, most supporters reluctantly accepted the re-branding. There was more controversy when the Cardiff Blues Rugby Union club had their CCS tenants' agreement terminated early by mutual consent after failing to draw big enough crowds, the scenario drawing eerie parallels with the ill-fated Cardiff Blue Dragons rugby League club venture in the early 1980s.

2012–13 season
Despite all the summer upheavals, the team performed well in pre-season as the new signings began to gel, losing just one game out of five culminating with an impressive 4-1 home win over Premier League Newcastle. The Bluebirds began their season ahead of the competition on Friday 17 August against Huddersfield, taking to the field in their new red strip for the very first time against the team for whom Anthony Gerrard was making his debut. The re-branding didn't seem to affect the attendance too much, as 21,127 turned out to see captain Mark Hudson snatch an injury-time goal to seal a 1-0 win, and offer the perfect remedy to any lingering murmurs of discontent. However, those murmurings were soon back when City drew a midweek tie

at Brighton then lost the first Severnside derby of the season 4-2 at Bristol City. A Whittingham hat-trick saw off Wolves, and the midfield general was on target again in the next game, a 2-1 win over Leeds, when Bellamy also scored his first goal of the season. He kept up his hot streak by breaking the deadlock at Millwall, with Noone's first goal for his new club doubling the lead just two minutes later to sink the Lions. A defeat at Crystal palace was quickly forgotten when City reeled off another three consecutive wins against Blackpool, Birmingham and Ipswich to roar to the top of the Championship. By this stage, 19-year-old 6'5" defender Ben Nugent was beginning to force his way into the team, along with fellow academy product Joe Ralls, and to a lesser extent Theo Wharton and Declan John.

The only downside in the early stages of the season were a career-threatening cruciate ligament injury to record signing Nicky Maynard, which would rule him out until the end of the season. After an international break, the Bluebirds (or Redbirds, as some people had begun to call them!) travelled to Nottingham Forest where they lost 3-1, but again they showed resilience to come back with two good home wins against Watford and Burnley. By now a pattern was emerging, City were proving very strong at home but vulnerable on their travels, and it was evident once more when City travelled to Bolton and Charlton at the beginning of November and lost both games. The latter was a 5-4 thriller, though the score flattered City slightly as Noone and Gunnarsson scored in injury time to add to earlier goals from Helguson and Mason which actually put them 0-2 up!

City regrouped to take five wins and a draw from the next six games, the highlight being a thumping 1-4 win at Blackburn on 7 November where Hudson, Bellamy, Mason and Kim were the scorers to consolidate top spot. They suffered a blip just over a week later in a 1-2 home defeat by lowly Peterborough, the match proving yet again how unpredictable a sport football can be; until that point Cardiff had boasted a 100 per cent record at the CCS, while Posh hadn't won for eight games and were rock-bottom of the League. To their credit, Cardiff roared back in style. A Bellamy goal was enough to win the next game at Leicester, before back-to-back home wins over Crystal Palace on Boxing Day and Millwall three days later. On New Year's Day 2013, City faced a difficult trip to Birmingham City, where they again triumphed thanks to a single goal from Mason, a result that stretched their lead at the top of the table to seven points. It was the first time Cardiff had completed a League double over Birmingham for forty-six years.

Off the field, the fans and media were beginning to believe that after so much disappointment, this could finally be City's year. However, drama was never far away. In October Alan Whiteley had been replaced as chief executive, though he remained with the club until January when he resigned altogether following an arrest for fraud. He vehemently denied the charges, and though there was no suggestion the club were involved in any illegal activity, it reflected badly on them. That month City suffered one of their most embarrassing incidents in recent years when they tumbled out of the FA Cup at the hands of non-League Macclesfield, who made the fourth round of the competition for the first time in their history at the expense of City, who had taken the gamble of fielding a weakened side. The defeat meant that by January, all City had to play for was the League, having already been dumped out of the League Cup, now called the Capital One Cup, by Division Two Northampton in the very first round. They had taken the lead in both Cup ties, but failed to hold on and were ultimately overcome by inferior opposition.

Although it started promisingly, Rob Earnshaw's second spell at his hometown club had been disappointing, bringing a return of just four goals from twenty-two appearances, many of which as a substitute. Despite the injury to Maynard, Earnie found himself loaned out to Maccabi Tel Aviv, before sealing a permanent move to Toronto where he scored five goals in his first six matches. He remains the only player to score hat-tricks in all three divisions of the Football League, the Premier League, the FA Cup, League Cup, and at international level. In January, young French winger Kevin Sainte-Luce's contract was terminated when he was convicted of assaulting two girls in a Cardiff nightclub. The player, who was just beginning to make an impact on the first team squad, was lucky to avoid a prison term and soon found himself at AFC Wimbledon, where he was handed a lifeline by ex-City youth manager Neil Ardley, who had recently been made manager with ex-Cardiff and Watford team-mate Neil Cox being named as his assistant. Before the transfer window closed, Mackay moved to sign ex-Norwich left-back Simon Lappin as cover for Anthony Taylor on a free after the 29-year-old impressed during a loan spell. The biggest signing, however, was that of Frazier Campbell, who arrived from Sunderland for a fee of £650,000. Since breaking into the Manchester United team as a youngster, the skilful striker had enjoyed mixed fortunes. At his most productive he notched twenty-four goals in thirty-eight games during a loan spell at Royal Antwerp, but most recently had spent four years at the north-east club where he managed just ten goals from sixty-seven games.

City returned to League action on 12 January with a goalless draw with Ipswich, but got back to winning ways a week later at Blackpool, where Tommy Smith scored the winner. After a home tie against Leicester was postponed, City travelled to Leeds, where Frazier Campbell won the game with his first kick of a ball in a Cardiff shirt, helping City clock up a fifth successive away win and open up a ten-point lead at the top of the table. After a goalless draw at Huddersfield, Campbell was on target again on his home debut, plundering both goals in a 2-1 win over Bristol City before City's form slumped slightly and they registered just one win from the next five, a 2-1 win at Wolves on 24 February where Campbell again scored both goals to continue his fantastic start at his new club. Even so, what was once an eleven-point lead over second-placed Hull had been eroded to just four points by the time City travelled to Sheffield Wednesday on 16 March, where they won 0-2 with goals from Cowie and Connolly to nudge Dave Jones' new employers closer to the relegation zone. The Cardiff team had been strengthened defensively by the arrival of Leon Barnett from Norwich on loan. That month there were changes at boardroom level, as chairman TG resigned to concentrate on other business interests, and was replaced by Simon Lim, who planned to combine the role with his existing one of chief executive. He told BBC Sport, 'TG leaves a legacy that we can all be proud of and should all work hard to see continued.'

An unexpected defeat at new bogey team Peterborough was quickly remedied with the help of a classy 3-0 home win over Blackburn, when Campbell, Mason and Whittingham scored the goals, and subsequent draws against Watford and Barnsley moved Cardiff ever-closer toward their target of achieving automatic promotion. Rudy Gestede scored twice against Nottingham Forest at the CCS on 13 April to add to Helguson strike in a stunning 3-0 win, which put City twelve points clear at the top of the League with only four games left to play, thanks to second-placed Watford losing at Peterborough.

Three days later, Cardiff finally secured promotion to the

Premier League, and the financial windfall that comes with playing in the most popular division in world football, with a 0-0 draw against Charlton at the CCS. The final whistle triggered a pitch invasion and scenes of jubilation as fans rushed to celebrate with their heroes, ecstatic at the prospect of Cardiff City becoming the forty-sixth club to grace the Premier League since its formation in 1992, and playing in the top division of the English Football League for the first time in fifty-one years. From the eleven players who won promotion, only two, Marshall and McNaughton, remained from the side that lost the 2010 play-off final against Blackpool. Suffering from fatigue and loss of form, Whittingham had lost his place in the side to Kim Bo-Kyung, who made up an extremely effective midfield triumvirate with Mutch and Gunnarsson.

Promotion assured, the next target was to end the season as League champions. They were almost thwarted in their efforts in the next game at Burnley on 20 April, when an injury-time leveller cancelled out Conway's opener, but the point turned out to be just enough to win their first League title since the 1992–93 season. Amidst the celebrations, Mackay told BBC Sport, 'I'm delighted that we've had the mental strength and character to have that consistency and just keep going, being relentless. That's what we were this year – relentless. I spoke to (the players) about how most people get to watch history happen, (but) very few people get to actually make history. For them to do that today for the city of Cardiff is something that I'm very proud of.'

The Championship trophy was presented to the team after a 1-1 draw with Bolton in the next match, cheered on by some 26,418 spectators. Interestingly, the crowd that day also contained Sam Hammam and new owner Vincent Tan, as past and future collided. The final game of the season on 4 May at second-placed Hull City, who needed a win to guarantee promotion, was full of high drama. With the score 2-1 to the hosts, Hull were awarded a penalty in injury time. The kick was missed, and Cardiff raced to the other end where they were awarded a penalty of their own, converted by Nicky Maynard, who was making his return from the injury that wrecked his first season with the Bluebirds. It was a lucky escape for Cardiff who finished the game with ten men after Andrew Taylor was sent off for two bookable offences. The game made little difference to the hosts, who took the runner-up spot after Leeds beat Watford. It all meant that Cardiff finished eight points clear of their nearest challengers on 87 points with a goal difference of twenty-seven.

It was a record-breaking season for Cardiff in many respects. They won twenty-five League games, beating the previous best of twenty-two; failed to score in only six; and kept eighteen clean sheets. They conceded only forty-five goals, beating their previous record of fifty-one, which had stood since the 2004–05 season, and the average 'goals against' fell to just 0.98 per game, their lowest since winning promotion to the Championship. Remarkably, not a single Cardiff City player managed to get into double figures on the goal-scoring charts, Heidur Helguson ending the season as top scorer with nine, eight of which came in the League. However, the team did boast no fewer than seventeen different scorers.

The next day the team enjoyed a triumphant promotion parade in an open-topped bus from Cardiff castle to Cardiff Bay. Long-serving Kevin McNaughton said, 'This is our time. We are the champions and heading for the Premier League.'

Immediately after the season's heroics, the largest-ever fans' survey, carried out by MediaWales, named Malky Mackay as the best-ever Cardiff City manager with a massive 59.6 per cent of votes. A high accolade, indeed. Second on the list was Jimmy Scoular who polled just 15.7 per cent. The top three were completed by Eddie May on 11.4 per cent. Korean sensation Kim Bo-Kyung was voted Mackay's best signing, commanding 44.2 per cent of the votes ahead of Craig Bellamy on 25.1 per cent. Tellingly, in the fans' eyes, the biggest disappointment of the season was the injury to Nicky Maynard, ahead of the club's re-branding policy. Directly addressing the controversial re-branding initiative, 64.9 per cent of supporters said that following promotion, the turmoil and upheaval was worth it. When asked by the media in a subsequent interview whether he would be happy to lose both south Wales derbies but stay in the Premier League Mackay himself responded, 'I'm going to have to be greedy: I want both!'

With promotion to the Promised Land of the Premier League finally achieved, exciting times lie ahead for the city of Cardiff and on a wider scale, the country of Wales, which is sure to benefit from increased tourism and a rare opportunity in the spotlight. Whatever the next chapter in the illustrious history of Cardiff City football club holds, it is almost certain that there will hardly be a dull moment.